From Teaching to Mentoring

From Teaching to Mentoring argues for a simple educational idea: people, particularly adult students, learn well when they are full collaborators in deciding what, how and why they learn.

The authors advocate a sound, comprehensive, and lifelong education, shifting the emphasis of the learning process to students' understandings of their personal, professional, and academic needs. Whilst heeding traditional criteria of educational excellence, they ask for profound educational and political transformations, such as:

- teachers to become collaborative inquirers with their students;
- students to become skilled and lifelong independent learners;
- academic institutions to become learning communities embracing the full diversity of human curiosity and experience.

The book discusses what mentoring is, and why it is now so much in demand. Drawing upon two decades of extensive research and practice, and using a variety of illuminating case studies, the authors offer a stimulating and thorough examination of mentoring, integrating theory and practice throughout. It will be invaluable to anyone involved in the teaching of adults in further and higher education, as well as university administrators, programme directors, and development and training officers.

Lee Herman and **Alan Mandell** are Professors and Mentors at Empire State College/The State University of New York. Dr Herman was cofounder of the Empire State College Mentoring Institute, which Dr Mandell currently directs.

From Teaching to Mentoring

Principle and practice, dialogue and life
in adult education

Lee Herman
Alan Mandell

 RoutledgeFalmer
Taylor & Francis Group

LONDON AND NEW YORK

First published 2004
by RoutledgeFalmer
11 New Fetter Lane, London EC4P 4EE

Simultaneously published in the USA and Canada
by RoutledgeFalmer
29 West 35th Street, New York, NY 10001

RoutledgeFalmer is an imprint of the Taylor & Francis Group

Typeset in Times by Wearset Ltd, Boldon, Tyne and Wear
Printed and bound in Great Britain by TJ International Ltd,
Padstow, Cornwall

British Library Cataloguing in Publication Data
A catalogue record for this book is available from the British
Library

Library of Congress Cataloging in Publication Data
Herman, Lee, 1950–
    From teaching to mentoring : principle and practice, dialogue
and life in adult education / Lee Herman and Alan Mandell.
        p. cm.
    1. Mentoring in education. 2. Adult learning. I. Mandell, Alan,
1950– II. Title.
    LC5225.M45H47 2004
    374—dc21
                                                      2003013095

ISBN 0-415-26617-3 (Hbk)
ISBN 0-415-26618-1 (Pbk)

For A.G.

For Seymour and Florence Mandell, for Jonah Mandell
and for Victoria Shick

Contents

Acknowledgments

Extracts from Hamilton, E. and Cairns, H., *Plato: Collected Dialogues*. Copyright © 1961 by Bollingen Foundation reprinted by permission of Princeton University Press.

With thanks to Random House for permission to quote from *Nobody's Fool* by Richard Russo.

Every effort has been made to contact the holders of copyright; in the event of any inadvertent omissions, please inform the publisher.

Chapter 1

What is mentoring?

> Where do you come from, Phaedrus my friend, and where are you going?
>
> Plato, *Phaedrus* (227a)

"What do you want to learn?"
"Why do you want to learn these things?"
"How do you want to learn them?"
"What do you believe you have already learned?"
"How do you decide that you have done so?"

We ask our readers to consider that these five questions can germinate and shape an entire education. We suggest that the dialogues initiated and sustained by these questions will sufficiently provide both the content and process of learning in academic, workplace, community, and personal life. Moreover, these questions, when asked of oneself in self-reflection, create a lifelong course of learning which is at once entirely coherent and meaningful and yet entirely open to endlessly diverse and unexpected discoveries. The name we apply to the people whose vocation it is to ask such questions is "mentor." The deliberate practice of learning, through asking them of one's students and of oneself, is "mentoring."

We work in an academic setting, a degree-granting, public university. We are professors who work mainly with adult students. They are busy and pre-occupied with the responsibilities and commitments of adults to their jobs and careers, to their families and their communities. They usually want university degrees to serve their success and prosperity. They want their academic learning to be efficient and convenient: that is, to move quickly but also to flexibly accommodate the other demands on their time and attention. Adult students want their learning to make them more powerful in the world beyond the academy. And, once they are assured that the content and organization of their learning will suit these practical needs, our students also want to address the more contemplative issues which almost invariably underlie, suffuse, and trouble the daily business ordinarily consuming their attention: Who am I? What sort of life do I want to live? How can I be free? How can I treat others and be treated respectfully? What excites my curiosity, wonder, and delight? That is, our students want their learning not only to help them succeed but also to help them become something rarely attended to in their workplaces and equally busy domestic lives: they want to be happy. Our work, the work of mentors, is to help students, each one and one at a time, conceive and complete an academic education that responds to these practical and contemplative needs.

This book is about how mentors do this work and about the principles which govern its practices. We will show how we and our students enter into and sustain academic dialogues evoked by the five questions above. We will show how these dialogues address the usual requirements of a good undergraduate education, as well as our students' individual practical needs. We will also show how the dialogical relationship itself creates a little community that is truthful, just, and beautiful – that is, a learning experience enabling both mentors and students to care for their frequently reciprocal, even universal contemplative concerns. The work of mentoring and the dialogical learning it generates are moved by what Kurt Wolff calls "cognitive love" (1976: 20). This spirit is not different, we believe, from the Eros or love which Socrates claims to animate every effort to learn to live a good life (Plato, *Symposium* 212b–c).

Before we explain the organization of this book and then in subsequent chapters illustrate and explain in detail the practices and principles of mentoring, we offer a glimpse into the beginnings of dialogue with two students. Their particular needs and purposes are individual, even idiosyncratic; but these people are also in many ways typical adult students seeking bachelor degrees from a fully accredited university.

Doris

As soon as I ask what I can do for her, Doris quickly reels off her "resume." After completing high school, she found a secretarial position at a local bank, and then, while raising her three children, she continued to work in various office capacities on a part-time basis. She is quite proud of what she has accomplished. But when I ask her why she has decided to come to university now, she begins to describe a difficult divorce and the need to find a way to support herself. Two years ago, she found a full time job in the personnel department of a food conglomerate that recently moved its administrative offices only a short bus ride from her apartment. Doris also discloses another part of her life: for more than twenty five years, she has been devoted to her church and to its many community activities. "Almost every weekend, I'm off to another church event. People are always asking me to pitch in, and I'm happy to do it." As she talks, I wonder what skills Doris might have learned from all this "pitching in" and what important meanings these activities might have for her.

After two meetings in which we continued to talk about Doris's life and academic learning, it became clearer and clearer to me that even though she was discouraged by the end of her marriage and worried because she didn't have a professional credential, many aspects of her life have been fulfilling. She had indeed accomplished a lot and had gained the respect of everyone with whom she had worked. I learned that whether in the local business office or in the parochial school where she had been volunteering for years, co-workers and supervisors knew she was very capable. When she "pitched-in," she in fact was the person to whom others turned to take charge. With more than two decades of varied work experience, Doris could, I was sure, earn college credit for the skills and knowledge she'd acquired along the way. But right now, both Doris and I understood that she was really stuck without a college degree.

Doris had never been to university. Indeed, no adult of her generation in her family had. She worries that her age and her lack of a formal academic background would impede, if not completely block, her success. And though with the support of her kids, she has arrived in my office, she also worries that she isn't "real university material." But I sensed that her enthusiasm, her strong religious values, and her experiential learning would all serve her well as she pursued her university degree. Even by our second conversation, Doris and I had identified clusters of learning, both past and future, which, although still unrefined, would quite easily form major elements of the curriculum, the bachelor's degree program, she would eventually design. Her apparent competencies in secretarial skills, office management, event planning, and in effectively dealing with people would nicely fit a variety of educational plans. And certainly this experiential learning would serve what Doris, during this second meeting, reveals to be her life's goal: managing a church-based service agency for children.

Shifting our focus from these practical learnings, I wondered aloud:

"Anything else?"

"Well, I do like to listen to the radio a lot. Old radio shows."

"Really?"

"Yes. I buy tapes of the Golden Age of Radio. Sometimes I record re-broadcasts of those old shows. Actually, I've collected hundreds of hours of tapes."

"You could get credit for what you already know. And, you might even want to learn more about the Golden Age of Radio as an additional study."

"I didn't know I could do that."

We have discovered something else that could become part of Doris's degree. And I have found another example of the expanse of Doris's inquisitiveness. I'm sure she can make it.

But we both knew we were not operating in a vacuum. Her circumstances impose constraints on her learning. First, Doris needs financial support, and her new employer will fund her university education only to the extent that her degree focuses on business. So too, her very busy life – filled with work, family, and church – conspires against the pattern and pace of any typical academic calendar. Yet, however much her situation might constrain her, Doris has always embraced the learning afforded by the roles she's taken on. She learned how to be a parent; she learned the skills needed to effectively work in diverse office arrangements; she learned how to run complex events and to set up and fund new programs; and she learned the traditions and the theology of her faith. Thus, whatever the force of circumstance, Doris has also acquired a rich general education from her history.

At this moment in her life, Doris wants to make her own path. Even though she is anxious about achieving university-level learning and about how she will manage it, she wants to learn whatever she can that will help her attain her goal and to explore whatever she's interested in. She is looking for guidance, and she knows she needs support to make her way on this alien academic terrain. She is depending on me to get her through the rules of the academy, even though she was quick to let me know that she intends to be "a little rebellious." That is, despite the impositions of her workplace or the academic requirements she sees she might encounter, Doris intends to concentrate on the questions and topics which matter to her. She knows that it was thinking about those things that really got her excited about going to university.

Alex

Alex walks nervously into my office to learn how our college works and to plan a first independent study with me. I ask him, as I do every student, what he wants to learn. He tells me, "I just want to learn. I need a degree." And then, in clipped, jittery sentences, he quickly gives a history of himself: Now in his mid-twenties and living on his own since he was fifteen, he had never graduated secondary school, but managed to pass an exam, which secured him a diploma. Alex then enrolled in several liberal arts courses at another college. These were required of all first year students and seemed, in Alex's view, to have been taught by formula and without much regard for the students' interests or participation. He did poorly in all of them. Nonetheless, Alex was and remains interested in the topics of those courses: psychology, sociology, and writing. "Everything," he says, "I want to learn everything."

While I am wondering what he means, Alex also tells me that for the past few years he's worked in a local steel mill (one that is profitable, quite modern, and, for this largely rural area, quite well-paying). He doesn't much like the work because it's dangerous and he knows that over the long term it will damage his health. (I've had students before who work there; most were frequently afflicted with colds and other respiratory ailments.) Alex gets along with his co-workers and bosses, but he feels distant from them: "I'm not interested in most of the things they like to talk about." However, he enjoys their company when conversations turn from money, women, hunting etc. and become "philosophical" about religion and politics. Even so, his views on those matters – which seem to be critical and liberal – tend to make him feel isolated as well. Alex tells me he likes to read about these topics, about "everything" concerning human behavior and that he sometimes keeps a journal of his ideas.

I feel a pressure from the nervous rush of Alex's presentation. He's skillfully self-supporting in, and well-informed about, the practical world. But he's also alienated from it. His alienation, perhaps, makes him critically reflective and contemplative. He wants to form and find his place in the world, but not just anyplace, not even a simply prosperous one, will suit him. Alex has many desires, and he searches but is certain that he does not yet know what he needs. I want to respond helpfully to his specific and individual purposes, but I also need to make sure our connection is appropriate: friendly but not too personal, academically helpful but not psychotherapeutic. So, when he pauses, I ask him, hoping to project a calm but genuine curiosity, to tell me more about some of the books or authors he's read.

He becomes even more agitated, his pale face and close-cut scalp flushing pink. He mentions Freud and "Fost." I realize he means *Faust*, and worrying that I might embarrass him, I try to causally mention the correct pronunciation while saying admiringly, "Oh, you've read *Faust*?" Alex flushes more deeply, and then says, "There are lots more. I can't think of them all now." And he then rushes on to tell me more about his personal life: "I need to get a degree so I can get out of the mill someday." He and his fiancée have a child; they plan to have another. He wants to provide for his family, which his factory wages enable him to do; but he wants to do something different, "so I can use my mind," and he's not interested in becoming a manager or a technician. The twelve-hour rotating shift work the mill requires of its laborers prevents him from attending regular university classes. Moreover, although Alex seems to love learning, because of the regimented and condescending expectations he experienced, he simply hates "school." Furthermore, although Alex clearly takes his thoughts, his reading, and writing seriously, he doubts that anyone else will; "I don't know if I'm good enough to go to university."

I've become familiar with some of Alex's practical dilemmas and self-doubt from many other adult students. He needs a university degree to get on in the world, but he's not sure how he can manage doing so with his work schedule and other responsibilities. His eager and explicit intellectuality may set him apart from many "typical" adult students. However, he is also as concerned as they are about obtaining practical value from a university education; and he is as doubtful and anxious as they are about both his ability to succeed and the university's ability to respectfully accommodate his needs.

While I continue to wonder where the point of useful and successful connection with him might be, Alex gives me more detail about his own quandary: the mill will pay for his college studies, Alex tells me, but only those which are "work related." He understands his dilemma: "I want to learn what I'm interested in. I'll just pay myself." Then, a few moments later, "But I want them to pay. That would help me support my family." Alex isn't sure what to do about this, and he's not sure what to study or even if he really can do "university" learning. His words slow down and his voice slides into silence with a question: "I don't know. What do you think?"

Who are these students? What do their mentors do? Some observations

Both Doris and Alex desire academic degrees for practical reasons. She needs to support herself and wants a position for which the skills she already has nearly qualify her, but for the lack of the degree itself. He needs to support himself and a small family, in a position at least as lucrative as his factory job but more healthy; Alex knows that an academic degree is almost certainly necessary to be considered for entry into such a career. But both he and Doris are motivated by other kinds of purposes. Alex hopes for a career that will engage and stimulate his ebullient intellect; and he is interested in huge topics – literature, philosophy, human behavior – for their own sake, regardless of their usefulness in a career. Somewhat similarly, Doris has a dream, not just of a job suited to her skills, but one originating from her earnest spiritual life, which allows her to be a leader in serving people in need. She is also interested in pursuing her curiosity about the Golden Age of Radio, just because it delights her.

Another common feature of these students is that it seems that they have already acquired, through their work and other experiences, substantial learning which is very likely identical to university-level learning. Doris possesses supervisory, administrative, managerial, and leadership skills; she also probably already knows a lot about community-based social services, and of course her knowledge of radio programming may prove to be deep and extensive. Alex, though he may not be very interested in his current job, might well have learned much about factory operations and steel-making; and his wide, if eclectic and academically ungrounded, reading will likely be comparable to the liberal arts learning expected of a beginning undergraduate. Moreover, his intellectual passion for what he's read and the themes which interest him suggests that he has understood and appreciated them, perhaps significantly more so than the many uninterested students who have been required to take such subjects and managed to "get through" them with passing grades.

Finally, both Doris and Alex experience tension and conflict between their practical and contemplative purposes. Their socio-economic status and goals demand that they complete their degrees expeditiously and cost-effectively. And there is their assumption that the university will impose requirements upon their time, interests, and abilities, which they will find taxing and constricting. They are afraid and anxious.

Their mentors are not merely aware of these features; we pay close attention to them and we care about them. We want to understand who Doris and Alex are. We want to know what they want and need to learn; we want to understand why. Moreover, we are eager to help them discover, articulate, and shape into individually appropriate curricula what they might already know, what they intend to learn, and what they might be required to learn. The mentors are beginning to help Doris and Alex create degree plans that express and satisfy their purposes, and meet normal university standards. They also want to help Doris and Alex satisfy the academic preparations typically expected for entry into the fields in which they decide to make their careers. In addition, we are looking for entry or "connecting" points from which we can create, with Doris and Alex, studies or tutorials which both engage the informed curiosity they already have and expand their learning into new but individually meaningful topics.

We are also mindful of the constrictions, conflicts, and anxieties Doris and Alex are already experiencing and anticipating. We are trying to be attentive to the ecology of their learning. This is a complex and dynamic mixture of social, economic, institutional, psychological, cognitive, and spiritual pressures and aspirations which determine what they will learn and how they can reasonably do so at the university.

And we ourselves inhabit and represent such a complex environment. We are professors in an "alternative" but fully accredited college of a large state university. We are officially called "mentors"; our college is administratively and academically designed to accommodate the needs and purposes of adult students such as Doris and Alex. Our college, Empire State College, is relatively non-selective and flexible in schedule, open in curricular opportunities, and diverse in modes of learning (e.g. group and individual tutorials, distance and in-person communication). However, as university faculty, we are responsible for counseling our students and for helping them learn not only what they individually desire, but also the content and skills typically expected of a university graduate. Our role is to help our students, each one, learn to integrate and manage the complexity and tension of these multiple contexts – their own and ours – within which they seek academic degrees and a "higher" education.

This book is about the principles and practices which enable mentors to fulfill these responsibilities. The many case studies offered in subsequent chapters will demonstrate, we hope, how mentoring is done and why it should be done. Already, the brief encounters with Doris and Alex we've offered should suggest several governing ideas.

- Mentors engage in dialogues with their students.
- Students are invited and expected to become full and increasingly autonomous collaborators in their learning.
- Mentors, although authoritative representatives of their academic community, do not presume to know all or even most of what is best for their students to learn or how to do so.
- Mentors, as well as students, are therefore learners; and, in order to engage in their collaborative inquiries, they must carefully reflect on what they believe they already know, what they need to learn, and how and why they will do so.
- This on-going process of reciprocal self-examination embraces traditional academic material (e.g. what is typically read in books and "covered" in classrooms). Our self examinations also embrace the essential "life issues" which may originate beyond the academy. These issues make academic learning meaningful for human beings who are attempting to flourish, practically and contemplatively, in the world.
- We believe that these student-mentor dialogues enable our students to complete a sound university education and to use that education to acquire the power they need to succeed in the world beyond the academy.
- Further, we believe that the very experience of these dialogues, conducted as we've suggested, enables our students to explore the truths, the justice, and beauty everyone seeks for happiness. In other words, the small and diverse communities students and mentors create together are the germs of a "good society" in which people hope to live. This also is cognitive love.

The call for mentoring

Doris and Alex are typical not merely of the adult students we encounter in our college. Their needs and aspirations are common and not just in university programs suited for adult students: all of us want to succeed and want to live good lives. In response, there appears to be a call for people who have the interest and ability to help others learn to live integrated fulfilled lives. "Mentors" and mentoring programs are appearing in many contexts.

Our work as university-level academic mentors is very similar, for example, to Vivian Paley's with very young schoolchildren. She emphasizes listening to children, collaborating in the development of their ideas (even depending on them to participate in and conceive standards for classroom governance), and asking them to create their own stories as a significant part of their academic curricula (for example, Paley 1986, 1992). Mentoring programs, both academic and socially-oriented, abound for young people living in impoverished and otherwise dysfunctional communities. Members of service groups offer themselves as role models for the poor, the oppressed, and the alienated. Recently, the Harvard Mentoring Project ran a full page advertisement in the *New York Times*. It advises, in "a step-by-step guide to mentoring":

> Step one: Listen.
> Step two: Share what you know.
> Step three: Repeat step one.
> It can be that easy to turn a kid's life around. So turn your lifetime of experience into the experience of a lifetime. Mentor a child.
>
> (*New York Times* 5 January 2003: 30)

One might wonder exactly what wisdom, what sort of social vision these mentors will have to share. The work of Helen Colley on social and academic training programs for "disaffected youth" and teachers offers a critical perspective on the dominating or oppressive power relations which often exist in those programs (for example, Colley 2001, 2002). We too believe that essential social institutions – schools, businesses, service agencies, governments, families – often reproduce the very inequities and dissatisfactions they are supposed to prevent or alleviate. In our mentoring work, we have to be mindful of how the presence of these problems trouble our adult students' purposes and also influence our own academic expectations.

Non-academic mentoring programs for adults are also common. Businesses and other large organizations, including schools and community agencies offer "mentors" to their newer and/or younger employees. The mentor is supposed to help the "protégé" succeed within the organization and contribute to its effectiveness. Books, such as Lois Zachary's *The Mentor's Guide*, provide instruction in this organizational learning (Zachary 2000). An ad for "about.com" recently displayed on the #4 subway train in New York City reads: "If your mentor's mentor had a really good mentor, that would be us."

Whatever the differences in label, values, approach, and consequence, all of these programs are responding to a widespread call for guides and role models, someone who can genuinely care for each person's effort to learn to thrive in a world where it is tough not merely to succeed but to be wise. Information and instruction about how to succeed abound, as do self-help manuals about how to be happy. This abundance seems to respond to a dearth of people who can care and who know how to integrate the desire for learning that will help one be powerful in a difficult world. It underlies the desire for learning that will help oneself and others lead a good life. This kind of integrated learning seems hard to come by – hard enough so that special words, "mentor" and "mentoring," are used to name it.

"Mentor" is an ancient word, the name of a character in Homer's *Odyssey*. Athena, the Greek goddess of wisdom, disguises herself as Mentor, an elderly and respected man in Odysseus's kingdom, Ithaca. S/he guides Telemachus, Odysseus's son, in his efforts to make his way in a dangerous world. The father has been too-long absent, fighting the war at Troy. And Penelope, the mother, is absorbed and distracted in her efforts to protect her household and her virtue from the rapacious ambitions of suitors who seek her hand in order to control the kingdom. Telemachus needs to learn to become shrewd enough to survive and to learn the virtues of a prince who will someday be called upon to serve the prosperity and happiness of his people. This is the "higher" education Mentor is supposed to nurture. So it is perhaps a good name to revive now for a kind of educator in a world so caught up in ambition and violence that power and virtue appear to be an impossible combination (cf. MacIntyre, *After Virtue* 1981).

Neither Doris nor Alex represent the most disadvantaged groups in our society, and they have indeed done rather well for themselves. Nonetheless, they are uncomfortably familiar with a world of powerful and insufficiently nurturing social institutions or systems. Schools have left too many teachers and too many students to fend for themselves in increasingly unfriendly and unsupportive classrooms. Businesses demand "total commitment" from their employees, yet treat them as utterly expendable. Human resource departments have become repositories of regulations and rewards rather than trusted agencies of employee development. Social service agencies, bureaucratized and overwhelmed, have perpetuated the anonymity and rejection they were created to cure. In response, the call to mentoring can be seen as an effort to revive neighborly civility and affection in impersonal and oppressive environments.

Our role: from teaching to mentoring

We are not social reformers, therapists, or motivational consultants. We are university faculty, and people like Doris and Alex come to our college for academic learning and degrees. Above all, we are not sages or gurus. We do not possess, nor can we transmit to our students, the wisdom that will make their lives successful and happy. We *do* know how to help our students learn for themselves what is most important to them. This includes helping them understand the implications of their own purposes. These implications will have practical and traditionally academic aspects, such as the requirements of a university degree and professional preparation. And, almost certainly, our students' purposes will also be more or less subtly suffused with anxious philosophical wonder about what to make of their lives.

Although we, like all university faculty, have scholarly expertise in academic disciplines, we do not presume that the knowledge we believe we have enables us to determine what is best for our students to learn. To be sure, mentors make use of what they know (for example, from their disciplines, from their familiarity with university expectations, and from their experience with other students). However, we begin from the principle and constantly try to remind ourselves and our students that beliefs, theirs and ours, about what is true, including what is important and good, are incomplete and provisional. From this principle, the first principle of mentoring, follows an inquiry or dialogical approach to education. We mean that all learners, both students and mentors, best serve their curiosity by continuing to become informed about what they want to know and about what they believe most deeply they already know. That is, we say to ourselves and to our students: "Yes, study, read, and write about whatever you want and/or need to learn. But also, listen to and examine yourself carefully about what you believe to be true, especially about what you believe to be important in the life you intend to live."

Our own "role model" is Socrates. Socrates insisted that he was not a teacher and certainly he did not work for an academic institution or otherwise seek payment for whatever good service others believed he performed (Plato, *Apology*: 31b, 33b, 36b; *Collected Dialogues* 1963). He claimed rather to be a "midwife" – someone who did not transmit knowledge to his companions in dialogue but helped them labor successfully to bring to life the wisdom they sought (Plato, *Theaetetus*: 150b–d). Our assumptions as academic mentors are nonetheless very similar to those at the basis of Socratic dialogue. Although we do not suppose that we are absolutely ignorant, we do believe, as mentors, that our knowledge is provisional and uncertain, that our "wisdom," such as it is, consists in our ability and willingness to detect our own ignorance. We are constantly learning not to believe that we know that which we do not know (*Apology*: 21d). Further, we believe that the best way for people to learn what is most important is to engage in critical, self-examining dialogues within themselves and with others (cf. *Meno*). We believe, in other words:

> that to let no day pass without discussing goodness and all the other subjects about which you hear me talking and examining both myself and others is really the very best thing ... and that life without this sort of examination is not worth living.
>
> (*Apology*: 38a)

The principles of mentoring

Our work as mentors is to translate these very basic (and perhaps puzzling) philosophical positions into specific educational principles, which in turn govern our academic practices. In brief, the following are the principles constituting Socratic dialogue in a contemporary academic setting.

1   Authority and uncertainty: Act so that what you believe you know is only provisionally true.
2   Diversity of curriculum: People learn best when they learn what draws their curiosity.
3   Autonomy and collaboration: Treat all learning projects, all studies, as occasions for dialogue rather than as transmissions of knowledge from expert to novice.
4   Learning from the "lifeworld": Treat all participants to an inquiry as whole persons – that is, as people who hope to experience even in their busiest and most instrumental activities, the virtues and happiness which are ends-in-themselves, and give life meaning and purpose.
5   Evaluation as reflective learning: Judge the quality of learning in the movement of the dialogue; expect that the content of individual outcomes will be, like all knowledge claims, incomplete and diverse.
6   Individual learning and the knowledge most worth having: Honor and engage each student's individual desire to know and every student will learn what is important.

We will explain these principles more fully in our next chapter, where we show how we apply them to our work with Doris and Alex. We will use this method of demonstration, reciprocally referring to (and thus integrating) principle and practice, for the remainder of the book.

We hope that readers are making connections between these educational principles and "ordinary" communication beyond the academy. The six principles of mentoring have much in common, for example, with Jürgen Habermas's analysis of "discourse ethics" within the "lifeworld" (*The Theory of Communicative Action* 1989; *Moral Consciousness and Communicative Action* 1990). Some readers may be reminded of Donald Schon's work on "reflective practice" for educators and other professionals (Schon 1983, 1990). They will detect the influence of his ideas in the remainder of this book; and we shall often use the term "reflection" in a way similar to his own. Most often we shall allude to Socrates's efforts to help himself and his fellow citizens learn, through self-examination, to be wiser in public and private life.

Whether we associate the work of academic mentoring with the ideas of our approximate contemporaries, such as Habermas and Schon, or with the Socratic enterprise of 2,500 years ago, we do intend to suggest that a mentoring approach to university education today can and should embrace learning which occurs far beyond and within the academy.

As we've said, the call to mentoring is not voiced in a vacuum. It responds to specific and harsh realities. These afflict both the academy and all the spheres of activity, public and private, in our culture. Fragmentation abounds: people are overwhelmingly informed, but lack reliable coherence. We have an extraordinary array of technical competencies, but don't know how to live. We provide endless products and services, but we are hunting for care. We create historically incomparable abundance, but institutionalize just as much unprecedented inequality. We celebrate a global society, but remain parochial enough to tolerate starvation, slavery, and genocide. Of course, mentoring does not solve these problems. However, to the extent that each of them stems from our ignorance – that is, to the extent that each can be understood as an educational problem – mentoring has something to contribute. Mentoring is about lifelong learning which helps people live well.

The organization of the book

In our next chapter, we continue to explain the principles of mentoring, by illustrating them in our work with Doris and Alex and then grounding them in the philosophy of Socratic or dialogical inquiry. In Chapters 3 through 8, we offer a detailed exploration of the practices distinctive to mentoring. Our many examples come from our own work with students at Empire State College. Some of these practices, such as "asking questions" and "planning," readers will find to be part of the familiar repertoire of any responsible teacher. The rest – waiting and teaching as learning, integrating the personal and the academic – are practices uniquely emphasized in mentoring.

Those six chapters represent academic mentoring in a particularly supportive university environment. However, we try to demonstrate that the integrated mentoring principles and practices discussed are pertinent to any organization, any context in which "knowledge claims" and learning are important. In fact, we argue that an "educative" dimension exists in nearly every human association and relationship, and that these are therefore to be treated with "cognitive love." Recognizing moreover that our college is unusual, in Chapter 9, "Access to and within the academy," and in the Epilogue, we explore how a traditional university might gradually evolve toward mentoring. There, we imagine a developing relationship between an adult student (based on one of our own) and a fictional professor (derived from our experiences and observations). We invent a series of encounters in which they both learn how to engage in dialogue and they begin to imagine transforming the academy into a more nurturing, inclusive, and profound learning community.

Sources and acknowledgments

Our book about mentoring of course does not stand alone. We are participants in a profession, in which the labels "mentoring" and "adult education" are used somewhat interchangeably. Our ideas have been influenced by some of the basic works in this field. These include:

Stephen Brookfield, *Understanding and Facilitating Adult Learning* (1991).

Patricia Cross, *Adults as Learners* (1992).

Laurent Daloz, *Mentor: Guiding the Journey of Adult Learning* (1999).

Malcolm Knowles, *The Adult Learner* (1990).

Jack Mezirow, *Critical Reflection in Adulthood* (1990), and *Transformative Dimensions of Adult Learning* (1991).

Even if we do not make explicit reference to these sources in the chapters that follow, the ideas of these authors have certainly informed our own efforts to describe, practice, and understand the work we do with adult students.

We have jointly written articles and essays from which many ideas and examples in this book derive (e.g. Herman and Mandell 1996: 57–72; 1999: 17–38; 2000; Mandell and Herman 1996: 3–18; 2003: 77–89; as well as in the Empire State College journals *Golden Hill* and *All About Mentoring*, the latter of which we have separately been the editors). Of course, trying to practice what we preach, we have learned from ourselves, often changing and, we hope, improving the understandings and words we offered in those publications.

In addition, we have benefited from scholarly and amiable conversation with Jack Mezirow, Larry Daloz, and our colleague, Xenia Coulter. Their years of experience and especially their sensitivity to the particular qualities and needs of adult learners gave us encouragement and a ground on which to build our own work.

Over the years, we've been privileged and delighted to participate in the "Cambridge Conference" series. This biennial meeting was created and has been sustained by Roger Mills and Alan Tait, of the Open University in the East of England, who also have read, invited, and actively supported our ideas. The Cambridge Conferences have introduced and allowed us to participate in a genuinely international community of adult educators. We had the opportunity to learn about practices other than our own. In addition, the amiable, open, and genuinely collegial character of these meetings inspires and manifests the fundamental virtues of truthfulness, fairness, and beauty, which, as we suggest throughout this book, are the most important qualities of a dialogical learning community.

At Empire State College, we have been fortunate to have "grown up" among colleagues, our fellow mentors, whose commitment to serving adult students is intense, imaginative, and persevering, often over decades. All of us, in varying degrees, helped to create a public academic institution, whose policies and procedures for a long time have been specifically intended to welcome and support the individual learning of our students. No other college (so far as we know) – especially among publicly funded and "open" universities – so completely organized and conceived itself to provide access, scheduling, and curricular flexibility, and the "room" for students to collaborate with the faculty as companions in inquiry.

Each day, our students have invited us into their worlds of experience and curiosity. And we have brought them into this book. The many, many examples we offer here are based on our records and memories of the students with whom we have worked. We report, reconstruct, and explain. We have masked the names and other identifying details of our students' lives in order to respect their privacy. In addition, we have invented composite conversations with and portraits of students so as to help our readers quickly gain a detailed and, we hope, vivid entry into the experience of mentoring. Most important, our students, as they do *their* learning, have given *us* opportunities to learn about so many things which we would not otherwise have known. This includes not only what they intentionally study, but also the meaning of learning itself. When we are trying to nurture someone's learning, mentors must think carefully about how well we really know what we claim to know. We are grateful that our students have both tolerated our efforts to be learners with them and, indeed, have insisted that we be so.

Finally, we want to write a few words about how we wrote this book. Certainly it has been a collaboration. Much of what you read, we have written, word by word, together. By speaking with one another as we wrote, we discovered new understandings of material and ideas which we, separately or together, thought we already knew very well, or which either of us by ourselves would have been unlikely to know anything about at all. This includes the principles of mentoring themselves. In our collaboration, we are indeed mentors for one another. This book is a record of our learning.

Chapter 2

The principles of mentoring and the philosophy of dialogue

It is only too likely that neither of us has knowledge to boast of, but he thinks that he knows something which he does not know, whereas I am quite conscious of my ignorance. At any rate it seems that I am wiser than he is to this small extent, that I do not think that I know what I do not know.

Plato, *Apology* (21d)

At the beginning of Plato's *Republic* Socrates talks with an old man, Cephalus, who is taking stock of the long life he has lived and pondering what might be in store for him when he dies. He is filled with "doubt, surmises, and alarms and begins to reckon up," to see if he has ever treated anyone unjustly and, if he has, to make sure that he has made proper reparation and atonement (ibid.: 330e–331b). His anxious curiosity is at once practical and philosophical. Cephalus does not want to be punished for whatever injustices he may have committed; and he desires the happiness which comes from self-respect and moral integrity. Socrates then asks Cephalus what he believes justice to be.

Thus begins an enormous dialogue. Some five people join Socrates in the inquiry. By the time the conversation ends, they have taken up, in their effort to learn the meaning of justice, psychology, sociology, politics and government, history, economics and business, literature, science and mathematics, music, theology, metaphysics and ethics. The *Republic* introduces methods of pragmatic and liberal education; it also involves the participants and its readers in this comprehensive tour of human learning. A single question, so long as it is important to the learners, can open the world.

Two contending world views create the intellectual and social drama of the *Republic*. Thrasymachus represents one: justice is "nothing else than the advantage of the stronger" (ibid.: 338c). Might makes right; and the more power one has, the happier one will be. As befits a person who is certain only that one does not really know as much as one believes and that wisdom lies in continuing the inquiry, Socrates's definition is less precise: Justice is rendering the Good that is due to everyone (ibid.: 433a–e). Much of the *Republic* is a demonstration that Thrasymachus's position is impossible, both philosophically and practically. Even the most rapaciously ambitious people depend for their success on a deep assumption (held by themselves and others), that virtue is something more than power alone. And a life devoted to power is in fact miserable, dominated by fear and emptiness. Nonetheless, Socrates acknowledges that life in a purely just human society that disregards wealth and other kinds of worldly power will be, as Glaucon (one of the interlocutors) says, a life fit for "pigs" and other subhuman creatures (ibid.: 372e).

What, then, would be a good life, both morally just and materially successful? What would be an education that would help one learn to live such a life in an imperfect and dynamic human society? And finally, how could such questions be answerable if one begins with the assumption that all knowledge-claims are provisional and incomplete, or, as Socrates insists, that human wisdom consists in learning that one does not finally know what one believes one knows? These questions also frame the work of mentoring and suffuse the conversations of Doris and Alex with their mentors. Like Cephalus, we are all "reckoning up," trying to understand the lives we have had and lives we intend to live in the time remaining to us.

Doris

As I thought about Doris between our second and third face-to-face meetings, I realized that in talking with her again I wanted to emphasize two things. First, I wanted to make sure that she understood that anything she might do during her first enrollment would begin to help her move toward her degree goal. Second, I wanted to find something we could do together (a "learning contract," as our college calls a plan of study for any given enrollment period) that would directly respond to some of the many interests she had mentioned and had begun to jot down in a notebook I urged her to use as ideas popped into her head. "Just write these things down," I urged her. "Don't worry if it doesn't quite sound like what you think a university course title should be. Just asking yourself a question could be really useful." Yes, there was the recognition of a practical moment here, but I wanted to show Doris that college could also mean defining and carefully pursuing a topic she created herself.

Something else was important too. Although I was not aware of this at first, I began to see that Doris did have a reasonable level of self-confidence. For some adult students, by contrast, speaking about what they have done in current or past work or community experiences is incredibly difficult. One has to carefully and very gradually coax this learning out, convincing students along the way that their "accomplishments" are not only personally meaningful but legitimate and valuable in the context of university study as well. But even with important trust in herself, Doris,

I felt, really wanted me to know her best interest. She wanted me to be a more caring authority than she had known, but to be an authority nonetheless. Without adding yet another layer of anxiety to her fledgling university experience, I wanted to see if I could encourage her to participate in a significant way in making the decision about her first studies. True, Doris never said a word to me about having chosen this college because she was attracted to the ways of an innovative student-centered educational alternative. She was primarily here because it was convenient. But I was excited to show her that she would like and benefit from a way of studying she probably had never considered.

"Any ideas?" I asked while Doris adjusted her papers. In preparation for this meeting, Doris had continued to make lists of activities in which she has been involved in the past, including a few work-sponsored computer training programs she had completed, a literacy volunteer course that prepared her for work at the neighborhood school, and annual week-long study programs sponsored by her church. I'm more and more sure that her life has been full and that "study" (which often focused on topics she cared about quite deeply) has been significantly intertwined with her daily life. Doris does not yet think about herself as a successful "student," but her spirited and thoughtful involvement in myriad learning projects jumps off her list.

"I couldn't stop thinking about what you told me about the radio shows. I never thought I could study that in college. It's something I just like to do to relax. I just like collecting those tapes. Are you serious about including something about radio in my college work?" I hadn't forgotten this either. It was one of the topics that came up at the end of our second meeting and Doris had introduced it with obvious tentativeness (as if it were a more private topic that really had no place in this university context). Nonetheless, it was something that Doris really cared about. Moreover, this potential study topic both intrigued me and gave me pause. I quickly gathered that Doris knew more than I would ever know about "The Golden Age of Radio." As her mentor, what could I offer her? But her desire and my curiosity outweighed my hesitancy. "Yes, I think it makes sense to focus on this topic as one of your first two studies in this college. Let's see if we can begin to outline what you will do."

Actually, we saw that it was not difficult to begin to structure this learning contract. Doris had a topic that she cared about; I saw my role as guiding her and helping her to learn about the rudiments of scholarly work. So our conversation turned to the library resources available to her, how she could learn about on-line research, how she would keep track of the information and ideas contained in what she read, and what it meant to develop an annotated bibliography. (I was pleased that in this way, Doris would also be gaining more comfort with the tools of scholarship that she could continue to use as her university studies developed.) Further, Doris realized that she could use this study as an opportunity to organize the radio tapes she had and to visit The Museum of Broadcasting (where she had never been) in order to listen to particular shows she knew of but had never heard, and to investigate materials with which she was not familiar.

Doris had another idea, which we decided to incorporate into the contract as well. She wondered about the "experience" of listening and about the memories of those who spent so many hours "glued" to the popular radio programs of the day. Thus, in another learning activity, Doris was going to develop a short questionnaire and carry out her own empirical research on people's experience of this Golden Age. And, there was a final component that I proposed. I thought it would be important for Doris to try to place radio within the context of American popular culture, a broad area of study I thought Doris would find fascinating. This would serve as an effective way for Doris to complete her project. She would take what she had learned about the influence of the radio in American life and link it to some key issues in American society. And perhaps those issues – such as how the media influence people's expectations might connect with the church-based social services to which she was so dedicated. To what extent, for example, were the troubles impelling people to seek those services caused by dashed hopes raised by mass entertainment and advertising?

But while we excitedly sketched out this study, I knew full well, as I continued to emphasize to Doris as we drafted the learning contract, sitting together at the computer, that the particulars of her activities would shift as she got more and more deeply involved in the reading and research. Her curiosity would evolve. I also knew we couldn't neglect the more practical side of Doris's university work. She still had to respond to the demands of her job and to its expectation that she earn a degree in business. Actually, Doris was genuinely interested in further business studies, particularly because she knew there were areas of personnel, management, and budgeting that not only responded to her employer's demands, but also that she wanted to learn as a part of her hope of designing and heading a social service agency focused on children and the services they need.

In the second study component of this enrollment, we thus decided to do a number of interrelated things. First, Doris was anxious about how many credits she could earn from her "work experience." At this stage, I really had little idea myself and wanted Doris to know that I wasn't hiding any information from her. What I did know was that Doris could now begin to effectively use the lists she had been developing as building blocks for fuller written descriptions of her "prior learning." That is, she could write about what she had done and learned over the years in her business-related formal trainings and through her experiences in local businesses. She could create a portfolio of her knowledge in the business area that could allow her to see what she had accomplished and that could provide a faculty member with an organized and well documented presentation of her knowledge and her skills.

The problem was, as she was quick to point out, she had no idea how to do this! "How do I know what I know? I don't know the words. When I think about my work, I have no idea if or what's worth anything." Thus, a second activity involved Doris in looking at other college programs in Business and at a general college text, an "Introduction to Business." In this way, she could begin to familiarize herself with the terms and divisions of the discipline, and thus begin to cluster her experiences around such categories. We both acknowledged that this work would be comparatively concrete and a good complement to her exploration of "The Golden Age of Radio."

As she was leaving my office, an odd occurrence gave us the final activity of this component of her enrollment. "Oh you have that book," Doris said pointing to Barbara Ehrenreich's new book, *Nickel and Dimed* that was piled on my table. "I read a review of it. Sounds interesting." "Would you like to read it now?" I asked. "I think it would nicely fit into this study. It could be another way to think about people's work experiences and the factors that influence the ways they try to balance work, home, bills, and relationships. It's actually connected to business and to your interest in poverty and social services, too." So we added Ehrenreich to Doris's second study and I felt, certainly for the moment, that we had created something together that would be fair, balanced, and manageable. It seemed like a good way to start.

Alex

During our first meeting, Alex had stopped describing his history and his hopes, to ask a question: "I don't know. What do you think?" I might have said the same: I'm completely fascinated by this complex person, but I don't really know what to make of him or how to respond.

I need him to help me make a workable connection between his dense matrix of desires and abilities (economic, social, intellectual, soulful, each of them openly and deeply personal) and the academic possibilities of the college I represent. I'm neither a therapist nor a substitute for the parents from whom Alex divorced himself years ago. (I remember, while I'm quickly thinking of what to say to Alex, that the mentor archetypes in Homer's *Odyssey*, Athena and Mentor, are the substitutes for Telemachus's distracted mother and his long-absent father.) Nonetheless, I can see that any educational composition Alex undertakes will, for him, necessarily resonate with tones much deeper within him than the notes written on an academic score.

Alex has an almost childlike neediness, as well as the fragmentary sophistication of an adolescent intellectual, to explore "everything." Many life possibilities are open to him to create and choose – many more openings than most older students believe they have. Yet, he has a child; he's about to be married; and he has a job which both supports and constricts him. Like most adult students I've known, he's as serious about learning as he is about completing a degree. He's uninterested in the social or "collegial" life of higher education. However, he contentedly inhabits fewer and thinner communities than older students do – workplaces, civic and religious organizations, circles of friends etc. Alex thus lacks their "general" learning and, to some extent, their more overtly instrumental attitudes towards further "higher" education. For Alex, the "fundamental questions" and the relevance of the "great books" and "great ideas" are very much at the surface of his curiosity. They urgently beckon him, almost unmanageably all at once. To be sure, for older students, these profound matters await attention too, but more implicitly, and they will usually emerge slowly and discretely, after the sifting and settling of much more practical issues. Like other adults, Alex wants to know how quickly he can complete a degree that will help him get on in the world, but, right at the start, he very deliberately and self consciously wants to use the academy and the guidance of a "mentor" to help him with a journey of the soul. How can I connect with these important facets of curiosity and learning which Alex presents to me? And how can I help make connections manageable within both my own and Alex's "systems" of work?

After an anxious couple of minutes of hurriedly identifying these issues, I tell Alex that I want to think about what he's said. I tell him about some of the flexibilities and the requirements of *this* college. Offering some examples, I explain that he can design his studies and his curriculum to suit his own interests and purposes, but that there are certain expectations of academic coherence and of academic "breadth" or "general education" he will have to meet. I tell him that he can set the pace of his studies and arrange his tutorial appointments to suit his schedule, but that my own busy schedule and the academic progress requirements of my college – however liberal they are – will not give him unlimited flexibility. I tell him that he can learn whatever he wants, however he defines his curiosity, but that if he decides to have his company pay, he will have to accommodate their expectations. And I tell him that if he chooses to acquire a degree in a specific academic "discipline" or as preparation for a particular profession for which there are strong, commonly understood traditional requirements, he will have to address those as well. However, I also emphasize to him that he does not have to resolve these issues now, and that in fact in this college we can begin by exploring them together, intellectually, and in fact as topics of academic study.

But, above all, I tell Alex that I simply don't know and, without his collaboration, can't know, what will be the best academic steps for him to take. I ask him to take some time to think about these things, just as I need to do. And I promise him that when we meet again soon, we will work together on creating a manageable tutorial study that helps us better understand and deal with the issues before us. Alex's body relaxes, a little; the flush has left his face. He looks tired but eager, and he agrees to continue.

A week or so later, Alex and I meet again. We try to find a focus for a first tutorial study. We are looking together for a topic, a question or theme, "a way in," that will respond to several criteria: something academically manageable (not the "everything" Alex wants to learn), but something genuinely engaging his curiosity and suiting his abilities; something "work-related" enough to be approved by his company, but not limited to the business of making steel; something that will address my college's "general education" requirements but not be intellectually constricting and superficial; and something both of us believe will be a good start on preparing an educational and possibly professional future still largely unformed and unknown to both of us.

Alex has clearly been thinking about these issues. He eagerly and fully participates in our conversation. He has no trouble understanding the pile of possibilities and criteria which both complicate and define our situation. And once I see this, I realize that he and I are beginning to identify and explicate a general theme which, usually much more implicitly, influences the educational experiences and choices of so many working adult students. Alex is a curious and autonomous individual trying to learn how to thrive in all the many aspects of his life, from the most intimately satisfying profound experiences to ones which seem to lack any but implacably demanding instrumental value. His life is both contemplative and laborious. He wants to be materially successful in a career to which he is committed, and he wants to be profoundly learned. Can he learn to do all of this? Can anyone? These abstract questions vibrate right at the surface of Alex's statements. In diverse forms and often much more implicitly, they are questions common to nearly every student I've encountered. These questions define our uncertainty – Alex's and my own. And they also begin to define for us an inquiry, a topic of *learning*.

I gradually begin to understand through our exploratory conversation that this uncertainty about, and tension between, the person as individual learner and the person as inhabitant of multiple roles can become "a way in," and could become an academic topic. And, in so many words, I tentatively put it to Alex as the subject of our first tutorial study. He catches on and brightens up even more. We can shape and name the theme to be relevant to his employers: "adults as learners and workers." It could easily address and draw from many of the interests Alex has expressed (psychology, sociology, philosophy, literature), and it can embrace what he likes to do: think, read, and write. And both the material he might read and the academic skills he'll be exercising will also begin to fulfill the "general education" requirements he'll have to satisfy (for example, in the humanities and social sciences, and in academic research and composition).

Each of us then draws from our respective reservoirs to make a list of readings to do. These include Plato's *Apology* (both literature and philosophy); Vivian Paley, *You Can't Say You Can't Play* (schools, individuation and socialization); John Dewey, *Experience and Education*, as well as E.D. Hirsch, *Cultural Literacy* (for a debate about what it means to be "educated" in a democratically constituted and workplace driven society); Freud, *Civilization and Its Discontents* (psychology and cultural anthropology); and various selections from Karl Marx for a critical and political perspective on economics. Alex will read his way along. We'll meet about every other week to discuss what he's read and connections he's made to his experiences and observations at work and elsewhere. From those discussions, he and I will devise topics for brief analytical and research-based essays. And, no doubt, when we approach the end of this study, some sixteen weeks from now, Alex will have formed more ideas and more questions from which we can plan further studies.

I will evaluate his learning on the basis of our discussions, his essays, and also on the clarity of ideas and questions he's posing at the end of this study. Perhaps Alex will have even begun to make some decisions about how he wants to shape the remainder of his education and what sort of career he wants to prepare for. I don't know for sure that this will happen, but Alex and I know how to begin.

System and power; lifeworld and wonder

We will return to the six principles of mentoring listed in our first chapter and show how they govern our work with Doris and Alex. Now, however, we want to describe briefly a conceptual perspective we've found useful in understanding the tension between pragmatic and contemplative concerns which frequently both disturbs and enriches the education of our students.

Like so many adult (and younger) students, Doris and Alex need university degrees to get ahead in the world. They need this certification to make money and to secure and enhance their status. To some extent, their educational pragmatism is forced upon them, but they have also internalized such expectations. They depend upon their employers to finance their learning, and their employers expect their learning to be useful. Almost any university, including our own, imposes additional requirements, regardless of student interest, consistent with its assumptions about what it means to be "educated." Doris and Alex look upon these diverse institutional demands with a mixture of trepidation, oppression, and ambition. More or less eagerly, they will do what is necessary to obtain the support, certification, and post-academic opportunity they desire. Like Thrasymachus, they expect to find happiness (including a kind of economic justice) in power. But Doris and Alex sense that such a view of life is insufficient; they are also inspired with wonder. They are curious, even passionate, about learning which will help them understand the meanings of their own and others' lives, regardless of its "use value." Their curiosity focuses on different particulars (Golden Age of Radio, for example, for Doris; for

Alex, reading Freud). Most generally, they want to understand what is true, what is just, and what is beautiful. However, they do not expect that this difference between practical and contemplative learning will fit well into the sort of coherent education, which Aristotle (who first articulated the distinction) supposed to be naturally appropriate for human beings (*Nichomachean Ethics* 1947: 1022–1036; *Politics*: 1277–1316). For Doris and Alex, as perhaps for most people in the modern world, the difference between practical and contemplative learning is experienced as a conflict, even a contradiction.

An historically and philosophically helpful way to understand this problem in modern societies is through the terms "system" and "life-world." We shall use them throughout this book. Much of our own learning about them comes from the work of Jürgen Habermas (*The Theory of Communicative Action* 1984, 1989).

Human beings control their environments, including each other, with systems. This is how we amplify and extend the powers of our bodies and minds upon the phenomena we experience. It is how we accomplish the instrumental projects and live in the practical dimension of our lives. These systems, whether social or physical, are constructed and controlled with tools, both physical devices and the technologies with which we invent and manufacture them. Further, systems are supposed to be entirely rational. That is, knowledgeable people, "experts," claim (and the rest of us tend to believe) that systems are constructable, operational, predictable, and controllable entirely according to intelligible rules and calculations. Far from being mysterious or beyond complete and certain comprehension, systems are either entirely known or entirely knowable.

Perhaps because we are so awed by the power systems bestow – wealth, information, political order, social infrastructure, ostensible control over the natural world – that we take such power to be an end-in-itself and to be completely extendable to all human purposes and objects of curiosity and desire. Just as with similar ease we confuse lust for love, we believe that everything on earth and in the heavens can be systemized, possessed, and transformed into both the necessary and sufficient conditions for our happiness. In consequence, we live in a world "colonized" by systems (Habermas 1984). And, as Socrates would have prophesied, we are not happy. We live in a "disenchanted" world (Weber 1946b).

Enmeshed in systems – schools, workplaces, markets, government, and other bureaucracies, even places of play and of worship – we feel, including the most privileged among us, confused and controlled. Violence becomes more barbaric; economic and other "quality of life" disparities become more extreme; and the planet is more toxic for the human species. To be sure, human life in a world without systems would be chaotic and poor; but in a world dominated by systems alone, by our desire for power, we would also find our lives to be "solitary, poor, nasty, brutish, and short" (Hobbes, *Leviathan* 1962: 100). These are ironic results for the enduring human project that is supposed to make the world intelligible and our own (cf. Beniger 1986; Gandy 1993; Tenner 1996).

People want to escape from these disturbing consequences. Doris and Alex are spared the savagery experienced by so many less fortunate people. But they are aware that their insecurities (for example, Doris's worry about making a living and Alex's about his unhealthy work environment) are not merely personal. They, like so many other students, hope that university degrees will protect them. However, they will have to struggle to manage the sometimes alienating curricular and scheduling demands of the academic system itself, along with constrictions imposed by other social and economic institutions. Moreover, they may not have considered yet whether their degrees will be sufficient for their modest and honorable ambitions. They live in a society where "lifelong learning" is celebrated, but also where, due to advances in technical knowledge and the "efficiencies" of a competitive economic system, most any particular set of intellectual credentials soon becomes obsolete.

Systems-thinking, however necessary, is insufficient for human purposes. Its acquisitive and controlling kind of rationality gives us neither the coherent understanding nor the freedom, and not even the reasonably secure material comfort we need to live meaningful lives. To follow our yearning and wonder for ends-in-themselves – truth, justice, beauty – we draw upon the "lifeworld." As deployed by Habermas and his predecessors, "lifeworld" refers to that aspect of our experience in which we allow phenomena, including all living beings, to disclose themselves, gradually and provisionally, as they are (Habermas 1989; Husserl 1970). From the lifeworld perspective, we do not seek to "grasp" people, ideas, or objects by reducing them entirely to data and rules (such as scientific theories or economic and governmental laws). We are not seeking the power to control things to suit our predictions and desires. Rather, we are seeking a kind of understanding inspired by wonder, through which we are always open to anything being greater than what we already believe we know.

The lifeworld is palpable in the joys we take in our daily encounters with and recognition of things before we have apparently complete explanations of them. Lifeworld learning occurs when we follow our curiosity for its own sake, because we are delighted by our discoveries and simultaneously by the awareness that there is always more to learn about whatever we are gradually understanding. And we experience the lifeworld when we treat ourselves and others with respect – that is, by recognizing that we are all intrinsically precious for our own sakes rather than for our "use-value," as mere instruments to serve our ambitions.

The lifeworld, in other words, is the domain of freedom. We do not control it; we never fully know it. But, by the same token, we can not exhaust or deplete it as a "resource." From the lifeworld perspective, nothing and no one is expendable; everything and everyone is a source of wonder. The lifeworld may therefore seem an irrational delusion to people who believe in only scientific and technological truths. But the necessity of the lifeworld is evident enough when, in response to the confusion and oppression of our lives when we try to thrive in a material and intellectual world dominated by systems alone, we know there must be something essential missing.

Mentors, therefore, are educators who try to help themselves and their students negotiate this tension between the lifeworld and systems. Just as we respect and serve the learning our students seek for their practical purposes, we nurture their efforts to reveal and understand their lifeworlds. Mentors help students complete appropriate academic degrees. Mentors also are adept at creating and sustaining learning environments in which the deeper anxieties underlying that ambition can safely emerge as opportunities for inquiry, as sources of wonder.

We ask our readers to return with this understanding to the principles of mentoring which we briefly identified in Chapter 1.

The principles of mentoring

1 Authority and uncertainty: act so that what you believe you know is only provisionally true

This is the most fundamental maxim of the six. We take it from the Socratic effort to learn wisdom – that is, the virtue of understanding how little and incompletely one knows even what one is inclined to believe one knows thoroughly and finally. Knowledge is provisional – a circumstance which might be frustrating but one which makes the world, everything, and everyone in it an endless wonderment.

And thus, among the sources of wonder, ignorance, and learning for mentors are their students. We do not and cannot know a priori what our students, collectively or individually, need to learn, what they are curious about or how they learn best. More than "diagnosing" or evaluating our students, mentors need to "learn" them; we need to pay very careful attention to them and listen to what they have to say for themselves. Indeed, we may well discover, and often do, that our students can inform us quite well about themselves as learners and, even more, that they possess more in-depth and extensive knowledge about their fields of interest than they realize. This is knowledge from which we ourselves can learn.

In order to know the provisionality and limits of our own knowledge, and to notice the openings into the learning others possess, mentors have to be keenly and vigilantly self-reflective. We engage in dialogue within ourselves, as though we were always accompanied by an inner questioning spirit, a Socratic *daimon*. Making an obvious practice of this virtue (for example, by asking questions of others for which we too should genuinely like to know an answer) encourages our students to do the same. We "teach" critical thinking by modeling it ourselves. We help students – who, after all, like to be as certain in their own beliefs as professors like to be in theirs – accept the provisionality of knowledge by taking the time to go back over things, to ask new questions, and to reconsider seemingly settled conclusions. When we are doing our work well, our students learn, as we do, that all learning is lifelong.

This fluid process of education does not exist in a vacuum. For mentors and students, it occurs within the multiple contexts of their lives, and particularly within the context where they share experience: the academic institution. By their nature, such institutions, as species of complex formal systems, gain their power because they are repositories of expertise, of, so to say, "settled" knowledge. Inevitably, faculties and administrators are encouraged to believe that they know more than they really do, especially when it comes to supposed knowledge about what students need. In this way, universities, even deliberately "innovative" ones, can too easily become poor environments for the practice of mentoring. On the other hand, the university also claims prestige and legitimate authority as a home to the life of the mind. It is a place of inquiry, of scholarship, whose entire nature is animated by the belief that there is always more to know and know better. In this regard, mentoring is simply the application of the principle of scholarship to the practices of nurturing student learning. The same values, freedoms, policies, and rules that encourage a life of the mind for scholars should apply to the work faculty and students do together.

Of course faculty and administrators will exercise power, but they must restrain this behavior. This restraint is especially important when they are exercising executive authority "for the good of the students," for "academic quality," for "efficient allocation of resources," and/or for the "political and economic necessity of meeting external requirements." It is just at those moments that faculty and administrators must take extra care to be critically reflective and scrutinize the grounds of their decisions. Exactly what are the meaning and basis of the "good" and the "quality" we are imposing? Does the "efficiency" we are seeking in fact compromise and constrict the educational freedom of inquiry, teaching, and learning we claim to serve? How "necessary" are the "requirements" to which we are called upon to respond? Would we not be doing better to question and challenge the powers presiding over us?

2 Diversity of curriculum: people learn best when they learn what draws their curiosity

Curiosity and thus learning thrive when connected to and/or emergent from contexts which are familiar and meaningful to the learner. John Dewey repeatedly demonstrated and advocated this vital relationship between education and "ordinary" experience (Dewey 1963). The "world as it is" does not necessarily impede learning; indeed, the one animates the other.

Carefully gathered empirical evidence but unintentional support for this claim comes from E.D. Hirsch's influential book, *Cultural Literacy: What Every American Needs to Know* (1987). Although he argues for a kind of "national curriculum," his research on how people efficiently and stably acquire accurate reading skills in fact supports the conclusion that people are more likely to become good readers when the content of their reading lessons is familiar. He uses the data to advocate a standardized curriculum: if everyone is required to learn the same cognitive context, to share the same "background" knowledge or "literacy," then everyone will have a better and roughly equal chance of quickly and thoroughly acquiring the basic skills of reading and writing (Hirsch 1987: 36–69).

Ironically, the results of Hirsch's research can serve just as well to support exactly the opposite conclusion: if students in the same classroom, the same school or even the same nation, have diverse "cultural literacies," it would be better for the teaching of basic skills to similarly diversify the content of people's studies so that they can learn those basic skills more readily in response to familiar and genuinely engaging material. Of course it might be a good thing for "every American" to know who George Washington was. But it also might be far more important for the teaching of basic academic skills to focus instead on what children are curious about in their diverse worlds. Perhaps they are already "expert" about baseball or soccer and passionately want to learn more. Perhaps their parents recently emigrated from Senegal and everyday disappear for many hours into the city to earn a living. Such children may deeply want and need to understand the geography and society of this environment at once so familiar and so strange. Surely all these topics and countless more can provide material for learning to read, to write and to do math. And, if it is the preservation of Western democracy that conservative educators care so much about, what better way for children to learn about democracy than by beginning to practice it at school, by having some say in their learning? Further, as Dewey suggests, if we begin with students by honoring and using the immediate contents of their curiosity, they will be all the more likely to happily expand their interests into unfamiliar places. Indeed, as Hirsch and many others have observed, children begin by wanting to learn anything and everything. Yet, "school" often constricts and stifles that very curiosity by imposing what "everyone ought to know." We miss the students' very reason for learning.

The first principle – the provisionality and incompleteness of knowledge – requires that we question and challenge proposals for standardized curricula. Who knows so much and so well as to proclaim that this information rather than that is most important for every person to know? Does not such a claim of expertise rest on the assumption that the persons making that claim know everything important there is to know about "America" or any nation in which one lives? How well does this claim take into account the obvious facts that, for example, Western societies have always been culturally diverse, are only becoming more so (especially as they proudly claim to be growing more "global"), and that this very diversity is a just reason for pride? Rather than presenting a grave practical obstacle to or morale problem for national unity, the diversity of our students' "literacies" should be understood as an opportunity to expand the legitimacy of curiosity and the practical likelihood that everyone will learn not only "basic skills" well but also unfamiliar topics. The second principle is a principle of equality amidst diversity: If each person's curiosity is valued as much as every other person's, then everyone will be more eager to learn anything. The second principle is a kind of academic application of "the Golden Rule." Thus, the greater the diversity of learning, the better served is everyone's knowledge. The more mentors appreciate their students' diverse curiosity, the more learned we all become.

To learn our students' curiosity, mentors must become very attentive listeners. And this takes time. If we see students not as generic vessels to be filled by the knowledge we believe we have to pour into them, but as complexly experienced individuals, we often find ourselves trying to "learn" them, to "locate" them precisely by the very features which are likely to be *un*familiar to us. Experimenting and exploring are important. Thus, the content of a curriculum for each student is gradually discovered rather than prescribed. Moreover, because mentor and student continue to learn more about the implications of the latter's curiosity as they proceed (as the incompleteness principle above suggests they should), a projected curriculum must be seen not as fixed, but as malleable, as subject to improvisation. Curricular diversity then means that no single program content will necessarily be appropriate for even a roughly homogeneous group of students. It also means that even individual students might very valuably change their curricular plans with which they began. Such revisions are also forms of learning.

So of course here too there is a tension between a principle of mentoring and the normal character of institutions. Universities, for example, are attracted to standardized curricula (just as other kinds of institutions try to standardize everything from training programs, production methods, and product lines through employee schedules, salaries, and social behavior). Yet, whatever the institution, a huge presumptuousness is required to seriously believe that one knows what is the knowledge most important for everyone to learn. However, with a self-critical eye on their own influence, administrators are responsible for preserving the ability of faculty and students to decide what a valuable education will be. And, in the same spirit, faculty are responsible for respecting and nurturing the wonder of each one of their students. A diversity of learning opportunities invites people to transform their curiosity into learning which is achievable, academically substantial, and lasting far beyond the award of credit.

3 Autonomy and collaboration: treat all learning projects, all studies, as occasions for dialogue, rather than for transmissions of knowledge from expert to novice

Principles 1 and 2 cohere with and suggest a third fundamental idea. People not only learn for themselves, they learn by themselves, not as solitary beings but as autonomous ones. All learning is active, an achievement of the learner. Even so-called "passive" learners, limply awaiting instruction at the back of the classroom, have made decisions: they will learn the minimum they calculate required of them, and they will do so by imitating what they hear. Some teachers disparage such students, but then only encourage their real or apparent submissiveness by treating them as empty vessels to be filled with whatever information the teacher chooses to pour therein. By contrast, mentors look for the locus of independent curiosity we believe exists, no matter how initially muted, in every student. This autonomy becomes the center of cognitive care. We ask, at every opportune moment and with every inviting variation we can muster, "What do you want to learn?" As we go along, we go farther, asking, "With what methods – such as reading, interviewing, writing – do you think you can best learn what you want to know?" And we continue to ask these questions with ever greater specificity until students (sometimes swiftly, sometimes slowly) become more deliberate developers of their own learning projects.

It is essential to note, however, that even these "open" questions (i.e. questions to which the mentor does not pre-possess the answers) are instances of collaboration. Learning implies a community, a dialogue. All knowledge, to be intelligibly distinguished from delusion, requires the active presence of the voice of an "other," a voice that questions and seeks to understand the meaning and basis of one's offered belief. Usually, this voice is literal and external; it is another person, sometimes more than one. Mentors, focussing their care and attention on each student, help their students comfortably participate in such dialogue and gradually internalize it. The questioning voice becomes internal and metaphorical. Hearing us asking them, our students learn to ask questions of themselves. Just as mentors must engage in reflective practice, so students learn to do the same. Listening carefully to one another, seeking to understand the meaning and the possible truth of what the other says, we – mentors and students – learn not only about the topic at hand but also nurture and listen to an internal "other," the Socratic "little spirit" or *daimonion*, which helps us learn for and teach ourselves. In this way, mentors in the very act of "teaching" and students in the very act of "learning," are acting as scholars. They take in all that they hear or read from others. They care for the questions they ask of themselves, because others have honored those expressions of curiosity. They apply all the intuitive, imaginative, and reasoning faculties of the mind to create new understandings, perhaps even ones which have never been achieved before.

Such collaboration creates not only learning but also a polity, a particular dynamic distribution of authority. As parents nurture their children to become stronger (rather than imitations of themselves or as extensions of their unfulfilled dreams), so do mentors help their students become autonomous minds fully engaged in the lives they propose to live. The mentor-student collaboration is thus like a continuously emergent democracy, in which every voice has the right to be fully heard and understood, and in which all participants are at liberty more and more to act as they choose.

The formal context in which these academic dialogues occur, the university, is also a polity. Its rules and procedures also imply ascriptions and distributions of authority. Thus, in order for the institution to be a good home for student-mentor dialogues, its rules and procedures must be loose, flexible and even ambiguous enough for students to develop and practice the autonomy customarily accorded only to faculty. Administrators need to be leaders of a community which supports collaborative decisions and does not mystify or abort communication. Faculty need to shape discussions so that students gain experience in a polity in which all participants are free to say what they really believe and can expect to be thoroughly heard. And students need to say what they mean and need to be, like every other "citizen," responsible for considering the implications and questioning the truth of their ideas. Inevitably, the faculty and administrators will be the final arbiters of credits and degrees. But they should be vigilant in looking after the culture of their institution so that differences of opinion between themselves and their students don't have to be arbitrarily settled. It is in this way that universities, in turn, can support the practice of democracy in the larger societies in which they participate.

4 Learning from the lifeworld: treat all participants to an inquiry as whole persons

Learning is multi-contextual. Adult students in particular simultaneously inhabit many spheres of life encompassing their academic studies: their work, families, neighborhoods, places of worship, and other public communities; their large fields of memory and, often, their anticipations of their children's futures. It is from these non-academic and non-bookish contexts that students create meaning and purpose for their studies. Far from subjective or idiosyncratic, these sources of intellectual motivation connect people to the larger world. Following their individual curiosity, students encounter the broad and powerful economic, political, aesthetic, moral, and epistemic structures and themes of their history and society. The academic system must welcome its students' lifeworlds.

This is a demanding requirement. Formal organizations acquire power with rules, steady fiscal streams, standardization, efficiency, and the specialization or divisions of expertise and labor. They sustain their efficacy with the sometimes helpful myth that the codification of those features in the form of policy can serve as the functional equivalent of absolute knowledge. This is a confusion (which, contrary to Principle 1, neglects the provisionality and incompleteness of human learning) perhaps all the more likely to occur in the academy, because we all – faculty and administrators – are the cultural leaders of the so-called "knowledge business."

The duty of self-scrutiny nonetheless remains. We are more likely to be responsible to it if we see our roles and our institutions not so much as sacrosanct but as nurturing. In such an institution, the formal codification of content and activity will be formally provisional, perhaps convenient starting points, statistically normal but otherwise not normative. That is, the normal academic expectations of the institution will not be taken as ends-in-themselves, but as material malleable to the students' lifeworlds. The place and time, schedule and sources of learning will easily accommodate the diversity of individual student needs. Efficiency of knowledge production within typical time frames and resource circumstances will not be confused with intelligence, aptitude, or seriousness of purpose. The required content of curriculum will be adjustable to student purposes and curiosity, as will the permeability of traditional disciplinary boundaries and academic specialties. In these ways, the university, or any learning environment, becomes not just an absolutist system of productive functions and functionaries, but a human community fostering an illimitable diversity of lifeworlds.

5 Evaluation as reflective learning: judge the quality of learning in the movement of the dialogue; expect that the content of individual outcomes will be, like all knowledge claims, incomplete and diverse

For all their collaborativeness, mentors must evaluate student learning; for all their flexibility and openness, academies alone award credits and grant degrees. Other reasons aside, were this not the case, students would have no practical need of the publicly certified learning the academy offers. Institutions require consistently identifiable, if not exactly measurable products. This is not only a requirement of the universities from which students seek degrees but also of the workplaces for which, so often, students need those degrees. How, then, is learning achieved in dialogue to be evaluated so as to be true to its nature and also understandable and credible to the world beyond the academy?

If learning is always provisional and incomplete (Principle 1), there is an inevitable arbitrariness in saying this or that shall be the outcome. On the other hand, if learning is collaborative (Principle 3), including the planning of its goals, then outcomes which the collaborators agree upon will be contractually constructed, not imposed. If, further, the collaborators, including the students, participate in the actual assessment of the learning, comparing what has been done with what has been intended, then the evaluation process will not only be collaborative, but also part of the diverse and reflective learning which occurs in dialogue (Principle 2). For these reasons, mentors involve their students in establishing the intended outcomes of learning projects and in evaluating what and how much has been achieved when the projects have reached the intended conclusions. In effect, mentors assess learning not so much in relation to a generically given or a priori "product," but in relation to a dialogically drawn line of developing understanding they and their students have traveled since the beginning of the inquiry.

What then happens to the consistency and standardization commonly demanded by academic and other workplace systems? The learning sought by adult students is richly contextual (Principle 4). They enter college loaded with the "real" world, not in retreat from it. In dialogical education, they have the freedom to follow their curiosity and the responsibility to accept the implications of their purposes (Principles 2 and 3). Their curiosity and purposes will inevitably connect them to the larger worlds implicit in their initially conscious thoughts and hopes (Principle 4). They will therefore encounter the formal learning and other preparations commonly expected of those who intend to enter and thrive in those larger domains of life. Perhaps those expectations will not be easily met – for example, the entrance requirements of a graduate school or of a profession. However, because they have begun with their own curiosity and purposes, students will have an intrinsic motivation to succeed, to discover for themselves they must learn. But what if those expectations are too many, too dull, too alien, or just too taxing? Then, students may reevaluate their purposes and revise their plans. This also is learning. The provisionality of one's understanding – in this instance, one's knowledge of one's own intentions – is a necessary and laudable part of the dialogical process (Principle 1).

We have been writing as though planning and evaluating were not only related but intertwined throughout the process of dialogical learning. And so they are. Taking stock, reconsidering, and revising what one believes to be true (Principle 1) assume that one is comparing one thing to another (a speculation to a fact, an intention to an outcome) and then making a judgment about the difference. These assessments are not suspended until the end of a study, but, as we say, recur throughout. The final or summative evaluation, the one "for the record," marks how far one has come over a longer but well-defined period, the formal beginning and the formal conclusion of the study. This idea applies just as well to planning an entire curriculum or to preparing for a career.

In the same way, the faculty and administrators of universities and other learning programs must vigilantly and collaboratively evaluate themselves. And they must include their students in these institutional and personnel evaluations (Principle 3). Further, because our expectations and evaluative criteria must not exceed what we really understand, because we must acknowledge our own ignorance and respect the diversity of our students' learning, we should be especially critical of rigidly standardized "outcomes assessment." Such assessments are seductive because they hold before us seemingly stable, unequivocal, and precisely quantifiable achievements. These are the simulacra of absolute knowledge. All the more reason to question them. Moreover, one's resistance to adopting such outcome expectations can be overwhelmed because they often emanate from powers beyond the university (e.g. economic and political institutions). The leaders of universities and the external powers to whom they answer must be brought into the dialogical process.

Every polity, every human system, not just the university, depends on learning. All human associations make claims and assumptions about what is true and important; they are therefore responsible for asking and listening to questions about those beliefs. Among these claims and assumptions are the demands made upon those over whom power and authority are exercised. Just like any other claims to knowledge, those demands, those "standards," must be seen as objects of critical, reflective examination, and thus as provisional and revisable. If we "standard-setters," whether administrators or faculty, demand as much dialogical learning from ourselves as we do from our students, we will be able to give to our students all the freedom and support they need to learn as much as they can. Moreover, we are likely to be happily surprised at how much they will achieve.

6 Individual learning and the knowledge most worth having: honor and engage each student's individual desire to know and every student will learn what is important

The academy worries that if students are left to their own devices and follow their own interests, higher learning will become hopelessly idiosyncratic, "the disciplines" impossibly chaotic, and humanity will lose access to the very best knowledge in its heritage and the most up-to-date skills for being productive in the world. The "culture wars" more or less formally initiated in the United States by Hirsch, Bloom, and others in the 1980s continue. And, at the moment, judging by the eagerness with which American universities (including, sadly, our own) and schools have adopted standardized curricula and rigid outcomes assessments, we admit that the traditionalists have the upper hand, for now (Aronowitz 2000; Mandell and Herman 2001). However, these expectations presume not only that the academy already houses all the knowledge most worth having, but also that "ordinary" experience is thin and that only experts lead students to intellectually deep and broad learning. We have asserted the contrary (e.g. Principles 1 and 4).

We do not agree with the claims of post-modernism that knowledge is merely a social construction of reality (Berger and Luckmann 1966), or that all knowledge is reducible to not truth but power (Foucault 1973). We claim rather that the illimitable provisionality and incompleteness of learning (Principle 1) means that mentors are obliged to be learners. This includes taking their students' curiosity (Principle 2) and experience (Principle 4) as legitimate and essential guides to education. By learning from our students what they want to learn and what they have lived, we help them and ourselves discover connections to everything human beings care to know.

That is, mentors help students see and create connections between their own seemingly fragmentary pieces of reality and, potentially, the entire universe and every possible way of understanding it. These expanding connections are not limited to pragmatic endeavors (Principle 4). They include all the academic disciplines, however they have been or will be organized. Any human experience can be meaningful in all directions. The would-be accountant, for example, may wonder about the numbers and formulas she learns. What are they? Why do they work? What makes "things" – natural or human-made – reliably countable and calculable? Will she be struck by the beauty of a universe at once so orderly and yet alluringly beyond absolute comprehension? She may wonder where her profession came from. Why have human beings come to love "money"? Why do we often try to make it look pretty or elegant (as well as hard to copy)? What makes a piece of paper or metal token (usually, in modern societies, nearly valueless in themselves) into "currency" and into such incredibly powerful instruments of economic growth? Is the flow and distribution of these monies not only accurate but also truly honest and just? What makes humans greedy yet bother so much about being fair? These questions will necessarily take her into history, sociology, and psychology. There are these and so many more questions and connections that we, her mentors, may have never thought of. This student's questions will stimulate our own.

Mentors must act on the assumption that in every grain of sand or seeming bit of trivia (as it might seem at first to us) all possible learning awaits. In every student's curiosity and experience lie potential universes of connections and curricula. These tremendous and splendid possibilities wait in every moment of dialogue. By the same token, they are inexhaustible; no curriculum can cover them all. (How preposterous then to impose a "general" education on everyone, which claims to "expose" people to something just like that!) But because these possibilities always wait everywhere, mentors learn to wait too, helping students to become more confident and even more eager to follow their curiosity wherever it leads. This nurturing of wonder needs only someone to show the cognitive love of paying attention and continuing to ask of each learner "Why do you believe this is so? Why do you think this is important? What do you want to learn now?" We thus free ourselves and our students to grow the tendrils connecting every person to every source of wonder, even to ones we'd never imagined. It's all there for the asking.

Doris, Alex, and the principles of mentoring

Neither of us mentors knows what is best for Doris and Alex to learn. We do know what our college will require of them, and we have learned from Doris and Alex what is demanded of them by their workplaces and by other exigencies of their lives. We have also learned from them something about their interests and the questions that motivate their learning. Thus, stimulated by what they've offered, we have formed our own ideas, based on our education and professional experience, of what might be helpful for them to learn and how they could do so. However, we are very aware that these beliefs, theirs and ours, are themselves speculative and contingent. They are so embedded in different histories, traditions, habits of thought, and current practical considerations. It's just not possible for any of us to know now exactly what learning will enable Doris and Alex to create the lives they want to live. The first principle of mentoring requires that we acknowledge our ignorance and the provisionality of our opinions, but also that we make use of this understanding to explore together what we don't yet know but hope to discover.

Doris is uncertain, for example, about what she has to learn in order to achieve her goal of managing a church-based childcare agency. Her mentor also does not know exactly what she needs to learn for this purpose, nor what she already knows from her volunteer and business experiences that could be turned into a strong academic foundation. Some of the suggestions her mentor makes (e.g. that Doris peruse a general business text and that she read Ehrenreich's book) are simply "ways in" for both of them to find out more. They are thoughtful hunches (not infallible pronouncements), based on the mentor's repertoire and on what he has thus far learned from Doris herself. Even at this earliest moment of Doris's formal studies, she and her mentor have begun a collaborative inquiry (cf. Principle 3, autonomy and collaboration), which might move in any number directions, but which both mentor and student have their own good reasons to believe will help them build an education for Doris.

To be sure, Doris has turned to her mentor for authoritative guidance. After all, she has paid tuition to receive services from someone who is supposed to be qualified to help her. And her mentor wants to fulfill his responsibility. He is paid by his college to put his informed understandings at the service of his students. Of course, the mentor is tempted to profess more than he really knows, and thus establish his authority. However, his knowledge of his ignorance should restrain him (cf. Principle 1, authority and uncertainty), and therefore he should see that what he suggests is merely one of many possibilities (cf. Principle 2, diversity of curriculum). And his acknowledgment, to himself and to Doris, of this provisionality creates the opening for her to learn to be a more fully active participant in the inquiry. The diversity of academic content or curricula in collaborative inquiry is not a chaotic or a quirky oddity, but rather arises from the careful inventiveness to which both mentor and student must contribute.

If Doris and Alex are to be full participants in shaping and completing their education, we shall see them as "whole persons" (cf. Principle 4, learning from the lifeworld). They will bring into our offices issues, hopes, fears, and questions which do not fit neatly into traditionally "legitimate" topics for academic business. This full presence makes itself felt from the very first conversation on, and influences the process of individual studies and the course of an entire degree. This is how the learning becomes meaningful; that is, this is how academic study becomes an part of the student and mentor's lifeworlds.

Alex, for example, presents many different "life issues." He needs to learn how to change his failed academic experiences into successful ones, and how to make his interest in "learning everything" into manageable academic learning. He is worried about how he can pay for college, especially given the restrictions his company has imposed and given the new responsibilities he has as a father and spouse. He knows that he wants a career that will stimulate his mind, but he does not yet know what that career will be. And, his mentor can sense that while Alex has done so much to create his own life, he is nonetheless looking for a kind of paternal authority figure who will notice and praise what he's accomplished and caringly help him find an acceptable place in the world.

Certainly, Alex's mentor is aware of him as a multidimensional, complex person. Moreover, the mentor, from the start, opens the way for Alex to present himself as he chooses. And as the mentor gradually learns who Alex is and takes his different facets seriously, Alex's mentor needs to invoke different roles. He is acting as a guidance counselor in explaining how the college will serve some of Alex's interests and not punish him for his past academic record. He is acting as an administrator and a clerk in making a plan with Alex to enroll him. And, the mentor acts therapeutically in attending to Alex's obviously powerful feelings, and then in honoring Alex's desire for independence while supporting his need for reassurance in the midst of his alienation. However, what integrates all of these different responses and roles is the mentor's concentration on Alex's intellectual journey (cf. Principle 4). No doubt, the conversations that will occur between Alex and his mentor about Socrates and Freud, Paley, Marx, and the rest will touch on many of Alex's concerns (cf. Principle 2, diversity of curriculum). Yet the focus of those conversations will constantly be the question: "What are you learning?"

How should their mentors evaluate what Doris and Alex learn in these first studies? As we have earlier noted, the question of evaluation is typically the prerogative of the professor. However, in the mentor-student relationship, it is entirely appropriate that, at the outset, neither mentor nor student knows precisely what the outcomes ought to be (cf. Principle 1). It would be intellectually presumptuous to prescribe them. Thus, just as the learning activities had to be created collaboratively, so too do the reasonably anticipated outcomes, including the methods and criteria of evaluating them, become topics for the inquiry itself (cf. Principle 5, evaluation as reflective learning). The students thereby gain important experience and practice in reflecting on and assessing the results of their own efforts. That is, the students thus become participants in and reap the benefits of the intellectual freedom of the university.

Like most college students, Doris and Alex will be reading books, writing essays, and researching questions of interest. Throughout, they will be regularly discussing what they have learned – what they've read, written and researched – with their mentors. These dialogues are central both to furthering the learning and to assessing what's been accomplished so far. Testing regimens presuppose that all valuable and legitimate learning outcomes can be known from the start and can be completely separated from who the students are. But, in the mentor-student relationship the evaluation of learning is part of the collaborative learning process itself and depends on the purposes agreed to by the mentors and the students. The educational principles at work remain constant; however, the particular contents of the learning and the criteria for evaluating it will necessarily vary.

The six principles of mentoring emphasize provisionality, diversity, collaboration, autonomy, integration, and the incompleteness of knowledge claims. Staying true to these principles does not mean that Doris and Alex will learn everything important, not even everything important for them in particular to know. But neither does it mean that their learning will be idiosyncratic, chaotic or small-minded. All their faculties will be engaged, and their pragmatic purposes and their lifeworlds will be involved and integrated. Doris and Alex will become more mindful participants in the world as it is, and the care their intellect receives (however different and variable in the particulars of its content) will help them begin to embrace the fullness of the world which they perhaps did not know waits within their experiences and ideas (cf. Principle 6, individual learning and the knowledge most worth having). What could be a more important or universal theme of education than that? And so, we ask them what they believe and what they want to learn and how they might go about learning it.

Mentoring and dialogue

These principles of mentoring constitute what we mean by dialogue. We begin, continue, and end our conversations with our students by inviting them to say what they believe to be true and then asking them to give the reasons for their beliefs. We take our students' conclusions and reasons seriously; but we also take them provisionally – that is, as sources of further questions and more learning. At the same time, we are using what they say to stimulate our own questioning of ourselves, our self-reflective dialogues. Reflection, in other words, thinking-as-searching is inherently dialogical and double-voiced (Baktin 1989). Socrates is always listening for his *daimon*, the inner voice which challenges him to consider if his current beliefs are really true (*Apology* 31d). Mentors expect that by modeling our efforts to take our own beliefs provisionally, we are encouraging our students to do the same for themselves. In this way, they learn to become increasingly independent learners.

This dialogical practice is not unique to our college. Burbules, for example, recommends something similar for academic institutions in general (ibid.: 1993). Moreover, it is applicable, we believe, to any situation in which human communication and thus learning can occur. Dialogical learning somewhat similar to our own meaning has been, for example, recommended for business communication (Ellinor 1998) and described in spiritual exploration (Bohm 1996). We hope that readers will make their own extrapolations and applications from the many examples we offer in subsequent chapters of the academic dialogues we have with our adult university students.

Uncertainty, learning, and freedom

But we must return to a question we asked at the beginning of this chapter. How does an educational process which depends so much on the provisionality and incompleteness of knowledge claims enable anyone to learn anything at all of either a practical or contemplative nature? If people are always questioning themselves and so discovering their ignorance, how they learn even pragmatic truths (i.e. what "works"), let alone what is fundamentally true, just or beautiful?

Meno, for example, rushes to Socrates in order to learn whether "virtue can be taught." He wants to know about this seemingly abstract point for highly practical reasons. If Meno can learn how to teach others to be virtuous, he believes he can profitably influence other young men who want to achieve honor and power in public life. Socrates reasonably suggests that if he and Meno are to learn whether virtue can be taught, they must first see if they know what virtue is. Socrates insists that he, Socrates, doesn't know. Meno plays along in order to get what he wants from Socrates, namely clear and certain instructions. But of course Meno, in responding to Socrates's questions, is soon reduced to "a mass of helplessness." He eloquently describes his frustration:

> I consider that both in your appearance and in other respects you [Socrates] are extremely like the flat torpedo sea-fish; for it benumbs anyone who approaches and touches it, and something of the sort is what I find you have done to me now. For in truth I feel my soul and my tongue quite benumbed, and I am at a loss what answer to give you.
> (*Meno*: 80a)

And Meno then turns his frustration into clever questions, famously posing a paradox about whether it is possible to learn anything at all:

> But how will you know to look for something when you don't in the least know what it is? How on earth are you going to set up something you don't know as the object of your search? To put it another way, even if you come right up against it, how will you know that what you have found is the thing you didn't know?
>
> (ibid.: 80d)

Ironically, this shift from helplessness to skeptical questioning allows the dialogue to proceed. Socrates and Meno begin to investigate the meaning of learning itself, entertaining the hypothesis that it is nothing else than a kind of "recollection," or, as we might say in more modern psychological terms, that all learning ultimately comes from within or what one teaches oneself (ibid.: 81b–86b).

But what makes possible this continuation of dialogue so that actual learning occurs? Our answer will be incomplete and equivocal from a "scientific" or "systems" viewpoint, because it is really a response to "life-world" questions: How can one know what is true? What are "truth" and "knowledge" in themselves? However, the dialogical responses follow rigorously and logically as the only alternatives to two fundamentally self-contradictory assertions or paradoxes.

First, one might assert that there is no absolute truth or certain knowledge; and that everything is merely a matter of opinion and having one's way with people whose opinions differ from one's own. This position is often called "relativism" or, emphasizing its subjective and wilful implications, "emotivism" (MacIntyre 1981). It is appealing because it appears to support freedom of expression and lifestyle. However, it is simply false, because it is self-contradictory: to assert that there is no truth and no knowledge is to assert that these very claims are absolutely true and knowable. It follows, therefore, that at least some truths must exist and some knowledge must be possible, even if one can not say about any other truth or knowledge claim at any particular moment that one knows with complete and final certainty, "I know this to be true." In other words, we have to keep inquiring, keep learning, articulating our beliefs and our reasons as best we can and then asking, testing, how complete and how tightly grounded they really are. The impossibility of relativism seems to demand dialogical learning.

But, second, one might take a different sort of position: that there are indeed knowable, certain truths, but these are not the fuzzy, indefinite sort gradually and not ever completely disclosed through dialogue. Rather, truth is obtained fully, albeit gradually, through the application of scientific method, a kind of systems approach to learning. By experiment, we extract data from what we choose to observe, and by means of logic, mathematics, and further experiment we formulate unambiguous, precise rules that explain the data. These rules are laws, and everything within their view is reduced to a system of necessary relations, specific causes, and calculable, predictable effects. Eventually, we shall have a "theory of everything" which explains all phenomena in the universe, including human behavior (Weinberg 1992). In this position, ambiguous and persistently incomplete or ungraspable principles, such as freedom and beauty, are merely empty ideas. They explain nothing and are merely the illusory, dreamy effervescences of our busy brains.

But from what vantage-point, we must ask, do we know that science is true and, moreover, the *only* way of determining truth? There must be a more fundamental knowledge than science offers, which allows us to answer such a question. Otherwise we would be assuming the absolute truthfulness of science itself in order to assert its own truthfulness! In his *Critique of Pure Reason* (1965), Immanuel Kant seeks this more fundamental or "transcendental" knowledge. This sort of knowledge makes possible the most basic cognitive human experiences, such as the very observations from which scientific inquiry begins.

Moreover, if we should assert, as scientific or systems thinking suggests, that "freedom" is merely an empty idea to which no reality corresponds, the intellectual objectivity upon which rational inquiries (such as scientific investigations) depend would be impossible. If all our actions, including the sequences of our own thoughts, were determined entirely by "laws" producing calculable and predictable chains of cause and effect, then we could not even say that anything is true. That is, in such a "deterministic" or "reductionist" worldview, even our own supposedly scientific thoughts would be forced upon us rather than learned from the evidence of our senses and the rigors of our reasoning. Indeed, the curiosity which allows us to ask questions in the first place, including scientific ones, depends upon freedom of action. The learning (including scientific learning) which our curiosity evokes depends upon the autonomy of our intellect.

In other words, we can no more "reduce" our thoughts and thoughtful actions to the physical and predictable activities of our neural system, than we can think without brains or move without limbs. From matter, we obtain information and power; but matter alone can not tell us what is true or what is best to do about it. Our ability to discover and test apparent truths (even that we might be merely helpless systems of molecules) depends on the reality of intellectual and moral freedom.

Thus, we understand truth and freedom as the logical consequence of the self-contradictions of relativism and scientific reductionism. This approach may seem pedagogically frustrating. After all, one wants to know exactly what truths to understand and what goods to freely choose. Defining truth and freedom, as it were, negatively, by paradox and contradiction alone opens a disorientingly illimitable field of possibilities. This, however, is exactly the basis of Socratic dialogue: learning begins and proceeds by repeatedly discovering one's ignorance, while at the same time being drawn forward by the fact that truths to discover and good lives to live are all but infinite in variety. And this is why our six principles of mentoring *open* learning – from university policies and curricular requirements through every aspect of "teaching" itself. These principles open learning to a world never completely defined or predicted but endlessly disclosing discoveries of truth and a good life.

Dialogue and the good life

To sustain this dialogue, the participants must be free. Though no one may be able to specify or predict the content of freedom, human beings know easily enough when they are not free: when our delights and questions, beliefs and needs, curiosity and purposes are belittled or ignored, we are being tyrannized by others' possession of power and their presumptions of knowledge. As we've said, human beings are necessarily able and free to learn what is true. However, because our beliefs about what is true are, at any given moment, incomplete and uncertain, we must not only continue to inquire but also suppose that any other inquirer may have something valuable to contribute – a question, an observation, and an idea – to our own learning. We must therefore respect or cherish others' freedom of action and intellect with the same regard in which we hold our own. Some readers will recognize the similarity of this maxim to "the Golden Rule" and to Kant's "categorical imperative" (*Critique of Practical Reason* 1956). We are describing a social world in which the qualities of life which human beings fundamentally value – the means to live, and the truths, the moral good, and the beauty for the sake of which we live – are necessarily grounded in our interdependent efforts to learn. Meaningful and loveable human community, within and beyond the academy, are founded in dialogical relationships.

Through such dialogical inquiry – the heart of mentoring practice – people can discover what they want to learn. They can learn how to succeed in the world as it is and learn to experience the virtues which will supplement that success with happiness: truth, justice, beauty. Moreover, we are saying that the process of dialogue is itself the experience of those goods. The dialogue is a kind of relationship in which people serve each other's practical needs, in which they help each other make their beliefs more truthful, in which they treat each other respectfully and justly, and in which they find delight and beauty in their association. Truth begins in the simple act of asking what someone means. In eagerly helping others disclose themselves to us, we feel wonder. Justice occurs in the reciprocated willingness to wait for others to answer and listen carefully to the answer. When we treat others this way and are so treated ourselves, we feel respect. And beauty takes us in the shapes and rhythms of collaboratively discovering and disclosing what or whom we had not previously noticed or understood. Drawn to these things, we feel love.

Of course, all that we have experienced and believed we have learned up to any point in the inquiry, as our first principle of mentoring pre scribes, is provisional and incomplete. The conversation may stop, but the call of dialogue does not end. Why should we want it to? Speculating that in death one might experience a sentient afterlife, Socrates sees himself eternally conversing with every soul he encounters there – a prospect he calls "unimaginable happiness" (*Apology*: 41c).

Academic dialogue thus offers practice in learning how to live a good life in an uncertain world. It is a world in which we constantly have to ask ourselves what more we must learn to survive and succeed, and what more we must learn so that we are free to continue to understand the virtues sufficient for our happiness. Mentoring makes room for wonder and reason in a world of power. Mentors initiate and sustain the dialogues in which this kind of asking and learning occurs and endures. In the remaining chapters of this book, we shall examine in detail the principles and practices of mentoring.

Chapter 3

Asking questions

Either then allow me to speak at such length as I desire, or, if you prefer to ask questions, go on questioning, and I, as we do for old wives telling their tales, will say, 'Very good,' and will not assent and dissent.

No, no, said I, not counter to your own belief.

Yes, to please you, he said, since you don't allow me freedom of speech.

Plato, *Republic* (350e)

First questions

Adult students begin or resume university study at the midpoints of their lives. They have been wondering how they can live their lives better. Mentors hear, often barely asking, something of their new students' lives as they have been and as they imagine they might like them to be. Listening to these accounts, mentors look for clues about which of the many experiences and hopes we hear are likely to provide the most fruitful places to resume an education. But of course first we ask versions of the generic questions with which we began this book: What do you want to learn? Why? How? What do you believe you already know? Why do you believe you know it? This is how the dialogical dance between mentor and student begins.

However, it's important for mentors to appreciate that the questions have begun far before these first encounters. Our new students have been asking themselves what they want to do with their lives and why. Sometimes literally for years, they have been mulling about returning to or beginning university: Am I smart enough to do this? How can I fit into my life yet another activity? How long will it take? Can I afford it? Will any institution welcome someone like me and understand my needs? Even if I start, will I ever finish? Beginning or resuming university study as an older student often means that a discomfiting revolution has occurred in settled routines and expectations. Mentors have to be sensitive to this turmoil, prepared to turn its pain into wonder, and to be respectful of its potential as a learning experience.

Mentors also have a generic repertoire of questions we ask ourselves.

These are about where and how a student will "fit" within the university and what accommodations the university might make for the student: What is the student's past academic record? What experiences has the student had which might contribute to completion of a degree? What area or areas of academic study might suit the student's interests or professional goals? How well equipped is the student to carry out academic work? Is this student, at this point, likely to succeed in this institution? Naturally, mentors make appraisals, based on the application materials the prospective student has submitted. These clues accumulate and then, usually in response to the very first moments of direct encounter (in person, by phone, by email), we form an impression of who this student "really" is. This impression is not solely descriptive, but also normative. It shapes a set of expectations about how to approach the student and what to look for, including what further questions will have to be asked. It is essential, therefore, that we immediately practice the first principle of mentoring (authority and uncertainty) and regard our first impressions as tentative and open to drastic modification.

Our generic questions and our first expectations do have certain validity, which derives from our own experience of other students, and from our understanding of how learning occurs in our own and, for that matter, any academic environment. Whatever the individual differences among students, we know that all of them will be entering our academic world. However, as Principle 1 requires, we also must keep in mind that our knowledge is incomplete and our expectations provisional. As thoughtful as we might be, we are still moved by stereotypes and assumptions about who our students are, what they've done, and what they might become. Doris, for example, presents herself in her application and during her first conversation with her mentor as a middle-aged, single parent, an office assistant eager to learn but doubtful of her ability to succeed in formal university study. And the clues Alex offers mark him as someone with a terrible academic record, and as a young man with immature intellectual ambitions and overly acute suspicions of authority.

From these impressions alone, our expectations are limiting. Doris's mentor believes that she might complete a degree, but not that she will likely achieve all she wants (her desire to create a church-based community service agency). However, the mentor is increasingly aware of how much Doris has already learned from her work experiences and how well that learning will serve her ultimate purpose. He is also surprised and delighted at how much she seems to have learned about the Golden Age of Radio. By the same token, Alex's mentor believes that he will probably reproduce his prior academic failures and that his goal of "learning everything" is much more a fantasy than a useful idea for beginning to learn anything. Nonetheless, the mentor happily discovers that Alex is intellectually serious, that he is thoughtful, and that he has read widely, including some challenging classics. We thus have much more to learn about who these students are and how we can help them. And we need them to help us learn about themselves. We must ask. Thus, from the very first moment of conversation, we must continue to be asking them what they are curious about (Principle 2, diversity of curriculum), and what they care about (Principle 4, learning from the lifeworld). And, we must be asking them to help us understand them, even as we are depending upon their answers (Principle 3, autonomy and collaboration).

An important way in which asking questions helps us correct our first impressions has to do with understanding the nature of our students' purposes. They often present themselves as concerned entirely with the pragmatic aspects of their degrees, but this focus just as often contains deeper meanings. For example, a credential is demanded, usually by some external source such as a current or potential employer. Although this requirement takes a very practical form, having to do with money, status and/or power, in fact, as we learn when we get to know our students better, something deeper has been shaken up. These people are wondering if they can sustain the lives they are accustomed to or achieve the lives they wish to have. They are asking about the meaning of what they've done and why it no longer seems sufficient for themselves, for their families and communities, and for those who have power over them. In this way, their seemingly practical questions, difficult as they are, hold within themselves even deeper and more vexing concerns. With hope and fear, these potential students are already engaged in a revolutionary or transformative dialogue with themselves about who they are and what others will think of them (Principle 1).

Thus, our interest in student learning must be informed by our appreciation for the delicacy and drama of what's already been happening and what can follow. When mentors ask questions about what has brought students here and what they want to learn, and when these questions are not just polite talk but serious efforts to form the ground for study, a important rite of passage occurs: The private and subjective learning a student has done becomes public and academically legitimated. Moreover, the learning already achieved at least starts to define the learning to be accomplished. In this way, individual learning experiences become intellectual topics, and the student becomes a collaborator, the "professor," a mentor. (See Chapter 9 "Access to and within the academy" for a very detailed example of this process.) A profound shift in authority has occurred. Students can follow their own curiosity (Principle 2). They can define the learning most valuable to have and to achieve (Principle 6, individual learning and the knowledge most worth having). And, the struggles students have experienced over how they shall live and what they shall live for, are not put aside after courteous acknowledgment and possibly useful profiling for curricular advising. Rather, those fundamental questions of identity become catalysts of academic creation; the responses are honored as the lifeworld source which inspires the education of the whole person that ensues (Principle 4). A seemingly small question can reveal these big issues:

"No teacher ever asked me"

During our first conversation, I ask Tim to tell me about something he really wants to learn. He mentions the Second World War. When I tell him that we could make a substantial study of this, I'm surprised that *he* seems surprised and very nervous. As I continue to ask him about his interest in this topic, he not only demonstrates that he already knows a huge amount but also becomes more nervous and confused. I'm now confused myself, because I'd assumed I was asking simple and practical questions about how Tim and I might make a new study based on what he already knew about this ordinary topic. We weren't getting anywhere except caught in an old-fashioned student-teacher deadlock. I begin to wonder if I've misunderstood Tim's interest.

"Isn't this a study that would interest you?"

His answer startles me: "No teacher ever asked me what I want to learn, and I'm not sure what to say."

"Why don't you think about this for a few days and we'll talk again. Keep in mind that it's not only okay for you to follow your ideas, it's actually important for your learning that you do so and that you tell me what you want."

In the interval between that first appointment and our next one, Tim and I exchanged several emails. I began to understand that his intense interest in the war was fueled by some unsettling events in his family's history, and that Tim believed the more he could assimilate about the war, the better he could manage and accept that more private history. And Tim seemed to be understanding that he really could define his learning and that his curiosity about the war, however personal its sources, would be respected. When we met again in person, Tim was much more relaxed and prepared with a completely reasonable proposal. Since he already knew so much about the European theater of the war, he now wanted to study the "PTO," the Pacific Theater of Operations. And so he and I together began a search for appropriate readings for this guided independent study.

Exploring neighborhood and community

Sue stands at my office door, waiting for me to get off the phone. "I'm supposed to take a course on American society with you. I want to know what books to buy." "Why don't you sit down?" I offered. "And tell me what you want to think about." Clearly, Sue was not expecting this kind of exchange. She had truly hoped to receive instructions. I quickly realized that I did have some materials on hand that would start her off and ease her obvious anxiety. But I asked anyway: "Why do you want to study American society? Do you have any questions about it?" Sue explained that her degree was in computer studies and that she was adding an "elective" to round out her curriculum. She had never taken a sociology course and her advisor had recommended it.

Even though Sue was hesitant, she began to respond more directly to my questions about her interests. After a few minutes, we were talking about where she lived, the lives of her kids and her husband, and her feelings about being a woman who had recently moved to the suburbs from the city. Sue had many feelings about where she lived now and especially the difficulties she experienced as a relative newcomer who wanted to find something to join, but didn't quite know how. Sue seemed to feel that her discomfort was a result of her shyness, but I wondered if she was beginning to describe something other than a psychological impediment. This became even more obvious to me when I asked her to talk about the differences between the neighborhood she had left and the place she now lived. She surely had a lot to say about that. She didn't talk so much about her shyness, but about how everyone around her "was constantly busy." People were too busy, for example, to look after one another's children, to help out at school, or just to linger in casual conversation. I said: "What a great sociological theme. This is exactly the kind of experience people who study American society want to understand." Sue was very interested. While she didn't leave my office with a textbook and course guide, we did agree on a first learning activity: She would read an article I gave her by Robert Putnam on the deterioration of American communal life; and, she would begin a journal of her observations about her new social world. Our course had begun.

Both Tim and Sue are pursuing topics which respond to some important aspect of the people they are and the questions they have about who they are. Sue's study of the local community directly addresses the neighborly life she wants to live; and Tim's study of the Second World War resonates with his desire to make tolerable sense of his family history. Yet there is a difference. In Sue's case, the personal material is an overt part of the content of the study. In Tim's, the personal certainly propels his interest, but, whatever its power, his mentor senses that Tim's uncomfortable feelings about his family history will not be part of the public content of the study. Making an appropriate judgment about how much and how directly to address the personal dimension is a delicate matter. Sometimes, in the effort to be more engaging, mentors pursue questions about a student's personal interest and unintentionally upset the student or otherwise distract attention from the intellectual work to be done. By the same token, mentors can also utterly disregard a student's personal interest and miss an opportunity for a more profound intellectual connection. (See Chapter 6, "The personal and the academic" for further discussion of this important point.) Despite this difference between Tim and Sue's use of the personal, the judgments made by the mentors rest on the same principles: both students are encouraged to pursue a personally-driven curiosity (Principles 2 and 4); and, the autonomy and diversity of each student is given authority (Principle 3).

At the same time, these studies are clearly academic. Each builds toward a broad and commonly recognized intellectual context; there are connections to scholarly disciplines; the studies will be deliberate and orderly; and there will be demonstrable learning for evaluation. In keeping with Principle 6, these guided independent studies make connections, between very personally meaningfully topics, general themes, and several academic disciplines. The mentors' questions point the work toward creating these connections. We ask different versions of the same small and simple question: "What are you interested in learning?" And we look for sparks of curiosity in our students' responses, which can illuminate open ings for intellectual inquiry and which, over time, can shine back and forth between the personal and the academic. Both facets are necessary for learning to become meaningful. In this reciprocal way, legitimacy is conferred: the personal and individual are admitted into university education; and scholarship finds a home in students' lives.

After the first questions

Thus far, we have discussed how mentors and students begin their work together. We have focused on creating a topic of learning. Once that's done, students might work on their topics in a number of ways. They might, for example, work with other mentors whose academic areas best suit the topics at hand. The content of those studies might be very closely shaped to the student's particular curiosity, or, if the student's interest is more general, the study might look very much like a conventional course. (Tim's study of World War II falls in the middle of this range.) If it suits their curiosity and convenience, students might take a packaged Web course or participate in a group study whose content is relevant to all the participants. When we continue on with our students, after the initial conversations, we also continue to ask questions. So important in initially defining the inquiry, questioning continues to frame our conversations.

The on-going questions take many forms. Together, they comprise the repertoire of mentoring. Although we shall be describing many of the kinds of questions we use, our "taxonomy" is neither encyclopedic nor intended as a complete manual of practice. Instead, we are simply describing an array of questions which are at the heart of mentors' continuous engagement in inquiry with their students. There is no perfect question; there is no perfect ordering of questions. In fact, as we want to show, mentors are always making judgments about what questions to ask, when to ask them, when to offer their own answers, and when, simply, to keep silent. As Principle 1 requires, we try to question ourselves. This process of self-reflective questioning, sometimes prominently conscious, never goes away. Its purpose, always, is to ask ourselves how the dialogue can be served, and how we can help students achieve and sustain their own questioning.

The remaining sections of this chapter examine the kinds of questions we typically ask and encounter in our work with students. Some questions are "open," while others seek a specific answer or lead in a pre-conceived direction. Some questions, intentionally or not, reveal a contradiction to or within an opinion which has been offered. And some significantly and unexpectedly change the process and/or content of the inquiry. When and how these questions are asked will always affect the truthfulness, the fairness, and the attractiveness of the dialogical relationship between mentor and student.

Open questions

Even after the general topic or plan of a study has been determined, each meeting's conversation between mentor and student must discover a new beginning. Intense and long inquiries often begin with simple, "open" questions. The topic of the day's dialogue is not necessarily pre-defined; the questioner need not have a "correct" response in mind, nor need the respondent have a prepared answer.

Martin has been reading a book about the life of a young man, badly damaged by a neglectful family. He has chosen this book as part of his study, "Self and Society." His mentor asks, "What do you think was going on in this family?" His mentor wants to know what Martin has been paying attention to, and wants to find an opening to a more focused discussion on the formation of individual identities within families. Stimulated by Martin's lead, the topic of the day's dialogue eventually settles on how a child attempts to endure and how a child's character is formed within a dysfunctional environment.

During her study of organizational behavior, Sophia, who is the business manager of a small newspaper, has been experiencing and observing the confusing changes in her workplace caused by its incorporation into a much larger company. Naturally, she is pre-occupied with these events. Her mentor asks, "What do you think your textbook has to say about what you've been seeing at work?" Sophia's responses center their discussion on how the distribution of responsibilities becomes ambiguous and conflict-laden when an organization changes and its future is unknown. Her mentor's question is "open" because it is so broad. However, it is also a "leading" question in two ways. First, the mentor does assume that there *are* connections, innumerable though they may be, between the concepts in the book and Sophia's experience. And, the mentor also *intends* that she explore these connections, whichever ones she chooses, because that will allow Sophia to use her experience as intellectual terrain.

Open questions encourage the students to take ownership of the discussion – to follow their curiosity, as Principle 2 requires. And, they also show, in accord with Principle 1, that the mentor is not the owner of "the" answers. Nonetheless, the mentor, even in asking such questions, is also encouraging students to make connections, as Principle 6 requires, between the initial point of their curiosity, academic material, and one or more general themes. In so doing, mentors move open questions from inchoate conversation to focused inquiry.

Being expert and keeping "open questions" open

A mentor will not work with a student on any subject. Like all academics, we have our areas of normal expertise and focused learning or scholarship. Often, our students want to study something with a mentor who simply doesn't know enough, no matter how provisionally she or he regards her or his "knowledge," even to ask useful questions, especially if a student runs into intellectual difficulties. So, we ask an appropriately informed colleague or recruit a "tutor" (someone also qualified but not a full time academic) to work with the student. Nonetheless, mentors often find themselves "stretching" beyond their core of content expertise. In these cases, we are faced with the problem of deciding where the right boundary is between stretching appropriately and going too far. (In Chapter 7, "The mentor as learner," we will give examples of this stretching working well and working poorly.) But an interestingly different problem appears when we work with students on topics in which we really are quite learned: How do we restrain ourselves from overwhelming the student's curiosity with our own learning and interests? How do we keep "open questions" open? The following is an example of a mentor dealing with this problem.

Christina wants to study ancient Greek philosophy. Intending to become a history teacher, she's quite interested in this subject as an instance of connections between political and cultural history. She particularly wants to understand the *polis* or city-state within the classical period, how the Greeks (especially the Athenians) actually governed themselves, and the ideas they articulated about how they ought to govern themselves. Naturally, she is fascinated by the flourishing and decline of Athenian democracy, and by Socrates and Plato. During my own undergraduate and graduate education, I studied all these subjects and I have continued to read and think about them. I'm especially interested in relationships between philosophy, democracy, and education; I hope that Christina will be too, particularly since she wants to be a teacher.

Already quite familiar with ancient Greek history (she's read Herodotus, Thucydides, and Xenophon, as well as a number of modern scholars), Christina now reads some general histories of Greek philosophy. She also reads selections from the pre-Socratic philosophers, several of Plato's dialogues, and also selections from Aristotle's *Politics* and *The Nichomachean Ethics*. She's a good student: careful, thorough, thoughtful, and articulate. And, of course, her interest pleases me; I don't often have students who want to study these things. At her request, I've suggested most of the primary and secondary sources she's used. However, once she begins to study Plato, particularly his vision of the just state in the *Republic* and its corresponding educational system, Christina becomes increasingly critical and tells me that she wants to concentrate on other texts and writers. She sees Plato as an "irrelevant" utopian, an absolutist very like the tyrants he criticizes. And she sees Socrates as not all that different from the sophists who, in their own ways, abetted the corruption of democratic discourse. She considers Socrates's irony to be disrespectful; the logical contradictions into which he "pushes" his interlocutors as entirely manipulative; and his claims of ignorance as merely disingenuous. In the remainder of the study, which will be nearly half, she wants to focus on Aristotle.

I'm disappointed. I believe that Christina has not considered Plato's rendering of Socrates carefully enough on its own philosophical terms, nor appreciated that Plato's ideal state is a kind of speculative "myth" constructed for further examination rather than literal and absolute application. (However, as Christina points out, Plato seems to have taken his own ideas literally enough to try to turn the ruler of Syracuse into a "philosopher king." To which effort, Dionysius II responded by throwing Plato into jail!) I worry also that Christina has been too influenced by the accounts of Socrates she's read in Aristophanes and Xenophon, and a recent, very critical interpretation of his political and educational influence offered by I.F. Stone (1988).

I'm eager to persuade Christina to spend more time on Socrates and Plato. But, I also begin to hear my own questioning, inner voice:

Why is it so important to you that Christina stay with these philosophers when she wants to move on to Aristotle?

Because they're important, not just in Greek philosophy but in the whole educational/philosophical tradition she said she's interested in. This is an area that I really do know something about.

I'm sure they are important and that you do know a lot about this subject. But, do you know that Socrates and Plato are really more important than Aristotle? I know you've studied Aristotle, but perhaps you don't agree as much with his approach as you do with the other two.

That's true. I don't and I have good reasons.

Christina has her reasons too, doesn't she? And after all, she's not exactly straying away from what scholars recognize as the main lines of the philosophical tradition.

No, I suppose not.

And, how closely have you read Aristotle recently or the scholarship on his work?

Not that much.

Maybe then he has something to offer you, *not just Christina, which you don't realize?*

Maybe. But are you saying that I'm pushing Christina to stay with Socrates and Plato because of my own interest and familiarity?

Perhaps that's a question you should think about for a while. But let me ask you something else: doesn't Aristotle claim that all human questions and branches of knowledge are connected, that they form what came to be called an organon?

Yes.

And doesn't Plato claim that the Good *and all the virtues* – truth, justice, temperance, courage – *and even* beauty *are all really* one, *namely* knowledge?

Yes, all these things are connected, in both philosophers. And – I see where you're going now – this idea of the coherence of learning, which both of them assert, also has important educational and political implications.

Exactly. So...?

So given that Christina can't learn everything and given that she's really interested in Aristotle...

And given that maybe the questions you've wanted her to address about teaching and learning, and about ideal justice and education are likely to come up all over again, but now in the work of Aristotle...

Okay, okay. I guess I see what I should do.

When Christina and I meet next, I ask, "Christina, what do you think are the most important ideas you encountered in Aristotle's *Ethics* and *Politics*? What do you think we should discuss about them?"

Informational questions

These kinds of questions help mentors learn from their students what they have been assimilating from their reading and writing, their conversations and observations, and their reflections on all these activities. Although these informational questions are often used instrumentally for assessing or testing a student's comprehension, or to move an agenda along, they also become an opportunity for mentors to create and sustain a genuinely collaborative relationship with their students. In asking for information, mentors are "collaborative learners," as indeed they need to be to serve the dialogue (cf. Principles 1 and 3). That is, as mentors listen for responses, they are gaining insight into what's going on with the student and they are also treating the student as a reliable informant, an authority.

Cassie has been doing a study of contemporary African-American culture. She told her mentor that she wanted to think about how the use of language within that culture informs ways of understanding the social world. After reading Randall Kennedy's recent book, *Nigger: The Strange Career of a Troublesome Word*, Cassie becomes very interested in the use of the word "nigger" among young black men. Her mentor thus suggests that she read John McWhorter's, *Losing the Race: Self-Sabotage in Black America*. Cassie comes to a tutorial session extremely enthusiastic about McWhorter's analysis. She has found an author who has put into words what she feels as an African-American woman. Particularly, she points to the author's analysis of "the cult of anti-intellectualism" within African-American society. "What is his argument?" her mentor inquires. "When he uses the word 'anti-intellectualism,' what exactly do you think he means?" And so their conversation continues. Cassie has stated her curiosity or interest; trying to understand it better, the mentor also induces her to focus her interest more tightly and precisely. He suggests a connection (to another book) and then asks her, still trying to understand *her* meaning, to scrutinize and develop her own understanding of what the author means. Focussing on Cassie's curiosity (Principle 2), he also engages her in collaborative inquiry (Principle 3) and helps her reflect on her own responses (Principle 1) and to expand her repertoire of academic material (Principle 6).

For her study of legal and ethical issues in contemporary American health care, Maxine decided to become generally familiar with the range of those issues and then to select several for more careful scrutiny. Her main resource was a large anthology of articles and essays about this area. After Maxine summarizes her general understanding in conversations with her mentor, he asks: "What are a few different issues here that especially interest you?" Maxine identified several, including health care rationing, community services for the de-institutionalized mentally ill, and the politics and economics of universal health care. They agreed that these topics would be the focus for further research. Confident about Maxine's abilities but also wanting to understand them better, her mentor asked, "How do you want to do this research and present your learning?" They agreed that she would locate pertinent publications (including Web sources) on legislation, court cases, and ethical debates about each one of her topics, and that she would write detailed reports of her findings. After reading each one of Maxine's reports, her mentor would begin their discussion by asking, "What did you find out from this research? What do you think is important?" The same principles are at work as in the dialogues with Cassie. In addition, the mentor is also asking Maxine to begin to collaborate in assessing her own learning – "How do you want to do this research and present your learning?" "What did you find out?" – as Principle 5 expects.

Informational questions cover two different kinds of fields: they range from the general to the particular (from "What have you been noticing?" to "What does this author mean by...?"). They also range from the mentor seeking to elicit the student's curiosity ("How do you want to study...?"), through the mentor trying to make an informed judgment about the student's learning ("Tell me about the author's argument in this chapter."). And sometimes, the mentor is also trying to learn from the student about what the student has been studying. In this regard, it's noteworthy that by the midpoint in her research, Maxine almost certainly knew more up-to-date and detailed information about health care issues than her mentor did. She helps the mentor learn as well. In this way too, the authority is responsibly shared and the student has experienced what it means to be respected as an autonomous intellectual. These questions serve the truthfulness of the learning; they also make it more reciprocal, fairer. And, we believe, they make the experience more intrinsically gratifying, more beautiful, for both participants: mentor and student become intellectual companions. In their collaboration, they enhance their experience of the lifeworld (Principle 4).

Leading questions

Mentors ask "leading" questions when they have something in mind to which they want their students to attend. During his overview study of the natural sciences, Irwin has read Darwin's *Origin of Species* and, among other things, Ernst Mayr's *The Growth of Biological Thought*. He is almost gleefully taken by what he thinks to be Darwin's displacement of the existence of God with the law of natural selection. His mentor wants him to understand a fine but important logical point: that the truth of "natural selection" does not necessarily disprove the existence of God, for God might have created the universe so that it "evolves" by that very means. "Why couldn't there be a God, omnipotent and omniscient, who foresightfully created a world in which living things grow and diversify? Couldn't this be possible?" After a brief, puzzled silence, Irwin hesitantly says, "Yes." "Then," the mentor asks, "could the divinely created 'natural law' governing those changes in living things be the law of natural selection?" Again, after another pause, Irwin accepts the hypothesis the mentor has set up.

But the mentor's goal is not to undercut Irwin's enthusiastic efforts to understand something about science on his own terms. Thus, the mentor goes on to ask, "Is there something about 'creationism' which the law of natural selection, assuming it is true, directly disproves?" Brightening, Irwin says that if natural selection actually occurs, then it would not be possible for all of the species that have ever existed on earth to have been created all at once at the beginning, as many devout creationists claim. Irwin's mentor did indeed want him to see this particular point; however, the mentor was also hoping that Irwin would understand that scientific learning, whether or not it gratifies one's own beliefs, still calls for rigorous scrutiny of its own hypotheses and one's own expectations. Irwin did seem, at the end of the conversation, to understand this point about science and about taking care to scrutinize carefully his own opinions even when science seems to support them (Principle 1). The mentor, however, does not want to exclude Irwin from the dialogue, as the mentor realizes the first series of leading questions seem to threaten to do. And so he asks Irwin yet another leading question, which allows Irwin to discover for himself that his own religious skepticism is not merely to be regarded as foolish prejudice. The collaborative bond is not broken (Principle 3). Irwin has also become more involved in connecting and contrasting the different worldviews of science and faith (Principle 6); and he has developed a more carefully examined understanding of an issue – the existence of God – which is important in his lifeworld (Principle 4). Among other things, in this little dialogue, Irwin has perhaps learned something about justice, about willingly trying to understand the meaning of his own and others' deep beliefs.

Nonetheless, mentors make mistakes. In their confidence in their own insights, mentors can ask questions which are "too" leading. They can be premature or presumptuous, and instead of moving the dialogue along, such questions can stop it. Kathy, for example, raises the topic of abortion, during her study of contemporary political issues. She had already looked at privacy, and at the separation between church and state. And, in a recent essay she explored the debate about whether sex education should be legally mandatory and stated-funded. Abortion as a topic came up by chance. Kathy commented, "The government just shouldn't interfere with morality." Her mentor was sure from the edge in her voice that Kathy was strongly opposed to abortion.

The mentor believed that this was an opportunity to deepen Kathy's understanding of how political debate can turn on opposing moral positions. Taking advantage of what appeared to be a fertile "teachable moment," the mentor asked, "Do you think that people's public and political statements about the abortion question turn on whether or not they believe the fetus is a human being?" Looking suspicious and confused, Kathy asked, "What do you mean?" And the mentor replied, "Well, if someone doesn't believe the fetus is a human being, wouldn't that person also believe that abortion is not murder?" Not only did Kathy not respond to the question, the entire conversation, for all practical purposes, ended. The mentor completely mistook as an opening for discussion what in fact was a signal of Kathy's vulnerability. He was carried away with his desire to persuade Kathy to engage in some reflection on her moral-political assumptions about a topic *he* was concerned about but which, at that time, was not the object of Kathy's curiosity. Inattentive to the active presence of his own very different assumptions and curiosity, the mentor did not notice that his questions pulled Kathy into a topic so personally charged that she was silenced. The "leading question" was paralyzing.

Paradoxes and contradictions

The leading questions asked of Kathy led merely to her discomfort, not to learning. While the mentor pushed her toward what he sensed to be a limit of her understanding, he also provoked her to guard against an incursion into something very personal and precious. It didn't matter that the mentor's own response to his leading question seemed important and logically correct. What mattered in this instance was that the mentor's judgment was insufficiently attentive to Kathy's verbal and non-verbal cues. The mentor thus did not exercise appropriately delicate cognitive care. Leading questions that merely drop students into problematic aspects of their beliefs are very risky. This is especially true when those beliefs are related to lifeworld concerns important to the individual student (such as a particular religious or political stance) or simply important to anyone (such as not feeling helplessly humiliated). Sometimes, such moves can open a dialogue to new ideas, or, just close it down. The opportunities and risks are greatest when leading questions reveal paradoxes and contradictions within students' beliefs. For not only is the student confronted with a "problem," which perhaps a little more information and thought can solve, but with the prospect of having to discard the belief altogether. It's easy to feel trifled with and trapped. Nonetheless, these disturbing moments can open huge opportunities for unexpected learning. But mentors need to be delicate, and they need to be mindful that the logical dead end to which a student's idea can lead may not exhaust the fruitful meanings of that idea (Principle 1).

Les's study of business policy grew directly from his desire to understand more about a deliberately adopted change in the "culture" of the corporation where he'd worked for some twenty years. At work, he was receiving intense training in a very technical and sweeping methodology of quality control and productivity, "Six Sigma," that the most senior management had decided would become central to all areas of the company. Les very much wanted to include this on-the-job learning in his academic learning. He was proud to be among the first trainees, and thus to eventually become one of those who would lead the company through its transformation. The academic study was a clear expression of Les's enthusiastic curiosity and of the lifeworld he enjoyed at work.

The system Les was studying particularly appealed to him. And from the material and comments Les provided, the mentor also learned much about this managerial methodology. He also realized that Les's enthusiasm was in large part inspired by his faith in the leaders of the corporation, who, in turn, deeply believed in Six Sigma. It purported to be universally applicable to all aspects of work, and to rest entirely on mathematical analyses of objectively collected data. To the mentor's suspicious eye, this system, while claiming total rationality and objectivity, appeared to be an over-reaching "theory of everything."

The company's goal in deploying this system was to reduce costs, increase productivity, and "add value" to its employees, its shareholders, and its customers. Les was digging in: studying the material provided for his training, and reading a major text on business policy which his mentor suggested. Because examining underlying assumptions is a normal component both of the study of business policy and of its real world application (Magretta 2002), Les and his mentor spent a good deal of their conversation identifying and analyzing the basic tenets of this new system.

"How is value defined?" the mentor asked. Les quickly replied by quoting some of the mathematical formulas and axioms of the system. "But how did someone decide that these were the appropriate terms with which to measure 'value' as customers or employees, for example, might understand that term?" Les seemed uncertain about how to respond. So, his mentor asked, "It seems pretty clear, for example, that stockholders, who were interested in a relatively short-term profit on their investment, might be satisfied with the definitions you gave, but that investors with longer term interests, might not find those understandings of 'value' very suitable. In addition, employees likely to lose their jobs because of efficiencies gained in work-flow might not consider this to be valuable at all. So, how do you think value then might be defined in a way that suits all the interested parties?" Les now much more hesitantly responded, "I guess that everyone would have agreed on something." "Do the formulas you mentioned," the mentor asked, "rest on an agreement of the sort you have in mind?" "I don't think so. I guess everyone would decide what's valuable according to what's good for them. It would be hard to tell." "Then does this system really have a foolproof method? Does it maybe depend on some kinds of fuzzy assumptions about what 'value' means, even though the system claims to be absolutely precise and rational?"

Les was perplexed, but he did not shut down. During further conversation, he really seemed to appreciate the pertinence and significance of the apparent paradox he was encountering. Eventually, although he surely did not surrender his allegiance to or participation in the system he'd been learning, he did incorporate into his thinking, both at work and in this study, a more critical view than he originally held. For example, he began to wonder seriously if the system's assumptions about "value" were not heavily weighted toward the likely interests of relatively short-term investors. Further, Les observed that the system sought a rather low threshold of customer satisfaction, and that it all but completely ignored the interests of employees in their job-security. He even noted the somewhat cruel irony that because of the apparently participatory nature of the system, employees were expected to collaborate in planning for what might well be their own demise. The mentor was pushing Les to re-evaluate something whose truth and goodness he had taken for granted. The mentor thus risked simply stumping Les, undercutting their collaboration, while enhancing his own "teacherly" authority. But in this instance, the use of questions leading to a paradox worked well. Les was already an advanced and autonomous enough learner to be reasonably able to choose to grow from his disconcerting experience. Mentor and student continued their dialogue.

Mentors also work with students in groups. Perhaps because that context is reminiscent of the classroom, the mentor is more easily drawn to eliciting contradictions in what students say. This method is seen as an effective way to provoke deeper understanding – once again, to seize a "teachable moment." But it also easily, often too easily, asserts the teacher's authority, reduces participation, and silences dialogue.

A mentor, for example, is facilitating a group whose focus is contemporary poverty. One goal of this study was to examine understandings of the very notion "poverty." Another was to learn about several different kinds of historical and sociological descriptions of poverty. And a final goal was to place these discussions in the context of contemporary debates about social welfare and fairness. In addition, this group study would be a good exercise in critical thinking. Among other texts, students read Jacob Riis and Charles Dickens; they read Michael Harrington's classic, *The Other America*, and more recently influential works such as Elliot Liebow, *Tell Them Who I Am*; George Gilder, *Wealth and Poverty*; and Shelby Steele, *The Content of Our Character*. For a more global and theoretical perspective, they read Amartya Sen's *Inequality Reexamined*. To become more conversant with current debates, the students also read selections from an anthology of opposing viewpoints.

In weekly seminars, about a dozen adults (more black than white, more women than men) closely discussed what the texts literally said, as well as what they seemed to imply about the values and intentions of the authors. The mentor was less interested in convincing the students of any particular position, than in helping them learn to notice the descriptive language used, the information selected, and the turns of argument authors rely upon – all of which reveal their political and moral perspectives. The mentor wanted the students more to understand each other and the positions they learned about rather than judge them. But of course in such discussions, people do make judgments. The mentor wanted the students to see and understand both the differences among and the reasons for those judgments.

The anthology, in particular, permitted the participants to voice their own feelings and attitudes. While the group setting gave people some ease in expressing their opinions, it also made exploring the limitations and contradictions within those opinions somewhat problematic. Miles had been an articulate and avid participant in these discussions. He confidently maintained that poor people were to blame for their condition and further that, since what would be "poor" in one historical or social location would not be considered so in another, poverty had no objective basis at all. It was solely in the eyes and attitudes of the beholder. His opinions were not shared by nor agreeable to most of the rest of the group. But, like a good scholar, Miles brought in research and experience from beyond the assigned readings to support his positions.

"Do you believe there is no such thing as poverty?" the mentor asked.

"Only the poverty you think you have and saddle yourself with," Miles replied.

"So you believe that people make their own limitations and that they are entirely responsible for getting beyond them?"

"Yes."

"And you also believe that, for example, a person considered poor in New York City or London would, if living in the same conditions and with the same resources in Bangladesh, not be considered poor at all?"

"That's exactly right. I think that if only that New Yorker realized how much more he has than someone in Bangladesh, he wouldn't think himself so badly off and we shouldn't either. In fact, if the New Yorker thought about how much better off he is than so many other people in the world, maybe he'd stop complaining or maybe he'd even be motivated to make his own life better."

"So you imagine that the New Yorker would realize that he's not really poor at all, once he compares his situation to someone in Bangladesh?"

"That's right. If he were being honest, he couldn't believe he's poor."

"Do you mean that the New Yorker couldn't believe he's poor because the Bangladeshi is obviously so much poorer?"

"Of course the Bangladeshi is poorer!"

"Then you and our imaginary New Yorker are making some kind of comparison?"

"Yes. That's the only logical way to think about it."

"But Miles, what's your standard of reference? Based on what, are you saying that one person is poorer and the other less poor?"

"Well, here's what I think: the Bangladeshi doesn't have the basic necessities. He and his family don't have enough to eat; their house is too small and unsafe; they don't have medical care; the kids probably don't go to school for very long; and they have little hope that their lives will ever change for the better."

"So you have some idea about what people need?"

"I do."

"You've used your idea to compare the New Yorker and the Bangladeshi. Do you think it could be applied to pretty much anyone in the world?"

"Why not?"

"But if you don't believe there's really any such thing as poverty, except what people happen to believe about themselves, then your idea couldn't apply to anyone except yourself."

"That's not what I mean. Okay. If you're really so badly off that you and your family are starving and so on, then I would say and, yes, almost anyone would say, that you're poor. And that just wouldn't just be an opinion."

"Then what do you mean?"

"I mean that if you realize that you're poor and you really have any self-respect and really care about your family, then you're going to do everything you can to get out of your situation. That's your responsibility."

"And that idea would apply to both the New Yorker and the Bangladeshi?"

"For sure. Poor people in both situations have worked hard and improved their lives. I think it happens all the time."

"So Miles, you have to acknowledge then that poverty is real and not just a personal attitude?"

Reluctantly, Miles says, "Yes."

During what became an intense and exclusive dialogue between Miles and the mentor, the other group members reacted. A few dropped their attention. Some tried to participate. And others fidgeted at the spectacle of their mentor pushing Miles into the impossible corners of his ideas. Even though most of the group almost certainly disagreed with Miles's opinions, that seemed to matter less to them than Miles's growing public discomfort and isolation. The mentor was not entirely oblivious to this range of response. But caught up in his own certainty that poverty is real and in his awareness that he had found a seemingly perfect opportunity to show Miles and the other students an example of sharp critical inquiry, the mentor forgets to care about Miles and, for that matter, the community of the group. Instead of stimulating participation (Principle 3), the mentor produces silence. For the sake of getting quickly to a "truthfulness" important to himself alone at that moment (contrary to Principles 1 and 2), the mentor sacrificed, as the group sensed, the justice and delight of the learning experience.

In this example, questions leading to a paradox did not work well. The mentor was making a true and important point: A necessary condition of an in-depth understanding of poverty in the world is that one appreciate that poverty is a real phenomenon. However, in the circumstances of this discussion with these students, there were many equally true and important places to go. For example, the mentor could have seen his role as inviting others to join in and asking them to say what they thought about the reality and causes of poverty. He could have asked Miles to explain more thoroughly how poverty, though real, might *also* be a matter of self perception and how its thresholds might vary across cultures. But the mentor's choice asserted his authority, skewered Miles, and squashed the dialogue.

Though favored by "Socratic" teachers, exposing paradoxes in students' opinions is risky. When you are asked to say what you really believe and then are led to realizing that your belief is not just incomplete or doubtful but, apparently, utterly false, you can easily experience humiliation and shame. And it is too easy for the interrogator to say that the students are free to choose between holding on to their pride in what they have believed and reaching courageously from a powerfully discomfiting insight into the unknown. Of course students must take responsibility for their own autonomy (Principle 3), but mentors must also understand that they too have a responsibility to respect and support this freedom within the academic context – often a daunting one for students – where it is to be exercised. And the stakes are even higher when the discussion is about beliefs central to the student's view of the world, as was the case with Les and with Miles. When mentors go after such contradictions, they are exercising a power most distant from a student's collaborative participation. Those are the moments when mentors must be most careful and most caring, when "cognitive love" is most required (a topic we shall continue to explore in Chapter 6, "The personal and the academic").

Changing direction, experiencing wonder

Mentors also ask questions that, far from having an end in view, drastically and even unintentionally change the direction of the inquiry. These questions, when they are deliberate, often emerge from prior conversations in which the mentor has been deeply listening to the student. They are based on hunches and take leaps, using what the mentor has already learned about the student. The mentor may well not have anything particular in mind, except the feeling that there just might be some valuable opening to something new. When we ask questions that stimulate a change in direction, as distinct from "open questions" and "informational questions," we do not suppose the student is intellectually obliged to go along. They might not lead anywhere very important and the topic raised might be simply dropped. The mentor's hunch might just be off the mark. We must always regard our hunches as "provisional" (Principle 1). Or, the question might derive from a mentor's sharp insight, but the timing is premature and the mentor must wait. In asking questions that could change the direction of the dialogue, the mentor is reaching for something really quite unknown, feeling for expanding and deepening connections (Principle 6).

Vanessa's professional experience is varied. After high school, she pursued a career in music, and had some success as a singer, manager, and marketer of her own group. Over the last dozen years, Vanessa has succeeded in yet another area. She quickly learned the intricacies of an employer's computer system, and transformed antiquated and cumbersome customer service procedures into an accessible and accurate database. There was no doubt about Vanessa's diverse competencies, which were also reflected in the success of her first college studies.

Similarly, Vanessa rose to the opportunity to design her own college program (see Chapter 5 "Curriculum as collaborative planning"). Over many discussions between Vanessa and her mentor, it became equally clear to both of them that she would benefit from a quite conventional business degree. She had a well informed understanding (which the mentor heard and appreciated) that, along with her many demonstrated accomplishments, such a degree would prudently serve her need to support herself. But her mentor eagerly saw the prospect of a truly personalized and interdisciplinary curriculum design, one that would allow Vanessa to include and weave together the many threads of her talents and interests. The mentor saw that the artistry, the organizing, and the "people skills" of Vanessa's work in music were deeply connected to her artfulness and managerial ability in the business world. For the mentor, Vanessa could easily build a whole program centered on her abiding and expansive devotion to communicative arts and systems. But this was not Vanessa's view.

Typically, Vanessa, for example, would select several standard business courses. And the mentor would respond, "But what if you modified these courses to reflect some of your experience in music?" To this question, which the mentor hoped would help Vanessa see as eagerly as he did that her degree could be even more completely relevant than she'd supposed, she answered, "I want a business degree, and these courses are important. That's what I need right now."

The mentor's hunch was well taken. He had understood a great deal about Vanessa's skills and understandings and believed that she would be excited by his insight about how diverse studies could come together. But Vanessa saw it another way; she was sure that this was not the right time for her to be taking such academic adventures. Her mentor realized that Vanessa knew what she needed and he backed down.

Sometimes mentor "hunches" do create openings a student is ready to enter. At an orientation meeting, Patrick presented to his mentor a transcript of prior learning from another college and a written statement of his interests, goals, and work experiences. In addition to a customary variety of liberal arts and sciences courses, Patrick had taken a number of courses in computer and information technology subjects, a field in which most of his subsequent professional experience lay. It certainly seemed that this field was where Patrick's talents and interests were concentrated. Organizing his undergraduate program around his work seemed responsive to both his practical and personal needs. Moreover, during their early conversations, Patrick was clearly interested in learning how he could gain academic credit for the learning he'd acquired from his experiences as an independent consultant and sub-contractor in programming and in systems analysis. In addition, both in conversation and his written statement, Patrick had mentioned that he had training and experience as an emergency medical technician. He understood very well that a bachelor's degree concentrating in Information Technology would help him compete in a tight job market for computer consultants and would also help him become permanently employed as an IT specialist within a corporation.

But something made the mentor feel that there was another question waiting to be asked. Perhaps this feeling was stimulated by Patrick's not seeming all that anxious or impatient. Although he certainly understood that an IT degree would help him and although he was pleased to learn that he might receive substantial academic credit for what he'd already learned, he was not all that eager either. Unlike many students, Patrick did not ask, "How much credit can I get? How quickly can I complete this degree?" He was calm about the practical exigencies which so often drive adult students; and, although he spoke mostly of his IT work and learning, he mentioned several times during the conversation that he enjoyed his experience as a volunteer in emergency health care. Noticing Patrick's calm and his pleasure, the mentor became curious about academic and career options very different from those which they'd been discussing. He asked, "Patrick, if you could do a degree in anything you wanted, regardless of your background and your work in information technology, what do you think it might look like?"

In response, Patrick's demeanor changed. He spread his arms apart on the tabletop; a smile crossed his face; and he leaned back in his chair to think. Then he asked, "What do you mean?" The mentor replied, "I mean that you can design an academic degree in almost anything you want; it doesn't have to be in information technology." Patrick replied, "Well, there's no doubt health care has always been interesting and important to me." A few moments later, Patrick added, "Even though I know that a degree will benefit me, I'm not in a rush; I want to learn as much as I can."

Over the next weeks Patrick and his mentor continued to talk about the possibility of a degree which might focus on health care services, or in health care systems (which might integrate his interest in health care with his work with computer systems). The mentor's hunch led both him and Patrick to consider new academic and career possibilities. Nothing was settled; no transformation was completed; and Patrick began a study in theories of systems management (which he and his mentor agreed would be useful to his learning regardless of its ultimate direction). But they had opened up a possibility, which might not have emerged had the question not been asked.

Dancing lessons

Asking questions is at the heart of mentoring. Mentors look for occasions to invite participation, to welcome students into dialogue. Asking a question invites the collaboration on which the dialogue depends.

The inquiry moves forward, sometimes across places familiar to one or the other of the participants, sometimes into corners and onto prospects unfamiliar to both. The dancers revolve while they progress. They focus on the point between them and look at it from all round, in new ways. The tempo changes, sometimes moving slowly, lingering over a rich idea and sometimes quickly as the dancers rush along a line of shared thought whose destination they can sense. Rhythms can change as well, as unexpected questions and ideas alter the pattern and accent of the steps the dancers had first supposed they were going take in their inquiry. As they become more and more familiar with one another, the inquirers exchange the lead, first the mentor and then the student posing questions and offering ideas. Gradually, they no longer notice or care who is leading, who is following; neither need worry where either will step next. Absorbed in the movement of the dialogue itself, the dancers no longer know themselves apart from the dance. And, they are happy, suffused with this dialogical "flow," as Csikszentmihalyi would call it (1991).

Actual dialogues do not always achieve this graceful flow. As some of our examples demonstrate, even with the best intentions, mentors ask the wrong questions or ask the right questions at the wrong time. Mentors often fall back on professorial ways, and students, often not knowing of any other approach to teaching and learning, hold on to the expectations and rituals of being simply the recipients of another's knowledge. Further, the motions of inquiry are, especially at the beginning, naturally awkward and halting. After all, people who do not know each other well are trying to enter into an intellectually elaborate and often emotionally delicate collaboration. It will nearly always be the case that students are less familiar and will thus be slower with this kind of learning than their mentors are. And, even if gently and amiably invited to be partners, some students will resist for any number of reasons (e.g. interest, time, ability). Moreover, mentors, wanting to "help" their discomfited students, will all too comfortably begin to instruct and answer their own questions. These "mistakes" (from a dialogical perspective) are easy to make because, often, they don't feel wrong to either mentor or student; each is adopting an entirely familiar and conventionally legitimized role, the expert and the novice. To dance well, we have to know ourselves and our partners, and they must choose to do the same.

Winifred came to college, sponsored by a program that offered on-the-job training and money for higher education to people who had been on public assistance. She arrived with a very rough history and much trepidation. The success that she had been experiencing in her first full time position and the responses she had received from her supervisors gave her high hopes. She was learning in her job to help people like herself and she evidently had some talent for doing so. Indeed, her first two terms of study reflected her desire and ability to succeed in college. Winifred had completed conventional academic surveys of psychology and human services. At the time, she had made modest but real progress as a college-level reader and writer. Both she and her mentor felt that things were going fairly well.

However, something nagged at each of them. Winifred was struck, even amazed, at her success. She'd frequently wondered, sometimes aloud, how she could have got this far and worried that perhaps she'd just been temporarily lucky. Her amazement, while delightful to both Winifred and her mentor, expressed a still awkward self-consciousness about her learning.

She was not yet absorbed. Her mentor, while appreciating the progress Winifred had made, knew that she had a long way to go before her academic skills would become reliable and he worried whether she would be able to deal with increasingly challenging studies. So too, neither Winifred nor her mentor were naïve about the ongoing demands of her life: a rewarding but certainly stressful job, three young children at home she was raising by herself, and the weight of her own memories. Thus, both mentor and student were on a kind of plateau; the dance remained slow and movements still hesitant.

It was thus not surprising that Winifred was, for all her eagerness, a somewhat passive student. She very much relied on her "teacher" to tell her what to do. The mentor understood that she was still at a beginning college level. Nonetheless, he was bothered by a pattern of interaction in many of their academic discussions. He would ask a question that called on Winifred to work with a slightly general idea pertinent to her reading; and she would respond with a flood of details, in effect, reciting information she'd read. The mentor would feel Winifred floundering in these details, and he would become increasingly anxious to rescue her. Typically, he would then sort things out for her, explaining the idea in question and showing her its application. This procedure seemed to work quite well. Winifred would get the point, both of them would feel relieved, and the study would move along. However, during those moments of teacherly explanation, Winifred, while dutifully taking notes, would become uncharacteristically silent and would occasionally look up from her paper with a blank expression on her face. This pattern persisted through Winifred's first studies and probably contributed to her academic success. Yet, Winifred's silence and blankness lingered in the mentor's mind. He vaguely felt that he was enabling her passivity and perpetuating her dependence on his authority. Winifred was learning to read and write accurately, but she was not yet showing many signs of becoming an autonomous participant in dialogue. And, the mentor was complicit in this imbalance. His "rescue" efforts helped Winifred learn, but also helped her intellectual movement remain slow and halting.

For the next term of studies, the mentor decided to try a different approach. He hoped that Winifred would learn to work better with general ideas and analysis, and that they could organize the studies in a way that would change their pattern of interaction. He hoped that Winifred would become a less passive student, and that he would more effectively nurture her independence. Thus, the mentor drew upon his memory of topics which had seemed to particularly interest Winifred during her prior studies. He observed that she had been interested in the issues of race and class, drug dependency, neighborhood violence, and the experience of single parent families. He asked if she would be willing to pick one of these topics to learn more about in a study that they would design together. Winifred, although unsure what such a proposal meant, said that she was very interested in learning more about single parent families. He had invited Winifred to take the lead and she accepted.

He asked, "What would you really like to know about this topic?" Winifred thought for a moment and then eagerly replied, "Why don't more women get and stay married? Is it really worse for the kids if they are only raised by their mothers and grandmothers? Does this happen to black people more than other people? Why?" Winifred and her mentor discussed these questions and began to create a small outline for study, a collaborative choreography.

"What do you think would be the best way for you to learn about some of these topics?" After a time, Winifred realized that her mentor was telling her that she didn't have to follow a textbook. She said, "I guess I already know something about these things from my job and my own life." Seeing that Winifred had no trace of blankness on her face and that she was effortlessly jotting down a few notes for herself rather than trying to copy his words, the mentor suggested that she might keep a record of her observations and do some readings which might help her investigate her questions as they might apply to those observations. And so the study proceeded.

Typically, during their discussions within the study, the mentor would ask her to begin the conversation by saying what material from her journal she wanted to talk about and what had struck from the reading she'd done. Winifred's journal was full of detail and interesting observations. She had little difficulty talking about the content. When she selected and reported some of this material, the mentor would ask, "Do you see any connection between things you've just said and an idea you've read about?" Thus, for example, when Winifred described conversations she'd heard at her agency among women about boyfriends and husbands, and then mentioned that Stephanie Coontz (in *The Way We Never Were*) also wrote about those relationships, the mentor asked, "Do see any link between the conversations you've overheard and the reading you've done?" Winifred began to energetically compare the reasons those women had given for remaining single to the reasons Coontz explores. She found differences and similarities and even speculated that perhaps the reasons one offers in a personal anecdote might also be influenced by "bigger" factors "in society" which one wasn't aware of. She was not only connecting anecdote to the academy, Winifred was also clearly thinking in terms of her own experience as a single parent, her lifeworld. Winifred became increasingly adept at answering these kinds of questions; she was learning to use ideas – ideas which had meaning to her – to understand what she was observing. Winifred was learning to make good use of scholarship about families; the mentor was learning more about family experiences of a world in which he had never participated. At the same time, the mentor-student relationship slowly began to change. Winifred was beginning to learn to become a more independent student, and the mentor was learning how to ask the right questions.

In addition to Winifred becoming a more intellectually sophisticated and autonomous learner, she was also becoming more completely and unselfconsciously absorbed in the dialogical dance. As the mentor could tell from Winifred's increasingly relaxed and eager manner during many of their conversations, she was no longer concentrating her attention on whether he thought she was doing a good job or on worriedly searching for "the answer" he supposedly wanted to his questions. Her self-consciousness, rather, was now devoted to reflecting on her own ideas about the material she'd read, heard or written. She was thinking about the meaning of the questions and not trying to guess the mentor's response to her answers. Similarly, the mentor realized, that he too had become more relaxed. He no longer worried about "rescuing" Winifred or about whether his open or informational questions confused her (if she didn't understand his meaning, she would ask him to clarify, just as he had of her), or whether his leading and critical questions would paralyze her (for she could now take unexpected and critical conclusions as discoveries rather than as failures). Moreover, he too was learning, not just about Winifred, but also, from her, about the topic of their inquiry. Their dancing, at times, became graceful, and in their common immersion, they no longer bothered to tell the dancers from the dance.

Neither Winifred nor her mentor grew out of their customary habits overnight or without stops and restarts, wandering and backsliding. Trying to build genuinely collaborative relationships requires vigilance and it takes time. The vigilance is sustained by mentors' commitment to and institutional support for the principles that people learn best when they have the freedom to follow their curiosity and when they can arrive at ideas through connections they have made. The time this freedom takes to emerge is usually long. Mentors have constantly to learn to nurture this freedom not only through deft questions and other interventions but also by seeming to do nothing. Mentors have to learn how to wait. This is the topic of our next chapter.

Chapter 4

Waiting as learning

school ... f. Gk. *skholê* leisure
The New Shorter Oxford English Dictionary (1993: 2714)

Well, we started dinner, and still there was no sign of Socrates; Agathon still wanted to send for him, but I wouldn't let him. And when at last he did turn up, we weren't more than halfway through dinner, which was pretty good for him.

As he came in, Agathon, who was sitting by himself at the far end of the table, called out, Here you are Socrates. Come and sit next to me; I want to share this great thought that's just struck you in the porch next door. I'm sure you must have mastered it, or you'd still be standing there.

My dear Agathon, Socrates replied as he took his seat beside him, I only wish that wisdom *were* the kind of thing one could share by sitting next to someone – if it flowed, for instance, from the one that was full to the one that was empty, like the water in two cups finding its level through a piece of worsted.

Plato, *Symposium* (175c–d)

Not only can one not really impart knowledge to another, all of us take our own time to learn. Waiting, for ourselves and each other, is an essential aspect of dialogue. Does it seem very odd to think of waiting as learning, as one of the most important practices of students and mentors?

Wait less, acquire more

Within the modern tradition, speed and productivity are so customarily associated that it is easy to assume a necessary connection between them. We rush to our jobs, we are expected to work and complete our tasks fast, and then we move quickly on to the next ones. We ask questions or deliver messages and expect speedy replies. We look for the immediate results of our efforts, and we are often judged solely according to the short-term consequences of what we do. Everything zooms. As James Gleick says in

Faster, "We have reached the epoch of the nanosecond. This is the heyday of speed" (1999: 4). Computer-based tools, such as email networks and fax machines, are valued in good part because they accelerate communication, even to the point of instantaneity. Waiting is "down time," "lag time." Waiting is waste.

Even at play, we want to move quickly. We rush to and from our pleasures. The fun games and sports are the fast ones. Mountain hikers record how many peaks they can "bag" in a day. Popular films and TV shows contain lots of fast action and quick cuts; best-selling books, magazines, and newspapers are "quick reads." Should we be so unfortunate as to have to stand in line for an amusement park ride, our wait-times are often announced or posted at intervals and jugglers or magicians will move rapidly along the line to distract us with brief entertainments. Like work, play is disconnected from leisure (except when we guiltily indulge in "vegging-out"). Play has little to do with time that moves slowly, with offering room for contemplation and savoring.

It is not surprising then that we associate intelligence, the very ability to learn, with speed. Teachers want to "get through the material" quickly; and students want to get through the courses, get through school, get their degrees, and "get on with their lives" as fast as possible. Learning is like any object or commodity we own. It becomes something to be acquired, the quicker the better. "Accelerate your learning" some institutions proudly tout. It's a common marketing ploy and one attractive to many busy, hurried adults.

The common means of stimulating learning in the classroom is the assignment; the common means of evaluating learning is the test. These assignments and tests are always timed; and the time allotted for each is meant to both challenge and measure the intelligence of the students. Prior to receiving scores, students estimate the likely quality of their effort by how quickly they have completed these tasks. Passing means generating the minimum number of correct answers within the allotted time; superior learning is the highest number of correct answers within that time. When asking a question of a class, teachers often suppose the best answers will come from the mouths of the hands most quickly raised. And in the higher realms of the academy, quick productivity is readily taken as a sign of excellence. Faculty at research-oriented universities know that the more publications they generate within the allotted probationary period, the more likely they are to be granted tenure.

A simple equation might express these customary expectations: "Number of Correct Answers − Time = Truth." Perhaps when the matter is put so baldly, and in such caricature, the belief that high quality learning is fast will seem no less odd than our asserting that learning requires waiting. Several corollaries, equally questionable, follow from assuming a necessary connection between learning and speed: The "correct" answers are "the truth"; teachers possess the most important of these answers, know best how to acquire the ones they don't have, and know best how to transmit them; and of course good students are those who can produce those answers. In this view, learning and teaching are the mechanical components of a reproduction system. Knowledge is a possession grasped and used, not gradually explored and unfolded. The value of any "piece" of knowledge might be temporary, but until its obsolescence is forced, it is held on to absolutely. Provisionality and unsettling questions are unwelcome (Kuhn 1970).

We have cast doubt on this view and its assumptions (Chapter 2, "The principles of mentoring and the philosophy of dialogue"). If good learning is not necessarily speedy, if in fact it requires the slow time of leisure, then waiting is a crucial educational practice. In this chapter, we shall explore this idea.

Waiting and precious relationships

Waiting is the experience of distance between stimulus and response. It is the experience of slowed time between action and consequence, question and answer, between the glimmer of an idea and the assertion of it. There is something to do, something to understand, something to feel, something to communicate, but there is always a distance, a wait, between beginning and fulfillment.

For all the emphasis in our society on speed, on reducing waiting towards no time at all, it is surprising how much the relationships we value most deeply involve waiting: parenting, friendship, political associations, the relationships between therapist and patient, teacher and student. Perhaps even more surprising is that the waiting involved in each of these relationships, however taxing on our patience, can be savored for its interesting mix of suspense and serenity. We shall be arguing that along with the aesthetic and moral satisfactions waiting brings, there is an essential cognitive or epistemic virtue. Each of these deeply valued relationships requires and nurtures learning, and it is in the waiting that the learning occurs.

Parents wait for their children to grow. Friends wait for each other to appear. Therapists wait for their patients to achieve insight and to change. Politicians wait for their fellow citizens to speak. And teachers wait for their students to learn. Moreover, in each of these roles, we rely on the waiting for the satisfactions they offer and for the legitimacy of our participation. Parents must wait for their children to grow, and when this happens, they are joyful and realize that they have been good parents. Friends are patient with one another's eccentricities, needs and desires; and when they are, they offer and receive loyalty. Politicians who pause to listen acquire supporters and allies. They have reason to believe that their ambitions will contribute to a thriving polity of citizens governing their own affairs. Therapists who wait for their patients rather than cajole them to change, are professionally responsible, and they experience the gratification of increasing the autonomy and happiness of a suffering human being. And, similarly, teachers who wait for their students to discover answers for themselves, know that they are sending independent learners into the world.

Sustaining and appreciating the waiting required in each of these relationships both expresses our commitment to and permits our happiness at being embedded in the lives of others. Common to each relationship is a space for the reciprocal activity of persons who properly wait for one another to respond. We try to keep our distance, but not be separate. Our silence is in fact the respect we show for the autonomy of the others involved, and for ourselves in connection with them. We participate in these reciprocal relationships because they satisfy a basic human need – to become ourselves with others.

Imagine eliminating the waiting. The child would merely be a reproduction of the parents' wishes. The friend would only satisfy the companion's desires. The patient would wholly conform to the therapist's fantasy. The citizen would obey. And the student would simply copy the teacher. Removing waiting destroys these relationships. Preserving waiting sustains their inherent and reciprocal value. Alternatively, disregarding the wait or trying to remove it reduces each of these relationships to graspings for control and contests of power. The child fearfully and angrily rebels. Friends cease to trust one another and constantly, anxiously seek replacements. Patients become mortifyingly dependent and, if they are lucky, realize they have been abused. Politicians provoke suspicion and cynicism, and ever more desperately and emptily compete for support. And students become interested only in their grades, scores, and the piece of paper that will release them from school.

Waiting and learning

What is the cognitive dimension of these relationships? What does waiting have to do with learning?

In every relationship, between the stimulus and the response lie many opportunities. That space is filled by the particular expectations about the other(s) held by each party to the relationship. Those expectations not only define the character of the relationship. They are also beliefs, cognitive claims, about the other(s). These claims can be true or false, can presuppose prior learning, and can be open or closed to more learning. Waiting, in other words, is always filled with learning claims. The more insistently those claims are held, the more the waiting is experienced as something to be endured. The more provisionally or curiously the learning is entertained, the more the waiting is embraced and enjoyed. The eager willingness to wait is an opportunity to learn something new in relationship to another. This willingness to wait for what one does *not* know about the other, creates a reciprocal autonomy which integrates both the cognitive and moral dimensions of experience. Richard Sennett observes that:

> autonomy means accepting in others what one does not understand about them. In so doing, the fact of their autonomy is treated as equal to your own. The grant of autonomy dignifies the weak or the outsider; to make this grant to others in turn strengthens one's own character.
>
> *Respect in a World of Inequality* (2003: 262)

That is, waiting, whether in academic or any other kind of relationship, means that one is both respecting the autonomy of the other and respecting oneself as a learner (Principles 3 and 1).

Knowledge claims and the possibility of learning are immanent in every human relationship (Kegan 1995). How the parties wait for one another, or fail to do so, promotes or inhibits understanding among them. This principle applies to non-academic relationships among individuals, such as friendship therapy, parenting, and political leadership. We shall briefly discuss these and then examine the important and diverse uses of waiting in the work of mentors and their students.

Friendship

I patiently wait to hear my friend's desire. How warmly is this patience expressed? How genuinely is it meant? The particular qualities of the patience are influenced by my beliefs about my friend's desire. I have a belief about the compatibility of my friend's desire with my own. I have a belief about how truthfully my friend will express this desire. I also have a belief about how reliably my friend will act upon this desire. At the same time, my friend is making similar suppositions about my receptivity. All of these beliefs are knowledge claims. Moreover, because the relationship is reciprocal, we are assuming that each of us approximately knows the other's beliefs. Or, if my knowledge claims about my friend prove to be inaccurate, I expect that my friend will duly correct them, and we both expect that I will greet the correction with good will. The interplay of all these knowledge claims expresses and influences the strength of the friendship.

Such a dynamic also determines the relative comfort in which each is willing to wait for the other. In a relatively troubled or insecure friendship, I am uncomfortably impatient to receive my friend's response, because I anxiously want or need to know that it will be what I want to hear. In an easier friendship, I might also be somewhat impatient to know what my friend's response will be. But I am even more eager to know what my friend really thinks than I am anxious that my friend's response merely pleases or soothes me. So, even though I am impatient to learn what my friend will say. I willingly wait, knowing full well that I am ignorant of my friend's response until I actually hear it. In this waiting, I acknowledge and accept my ignorance (albeit not without tension), because I have faith that through our friendship I can learn something from my friend, which I had not known myself. I want to learn this for my own sake and also because that cherished person, my friend, thinks it. Thus, friendship is a complicated repository of understandings. It is an active field of knowledge claims about the beliefs we share, including the belief that our knowledge of one another is always unfinished and the belief that this incompleteness is good. The waiting of friendship attunes us to the recognition that we have more adventurous living to do together.

Therapy, parenting, and politics

What are the educative reciprocities of waiting in therapy, parenting, and politics? Unlike friendship, there is an inherent hierarchy in these relationships.

What, then, do therapists learn by respectfully waiting for their patients to make their ways to greater self-understanding and happiness? They learn the same things, and to do so, they are just as dependent as their patients are on the relationship itself. Every therapeutic relationship involves intimate engagements and "projections" of self, transference and counter-transference. (We examine mentoring as intimate engagement in Chapter 6, "The personal and the academic.") The sign of every successful therapeutic relationship (except the most impersonal and manipulative, if it can be said these are truly "therapeutic") is that both patient and therapist in their mutually intimate engagement "work through" this transference and counter-transference. In order to do so, *both* must achieve greater self-knowledge, both must learn to distinguish the false, fantastic beliefs from the true, appropriate beliefs each has about the other (e.g. Freud 1953). In every "case," therapists must vigilantly practice self-analysis. However knowledgeable and experienced they are, therapists thus discover their own ignorance and relieve themselves of being driven by false, wishfully charged beliefs. They free themselves to learn varieties of human experience with and from their patients, including ways of growing, which they had not previously known so well or at all. Thus, in therapy, embracing waiting means that therapists learn, in a very intense relationship, to respect and serve both their own autonomy and that of others.

Like therapy, parenting and politics are charged with powerful desires, including the desire for power itself. Parents are often torn between letting their children do as they please and controlling or disciplining their behavior. This conflict is difficult to adjudicate because one doesn't quite know what children are ready to responsibly do for themselves. And, more insidiously, it can be very difficult to distinguish which of one's desires for the children are really in their best interests and which are merely serving one's own frustrated wishes for oneself. Parents who let themselves get to know their children and let their children become themselves will manage this conflict better and be more successful nurturers. That statement is a cliché. However, it points to an important and difficult truth: serving the needs of others, especially when one loves them and has great power over them, requires engagement in the anxious, slow and never complete activity of learning about oneself. It requires waiting.

And the same is true of political relationships. The legitimate authority of those seeking or holding power depends upon "voluntary compliance" (Sennett 1980: 22), and neither followers nor leaders can enter or sustain such a social contract unless all are willing to learn about themselves and each other. Human beings, by nature, as Aristotle said, are political *and* they desire to know (*Politics*: 1129; *Metaphysics*: 689). These attributes, which bind us to others and draw us toward learning, are necessarily linked. It is in political associations of informed consent that we fully realize our capabilities. In learning with others, we fully become free. We depend upon our fellow citizens and they depend upon us to become complete. This perpetual and intrinsically valuable growing is moral, educative, and, to the degree we experience pleasure in the process, aesthetic as well. To accept and then grow from our incompleteness, we must wait. A world that always eliminates waiting in favor of efficient productivity is certain but thin. Parents, friends, therapists, politicians, and teachers who will not wait produce, in Max Weber's phrase, "the disenchantment of the world" (1946b: 143). A world in which waiting is savored is less certain, but a greater wonderment.

Waiting and the principles of mentoring

Schools and universities exist, obviously, for the sake of academic learning. They are also commonly regarded as environments in which students learn to become social beings. Just as non-academic human interactions contain an educative dimension, academic learning contains practical, moral and aesthetic implications. Waiting, in all it contributes to the richness of human association, would therefore seem a valuable practice to teach and learn in schools and universities. Perhaps all the more so because, nowadays, the homes from which young students come and the workplaces which often send adult students to university are, like the academy itself, so very busy. It is easy to understand why students, of whatever age and level, might see waiting more as an obstacle than a virtue.

In fact, a kind of waiting is normally taught and practiced in the academy. Students are admonished to wait their turns to speak, to receive service or gain entry and exit in line, and to ask questions. This custom of efficiency and etiquette is usually practiced by faculty and administrators as well. It is amusing to sometimes watch ourselves at meetings, eagerly shooting our arms into the air and then wearily holding them there, while we wait to be called upon, like so many schoolchildren. (Similarly, we tend to excuse the rude interruptions with which faculty sometimes impatiently pounce upon their hapless junior colleagues and graduate students as mere "childishness.") So, it seems that we both teach and practice waiting. But this kind of waiting is shallow, the mere behavior of passing time, until one's turn arrives. (We might ask, for example, while we hold up our tiring arms at faculty meetings, how often we actually listen to the people who speak in turn before us, rather than just impatiently hone our already pre-pared remarks before we deliver them.) This is not waiting as an educa-tional practice.

Waiting might not be a very valuable core skill for the professor in the lecture hall, but its importance for mentoring should be easy to see. We claim to practice student-centered, individualized education. How could we possibly do so, if we did not offer our students plenty of time in which to speak their minds?

We can understand more finely the importance of waiting by consider-ing it from the perspective of the six principles of mentoring:

Principle 1 calls upon mentors to rest their authority upon their willing-ness and ability to critically reflect on their own knowledge claims. That is how they are responsible to the provisionality of knowing, open to learn-ing, and to modeling these virtues for students. This practice necessarily slows the time of discourse. Mentors wait to present information, ask questions, and make judgments while they review the appropriateness of what they were about to say. Once they do speak, mentors wait for stu-dents to respond, giving them time to think and reconsider, time to learn.

Principle 2 expects diversity in the contents and approaches to learning. Waiting for their students, mentors give them the opportunity to become aware of and to articulate what they are genuinely curious to learn, why and how. Often, especially at the beginning of a mentor-student relation-ship, students are surprised and disconcerted that "the professor" would genuinely want to learn something from them. It is necessary to wait for students to formulate their ideas. It also takes some time for students to believe that their ideas will be taken seriously and respectfully.

Autonomy and collaboration, the virtues mandated by Principle 3, define dialogical inquiry. In order for mentor and student genuinely to col-laborate, as well to respect and support one another's autonomy, each has to wait for the other's idea or question. One can easily see here how the waiting creates and supports the intellectual reciprocity of the mentor-student relationship. In waiting, mentors suppose that their own know-ledge claims are provisional or incomplete (Principle 1). And, they assume that they have important things to learn from their students (Principle 2). Moreover, by waiting, mentors give their students time to work things out for themselves; they allow their students to express and develop their own capacities to learn, thereby supporting their efforts to be collaborators in the inquiry. This dialogical process takes time. It moves more slowly than a lecture and leads to places unmapped in a course syllabus. The waiting required of the collaborators allows them to discover what they had not anticipated and to begin to experience their intellectual relationship, the very process of inquiry, as an end-in-itself.

Principle 4 seeks learning from the lifeworld. By opening time, mentors allow students to bring into the learning relationship the matters which concern them most. They bring in themes, information, and questions from the contexts of their lives. When the academic discussion is integrated with these topics, it becomes meaningful and the learning achieved is remembered. Waiting allows connections between academic and social learning.

Academic evaluation is a particular kind of knowledge claim; it is a judgment about the quality of achieved learning. Principle 5, integrating both the principles of self-reflection (1) and collaboration (3), calls for evaluation to become part of the dialogical learning itself. Discussions about the means and criteria of evaluation are not only permissible but are important topics in the mentor-student inquiry. Student purposes and abilities have to be considered, along with common expectations (including university standards) necessarily related to those purposes. Mentors have to discuss with their students how far along they have come toward meeting their goals. And, if the dialogue has taken unanticipated turns and led to unexpected results, mentor and student will need to re-consider the goals and perhaps even the assessment methods they had originally agreed on. This approach to evaluation requires that both mentor and student *wait* to see where they go and to understand carefully where it is they've got to go before they can competently judge what, how much, and how well learning has been achieved.

Principle 6 means that if the other five are enacted, students will encounter the most valuable learning. They will learn what they had believed most important to themselves. They will have also revised and expanded those beliefs, making connections to topics and fields of which they had been ignorant, and developing skills which had been alien. And, the dialogue will also have stimulated and accommodated the fundamental themes and questions which motivate all learning: How shall I live? What is true? What is good? What is beautiful? Mentors and other academic authorities can not know in advance how this intellectual ecology of each student will evolve. They therefore should not *pre*scribe the knowledge most worth having. Instead, they must *wait*, holding their own beliefs about these matters up for critical examination, while students develop their intellectual lives. This takes time and the time should be as leisurely as possible, so that waiting becomes learning.

Waiting as mentoring practice

In this section, we shall illustrate the kinds of waiting mentors do. The cases are surely not exhaustive, but we hope they sufficiently suggest the diverse ways in which mentors use waiting to serve learning. We include waiting as giving students more time to complete their academic work; delaying criticism of work they present; waiting as an approach to conflict resolution; waiting as nurturing intellectual reciprocity; and waiting for the beauty of learning itself to emerge. This final example, in which waiting becomes beauty, serves well, we believe, as an image conveying all we have offered about both the instrumental and intrinsic value of "waiting as learning."

"I need more time"

Probably the most familiar use of waiting as a tool to promote learning is granting the student some extra time to complete a project. In mentoring, this sort of waiting can be helpful for months or even longer.

Marie, whom the reader will meet again (Chapter 6, "The personal and the academic"), is trying to figure out what to do with her several talents and interests. She is a subtle reader and fine writer of both prose and poetry. She is also a gifted pastoral counselor, a sensitive receiver of spiritual messages, and committed provider of spiritual counsel. Her health is fragile and further taxed by the many people who seek her help. Marie needs to make money. She knows that most of the careers suitable and attractive to her (e.g. counseling, teaching, editing, and writing) require that she have at least a bachelor's degree. In order to complete a degree, she will have to combine her interests into an intelligibly coherent program (see Chapter 5, "Curriculum as collaborative planning"). And this likely means that she will have to make some difficult decisions about which of her interests to pursue and talents to emphasize. In the midst of planning her program, Marie decides that she can't yet make those decisions. She needs more time. She asks her mentor if she can suspend her academic and career planning until she has made the decisions she is facing. He asks her how much time she believes she might need. She replies, "A month or so." He agrees.

Several months pass, between three and four. During this interval, Marie and her mentor attend to other academic studies, but occasionally and briefly converse about the planning project. The mentor is not concerned that this project is taking so long, longer even than Marie's estimate. However, he does take care to advise Marie that the more credits she continues to accrue before she finishes planning her curriculum, the more likely will she be constricted in making decisions about it. (In fact, as her mentor also notes, there's no guarantee that all the studies Marie will have completed can be accommodated within the program she eventually constructs.) Marie understands these advisories, and proceeds.

She finally announces one day that she knows what she wants to do, and she hands her mentor a draft of a complete bachelor's degree program. Marie intends to teach creative writing and academic composition, possibly at university level, part-time, and by means of Web-based study. Everything fits: Marie is going to prepare for a career involving her abilities to write and read sensitively, and to provide help on creative projects, which, as she knows, tend to stimulate troubled thoughts about much deeper issues than the writing itself. She has also made provision for some distance from the quality and quantity of work so taxing on her health: teaching writing rather than offering spiritual counseling; teaching at distance; and working part-time. Marie knows that she's not guaranteed to find a sufficiently paying job that suits her purposes and needs, but, as her degree program draft and her explanation of it make clear, she has made a well-informed and thorough preparation. The extra time, the wait, has been worthwhile.

Why did the mentor agree to wait? He took a risk. And he supported Marie in taking a risk. She might simply fall into confusion, procrastination, or just give up on finishing a degree at all. But he trusted Marie. He trusted that Marie understood her own abilities, purposes, and needs. His expectations were not clairvoyant or omniscient, but they were, like Marie's, well informed. Prior to and during the planning project, he had learned from Marie about her abilities, accomplishments, and the seriousness of her commitments. He believed that she could do what she said she intended and needed to do; he believed that her self-knowledge about these matters was reliable. Also, the mentor held his beliefs provisionally: he was ready to provide help and make a different arrangement if Marie learned that she was not up to finishing the planning project largely on her own. They stayed in contact so as to be open to this reciprocal and reflective learning. Waiting was not a passive experience for either of them.

Delaying criticism

Older students, new to university after long absences from academic learning, often present multiple academic deficiencies. When should these be addressed, how gradually, in what order? Which problems can wait and for how long?

Wally (who will appear again, in Chapter 5, "Curriculum as collaborative planning") returned to university after a very poor start many years before. Now, he was eager to learn and to complete a degree. He also doubted that he had the intellectual ability to do so. He occasionally mentioned his fear, but usually masked it with shrewd and assertively critical responses to assignments he was asked to do. The essays Wally wrote during his first studies contained all kinds of problems; disorganization, spelling and grammatical errors, leaps of logic, over-generalized and unsubstantiated assertions, absent or incomplete references. The essays were also highly intelligent. Wally had sharp eyes and words for other people's faulty ideas. And though not an obviously self-reflective critic, neither was he a supercilious one. Passionately interested in social justice in workplaces and communities, he drew upon considerable experience to advocate reforms in policies and programs. Moreover, he was eager to learn whatever he could that would help him be more effective.

His mentor was not sure how to respond to these essays. He was sure, however, after a few tentative efforts to combine praise with hopefully constructive criticism, that Wally's ability to tolerate such criticism, at least at this stage in his education, was fragile. How could he encourage Wally to continue and not ignore the problems? He decided to let some things go for now (references) and touch others very lightly (grammar), and concentrate instead on clarity (with the expectation that organization, logic, and evidence would follow). During their discussions, therefore, the mentor would ask Wally about the meaning of some of his key assertions and how he had arrived at them. The mentor waited for Wally to be ready for the rest.

Wally was happy to explain his ideas further and he agreed to revise portions and eventually entire drafts of his essays. He began to see them as steps in the progress of his learning rather an as final products on which the quality of his intelligence would be irrevocably judged. Organization, logic, and precision improved. Along the way, Wally became interested in and adept at writing on the computer. When he mentioned that he'd begun experimenting with the spelling and grammar tools, the mentor felt that Wally was ready to discuss the subjects themselves, which he introduced by demonstrating some of the limitations of the automated "checking" programs. Fortuitously, Wally's commitment to social justice also made him critical of the tyrannies automation sometimes made easy. His curiosity, both practical and contemplative, now aroused, he thus became interested in learning for himself the intricate customs and rules of English grammar and spelling.

A year or more into his work, Wally told his mentor that a research paper he'd written for a psychology study with another faculty member had been returned to be rewritten because the references were not entirely complete and had not been formatted according to the normally required style for that field ("APA"). He grumpily asked his mentor, "Why didn't you tell me to learn APA style?" The mentor apologized and smiled: "I'm sorry. I waited too long."

Waiting and conflict resolution

Sometimes, students and mentors don't like each other very much, and their dislike affects their academic work even though one or both know that it should not. Waiting can be a good way for them to gain some distance from one another and some detachment from their personal reactions, while still allowing the academic work to continue.

Lonnie wants to be an art therapist. When I began to work with her, I was trying to help her explore the academic preparations necessary for entering that field. Her investigation took the form of a research project. She would interview practitioners and become familiar with relevant professional journals. With this information, she would become an informed voice in planning her curriculum. Though I did not doubt the sincerity of Lonnie's interest, she often seemed to me to offer bravado instead of diligence. And, instead of focused and clear accounts of her learning, she often presented ideas and information in a scattered and incoherent way. She reacted to my criticisms by doubting whether I was really on her side. She was not convinced that I really wanted to help her learn.

Our mutual distrust became very serious. For example, she prepared a set of written summaries of journal articles on art therapy, which I thought rather careless and unclear. Both in her writing and in our conversations, she missed the main points and she misunderstood some of the central terms she used. Though I tried to express my criticisms mildly, Lonnie, I'm sure, detected the strong reservations behind them. She bitterly reflected aloud, "I sometimes think you are my enemy." As much as she must have worried about my attitude towards her, I was now skittish about her distrust of me. I was hesitant and frustrated about responding honestly to her work. I feared that she would take any criticism or even a suggestion from me as a personal attack. Indeed, I worried that expressing my concerns would be so distracting that they would actually impede her already limited academic performance. Lonnie and I were now dealing with two different problems: both the quality of her academic work and the quality of our relationship.

Each problem was exacerbating the other; our conversations became very tense. Lonnie did not believe that I would support her academic work, and although I did truly want to help her, I realized that Lonnie believed that I had lost faith that she would or even could do what was required – especially if *I* required it. I was sure that there were deficiencies and that I was applying normal academic standards. But, so long as we distrusted one another, I could not help her improve the quality of her work.

But was I being fair? I knew that I was sometimes annoyed by Lonnie's recalcitrance, complaints, and distrust. Had I become too particular, too demanding? Or, for that matter, in trying to make sure that my personal annoyance wouldn't harshen my professional judgment, was I too lenient, an "easy mark," as I cynically said to myself, for Lonnie's dislike? I could not confidently answer these questions.

How then could I do my job, which was to help Lonnie learn, but without "me"?

The question contained its own answer. At our next meeting, Lonnie and I suggested we take a break. Nearly interrupting one another, she asked for another mentor while I asked if she'd be willing to work with someone else. I arranged for her to complete with a colleague the study she had begun with me. And, at her request, she finished all her remaining studies with other faculty. We kept in polite touch, and I would occasionally ask my colleagues how Lonnie was doing. She happily told me that she was doing very well and my colleagues told me that she was doing well enough. They'd seen the same problems I had, but indicated that Lonnie had made improvements sufficient to complete her degree. Although I never understood the "bad chemistry" between us, I was relieved my professional judgment had not been very distorted and that I'd moved myself out of Lonnie's way.

The waiting here is quite simple. The mentor makes time and distance for Lonnie to proceed with her studies without the interference of their mutual distrust. *Their* dialogue, such as it was, never resumes. Lonnie, however, was able to collaborate effectively with other mentors. And her first mentor, examining himself, discovers that there are some dialogical problems he can not solve by himself.

Intellectual reciprocity

Waiting can also serve less conflict-ridden forms of intellectual collaboration. Students and mentors can help each other learn easily and richly in the academic studies they have undertaken together. Often this reciprocity requires time to develop, waiting. We offer two examples. In the first, the mentor reflects on a growing collaboration with a student. In the second, a mentor and a group of students create a small learning community.

In my first meeting with Michael, he told me about his experiences with prisoners and halfway house residents. He knew that he wanted to continue to work with these people. He also knew that there were things about their lives that he did not yet understand. He thought there were writings about history and society that might help him. This is why, he said, another faculty member had suggested that he work with me.

But Michael also was quick to let me know that while he wanted to know about sociology ("That's what you are – a sociologist, right?"), he was especially interested in the "development of the spirit." Within the first fifteen minutes of our initial meeting, he began to explain to me in great detail that he believed that those who had experienced the shock and deprivation of imprisonment had access to a kind of elemental dignity and forgiving understanding, which could become an antidote to "the insanity of our world." Michael was eloquent; his conviction was clear: If all of us could only "listen to the voices of those who live on the edge," we might be able to "heal ourselves" and "really change the world."

I was intrigued but wary. I wanted to follow Michael's lead but also thought he was asking me to teach him something different. I also felt that while he claimed to want guidance and the offering of another point of view, he was not particularly interested in the kind of analytical framework I would be able to provide nor in the kinds of readings and writings I would probably assign. Indeed, part way through a second meeting in which Michael read from a short first essay I had asked him to write about his ideas, I was convinced that Michael lacked any historical or reasonable conceptual perspective. At the same time, he worried aloud that the kind of approach he assumed I would want him to pursue would interfere with his efforts to "hear those voices" in their authenticity.

By the close of that second meeting, I wondered to myself if there was any way that we could talk to each other. I was actually more glued to my point of view than I had expected I would be. And, in response to what I thought was quite gentle questioning, Michael seemed to become that much more defensive and argumentative.

"OK," I said. "Suggest something for me to read."

"What do you mean?"

"Do you know of a book or an article that will help me better understand your point of view? Help me figure it out."

"I've read a lot on this topic."

"I know you have. I can lead you to sources on the social history of prisons, on the relationship between social inequalities, race, and incarceration, and on debates about victimhood. And that's what I thought you wanted to learn about. But I think we would do better together if you gave me something to study. I'll then think of something for you to read in response. We'll read each other's suggestions."

"I would do that," Michael responded with some glimmer of enthusiasm.

"It could be interesting. I'll have to do some thinking about the reading."

This agreement became the basis of our work together. Michael would suggest a reading to me and I to him. Michael's list focused on accounts of "prisons as places of potential self-transformation." Mine focused on prisons as "total institutions," which reflected a society's efforts to "discipline and punish." Over the next months, our meetings became opportunities to report to each other. We had many rich discussions about the prison system and about those inside. I learned a great deal from the new reading Michael had recommended. I particularly remember our conversation about the experiences of the Buddhist death row inmate, Jarvis Jay Masters (1997). I also learned from listening to Michael and reading the clear essays he wrote about selections I'd recommended from Foucault, Goffman, and David Rothman.

No doubt, all was not smooth. There were frustrating moments all along the way. There were, for example, those discussions during which I realized I was mounting arguments and looking for the weaknesses in *anything* Michael had to say. We'd crouch into our respective positions providing little room for any alien perspective. But I realized that what bothered me the most was that while I knew Michael was indeed looking at ideas that were discomfiting to him and most often could summarize what he had read, he rarely strayed from his point of view.

But something else was happening. I gradually came to see that there was something more important going on between us than the debates about "healing" and "social critique." There was something more compelling than our futile efforts to reach agreement regarding the most penetrating and conceptually sophisticated way to understand prisons and prisoners. Rather, although from the start I had thought Michael had only wanted to convince me of the truth of his insights, I was now feeling that he wanted something else. He really wanted me to be a partner who would agreeably accompany his efforts to work through his own thinking and get closer to those inmate experiences he so earnestly wanted to understand. From his point of view, I could become something of an analytical interlocutor who did not dismiss the authenticity of Michael's own approach to understanding.

"Do you agree with me?" Michael asked.

"What do you mean 'agree'?"

"Do you agree that a prisoner can 'find freedom' in prison?" "Don't you see that all of us live in some kind of prison and don't even see it?"

"Tell me what you mean. Give me examples."

"I am asking whether you understood Masters's feeling alone – 'the Lone Buddhist Ranger' – do you remember that image? Did you understand the experience he was having, realizing that he was seeing the world for the first time and understanding the violence in and around him, and knowing that we all don't have to suffer? It was an absolutely incredible insight."

"I see why you think so."

And he nodded, "I'm glad that you do."

As time went on, I often said little and Michael, I believe, came to trust that I was not trying to change him, not trying to reform his thinking. As a result, his experience of my acceptance became an important part of his learning. He discovered that school did not have to be a merely controlling institution as he'd read in Foucault. He discovered that here, unlike a prison, he was not under "surveillance" (Foucault 1977). We both came to understand that I was not waiting for him to become more like me, and that I would not judge his learning by its approximation to my ideas.

In many ways we were both waiting. I was waiting, sometimes anxiously, to see if and how Michael would engage the analytical readings I'd recommended. Michael was waiting to see if and how I would engage the more autobiographical and spiritual texts he wanted to read. Waiting was a quality of our discussions when we moved back and forth between our different ways of thinking. It was only by pausing to listen very carefully that we could learn from and with one another. I did worry about how to describe and evaluate what Michael was learning. I knew that Michael also worried that I would cut off our exchange. Each of us waited to see what the other would do.

For each of us there was, over the months of this study, a building of trust that supplanted the struggle for control over the terms of our talk. Waiting comforted us. It allowed us some freedom from our different worries about one another. My sense of the demands and openings of the mentoring situation helped me foresee and work with this roughly reciprocal relationship. The waiting enabled Michael and me to learn together, continuing to work at embracing our intellectual diversity.

Intellectual reciprocity can also emerge from waiting with a group of students.

A mentor decides to offer a group study on "the good life." (We will return to this group in Chapters 5, "Curriculum as collaborative planning" and 6, "The personal and the academic.") This topic frequently appears in discussions with students. Their concerns are usually immediate and practical: "What do I have to learn? What do I have to read or write? How soon can I graduate? How will I get a better job? How can I manage school, work, and family all at once?" But another kind of question often quietly rises to this harried, turbulent surface: "Why am I doing all these things? What sort of life do I really want to lead?" In fact the mentor himself experiences the same concerns. Burdened with everyday life, he often yearns for a clearer and more reliable understanding of what's really important and why.

He schedules the group to meet initially at an early evening weekday, a time he supposes many students are likely to be available. The group is open to whoever can and wants to attend. In the brief prospectus he writes, he says that the schedule of subsequent meetings can be created consensually by the participants. He also proposes a tentative set of readings – from literature, philosophy, political journalism, education – which he believes will be accessible to almost any student. Because the readings and the theme of the study itself are "liberal arts," they should fit almost any curriculum. Further, the prospectus indicates (as the mentor stresses during the first meeting) that the readings he's selected are taken from his own experience. They have helped him address the question of "the good life," but he encourages the students to add or substitute their own suggestions. This plan, the mentor believes, will serve both the collaboration of the group and the autonomy of its individual members (Principle 3) and will stimulate a diversity of ideas and resources from which everyone can learn (Principle 2, diversity of curriculum); the theme, obviously, pertains to an important life issue (Principle 4, learning from the lifeworld), and the readings and discussions should bring the students into appealing contact with "great works" and a variety of important ideas from several branches of learning (Principle 6, individual learning and the knowledge most worth having).

The plan looks good; the ten students are eager. Collaboratively making a schedule that excludes no one turns out to be quite easy. The mentor is a little troubled that no revisions are suggested for the reading list he'd proposed. Perhaps the students are too shy of "professorial" authority, and perhaps everyone is waiting to become more comfortable and get a feel for the developing group process. However, during their discussion of the first reading (Vivian Paley's *You Can't Say You Can't Play*), the students make comments and raise questions about "authority": Who should decide whom to include in or exclude from a group, in a classroom, at play, at work, in a community? What rights are necessary; what privileges are allowable? How does the experience of someone else's authority detract from, or, add to, one's sense of a good life? What does it mean to "have control" over one's own life? The mentor asks if this theme, these questions about authority, could be a sustained focus in their subsequent discussions of other readings. The students agree to try out this suggestion, although they also point out that other equally important topics might come up and that room should be left for them. They want to wait and they want the mentor to do the same.

Other topics do emerge: love, friendship, family, freedom of opinion and action, wealth and poverty, possessions and learning, solitude and community. By and large, the students do well. They listen to one another, offer different interpretations of the same material, and try to engage their differences. They write brief essays on common topics (usually proposed by the students and sometimes re-framed for clarity and manageability by the mentor) which have emerged during the discussions. Some students have difficulty keeping up with the group. The texts and/or discussions go beyond them; or, the circumstances of their lives require them to miss meetings. However, the mentor and the other participants offer individual help to compensate for academic problems and schedule conflicts. We try to wait for each other. Indeed, a little community of collaborative learning and "mutual aid" has formed.

The value of waiting never disappears, even at the conclusion of the group. A final project is to be done, the content unspecified in the learning contract but to be created by the group. During a discussion of what this final project could be, no one makes a suggestion. After all this time of working together, everyone is suddenly shy again. The mentor waits; tension mounts.

Someone says to the mentor, "Give us some suggestions."

He responds, "Why did you want to do this group study?"

Someone else says, "To learn about the good life."

And the mentor responds, "So, what have you learned? What's different now from when you started?"

And another student responds, "Couldn't this be our project?"

The discussion continues. The students decide to write reflective essays on some aspect of what they've learned about the good life, on one of the several themes – authority, freedom, friendship, etc. – which have been focal points of discussion. The students want to share their essays, both orally and the written versions, at a final meeting. The mentor makes one suggestion: that the students not place in their essays any personal information they would not want the other participants to possess. And he asks adherence to two criteria: that the students make explicit reference to the texts they've read and the discussions they've had about them, and that they give explicit reasons for any concluding beliefs and questions they've arrived at.

Two remarkable features emerged at the very end of the study. In their essays, the students offered a variety of conclusions about what they had learned. Some, for example, emphasized the importance of career, others emphasized family, closeness to God, or friendships as both instrumental and intrinsic values of "the good life." However, nearly all, citing both readings and their discussions in the study, highlighted freedom to be oneself, of learning for oneself, and of giving to and receiving from others respect for those freedoms. Their "primary source" for this claim was invariably their experience of participating in this group study of the good life.

Second, what the students asserted in their essays seemed to the mentor to be corroborated by their conversation during the final meeting. They did listen carefully and speak caringly to each other, even when strong differences of opinion emerged. They asked each other to elaborate meanings of statements. They hypothesized common grounds between very different perspectives (for example, the freedom necessary for genuine piety and the freedom necessary to fashion a meaningful secular life). They offered each other empathetic suggestions for enhancing the life each was trying to live. And, they seemed to delight in their intellectual association, their community of learning. The mentor concluded that all the participants, including himself, learned more about the good life, that everyone experienced mutual aid and respect, and that all experienced the deep satisfaction of an absorbing process of dialogical inquiry. The mentor was glad that he learned to refrain from deciding what the final project would be. He was glad that, despite the urging of the students and his own professorial impulse, he waited.

Waiting for beauty

We have claimed throughout this chapter that waiting serves fundamental human purposes: to discover and understand truths, to do justice, and to seek beauty. Of these, beauty is the most difficult to discuss. Its presence in dialogical inquiry is ethereal and rarely made explicit, and it is not commonly investigated. (For an exception, see Kupfer 1983: 24–39.) Once their practical academic anxieties ease, students will often reveal intense curiosity about fundamental existential issues and passionate moral questions. But unless they have undertaken art as a vocation, it is unusual for them to explicitly seek what they call "beauty" in or from their learning. Stella was therefore a surprise to her mentor, and waiting seemed to have everything to do with the wonderment that emerged.

When she resumed her university studies, Stella was already an accomplished nurse and health care administrator. With a professional nursing diploma and license, she had practiced in a variety of clinical specialties (obstetrics and gynecology, pediatrics, oncology). From there, she had moved into ward and departmental administration in a local hospital, and then into hospital public relations. Becoming more and more interested in the business side of health care, she wanted to concentrate the remainder of her undergraduate studies on management. Accordingly, she moved quickly toward completing a bachelor's degree.

Stella was studying business, she worked in management, and her manner was also "business-like": she was determined and focused; politely friendly, but rarely warm or ebullient. Moreover, she was not pleased to discover that the university's "breadth" policies would require that she do some non-business studies. But she expressed no interest in trying to shape this requirement to her curiosity; she just wanted to "get the job done." In this way, to her mentor, she was not the most interesting student, since she hardly ever raised anything but practical issues and questions about her studies and her career. On the other hand, the mentor also found Stella's single-mindedness and reserve fascinating. Almost always, students sometime along the way reveal some intense curiosity about a basic, often personal, human question. Stella never had. However, the mentor didn't ask, not wanting to violate the distance Stella kept. But he did wait to see if anything would happen.

Proceeding as a full-time student (while keeping her full-time job at the hospital), Stella quickly approached the final term of her enrollment. She'd become especially eager to finish the degree because, she mentioned in a rare personal aside, her husband and children had recently moved to another city, where he had accepted a very lucrative job. She longed to join them.

Stella and her mentor met late one day to plan her final group of studies, one in policy and the others in the required "breadth" courses which she had decided to select for simplicity and ease from a list of distance-learning "course-wares." Then, while she and her mentor were filling out the enrollment form, she said;

"There's something wrong with my education."

"What's wrong?" he replied, a little distracted and very curious.

"I don't know. Something's missing."

"What do you think is missing, a business course you need?"

"No, not that at all. It's something to do with ... I don't know ... with my soul." Stella was becoming upset, her normally even voice slightly trembling and her face flushing.

"Your soul?" The mentor was even more surprised that Stella had used such a word, in earnest, than he was that she was perceptibly distressed. "Do you mean that you want or need to learn something about the soul, like in a study of religion or philosophy?"

"No, I don't want to take a course in religion or philosophy."

"Can you tell me more about what you mean, what you want to learn about?"

This conversation continued for a long time and it seemed to oscillate between academic topics and surprisingly personal statements Stella made about her family and work life. The mentor didn't understand the connections, nor was he at all sure he should try. It seemed to him that Stella was experiencing longing, not exactly loneliness, but some kind of yearning to do something for herself, that, as she put it, "doesn't have to do with anything or with what anyone else wants of me. I want to learn something that will soothe me." The word "soothe" and the confiding way in which Stella uttered it, fascinated the mentor and also made him uneasy. What did Stella have in mind to learn? What did she want of him? Then, she abruptly added:

"Mythology. Greek mythology."

More than a little relieved to be on familiar ground, the mentor said, "Certainly. Of course you can study Greek mythology! You could read about the Homeric myths and others. They're interesting stories."

"No," she replied, returning to her normal, steady and cool voice. "I don't want to read *about* myths. I want to do this right."

"Oh, I understand. You could read Homer, the *Iliad,* the *Odyssey,* Hesiod, other authors. There are even some recent translations of Homer which try to give the feel of the original epic verse."

"No, no. I want to be close to the myths."

"Do you mean read Homer directly, in the original?"

"Yes, exactly."

"But you'd have to learn Greek, Homeric Greek."

"Fine. Excellent. I'll love it. Now, where do I start?"

Born and raised in Montreal, Stella was bilingual and could thus perhaps begin to learn a new language more easily than most Americans. Still, Homeric Greek was a long way from French or English. But she was determined. Stella and her mentor worked out a plan of study. She acquired an introductory textbook containing generous selections from both the *Iliad* and *Odyssey,* as well as lots of background discussion of the myths, the epic form, and the cultures of pre-classical Greece. She and her mentor also revised her degree program, entirely replacing all the remaining studies with a close exploration of the world of Homer. (See Chapter 5, "Curriculum as collaborative planning.")

And Stella did very well. She slowed her academic pace to part-time (even though this meant delaying her reunion with her family). She learned Homeric grammar, vocabulary, prosody, history, and mythology. By the time she graduated, she had read much of the entire first book of the *Iliad* and selections from other parts of both epics. She seemed especially delighted to read the Greek aloud, keeping the meter, and then slowly, haltingly translating what she'd uttered. The mentor had never seen her so exuberant and relaxed; and certainly he had never seen Stella do anything "slowly" or "haltingly," let alone with such pleasure. She was savoring.

Stella made no more personal or emotional disclosures. Upon completing her degree, she moved away to the city where her family had gone. The mentor received a holiday card from her, and then, nothing more.

He had many unanswered questions: Why the sudden change in Stella?

Why did Homeric Greek and mythology "soothe her soul"? What if she had wanted to study something the mentor or his colleagues couldn't offer? Fortunately, the mentor had studied Classics as an undergraduate and still remembered and enjoyed some Greek. Did Stella somehow know about the mentor's former pursuits (he rarely mentioned them) and was she seeking some kind of intellectual companionship, no matter what the subject? What meaning or consequence did this experience have for Stella after she graduated? Did she keep up her study? (As a graduation gift, Stella purchased for herself a complete edition of Homer in the original and a scholar's dictionary.) Was her life any different?

The mentor acquired answers to none of these questions. He realized that although he occasionally and idly asked, he wasn't really interested in the answers. For whatever reasons, Stella had decided to slow down the business and the busyness of her life. She was going to give herself this leisure, this beauty. And the mentor could also savor the beauty of her encounter with Homer. He will always remember the eager delight in her eyes and the relaxation in her voice as she slowly read aloud and then translated, utterly absorbed in a language and stories from the beginning of the world. Perhaps such things can't be fully understood or planned; one just has to learn to be open to them, to wait for them. The mentor was glad he had waited for her. She had given him a wonderment.

Chapter 5

Curriculum as collaborative planning and learning

> If our skeptic, with his somewhat crude science, means to reduce every [fantastic story] to the standard of probability, he'll need a deal of time for it. I myself have certainly no time for the business, and I'll tell you why, my friend. I can't as yet "know myself," as the inscription at Delphi enjoins, and so long as that ignorance remains it seems to me ridiculous to inquire into extraneous matters.
>
> Plato, *Phaedrus* (229e–230a)

We wait for wonder and beauty to emerge, but the preparation is not passive. Mentors and students plan learning: what to do next and what to do for an entire curriculum, all determined by the frames of references within which we work and live. Prominent among these contexts is the traditional academy itself. Students and faculty meet there to make curricular decisions among an array of choices, which are, as in any institution, more or less pre-set. Students search within catalogs to find courses they must take. Faculty teach those courses based on disciplinary expectations and departmental demands. For both, autonomy is defined by the range of freedom in that choosing. Students want to follow the proper rules and also to look for spaces to pursue courses that might interest them. As faculty gain status, they choose the courses they want to teach and have more say in determining the studies offered in their departments.

It is probable that among the lists, students will find something to which they will be attracted. It is also probable that faculty will be allowed to focus attention on a topic in which they have a scholarly stake. It is much less likely that an individual student and an individual member of the faculty will work together to fashion an entire set of studies, a curriculum, based on that student's efforts to follow his/her curiosity and to place his/her life experiences within a meaningful academic context. It is just such a demanding and intellectually rich activity, one that combines complex research and reflection that describes curriculum design in a world of mentoring. In keeping with the spirit of Principle 3, educational planning becomes yet another occasion for dialogue.

Of course, academic mentors and their students are beholden to the university and other institutions. As we've seen in our first and second chapters, these institutions shape and sometimes constrict and trouble learning. However, we've also said that these encounters are occasions for learning, for both mentors and students to reflect on what's really important to them and why. Even troubling encounters often provoke us, as Cephalus from the *Republic* does, to take stock and reckon up. In this chapter, we present curriculum planning as a self-reflective learning activity. When one's educational goals encounter the demanding conditions of fulfilling them, we, both mentors and students, begin to learn not only how to do so but also how to reflect on exactly why we should or should not. Curriculum planning, including everything relevant to one's educational purposes – from one's past and the life one leads now to the life one hopes to have after completing a degree – becomes consciously provisional (Principle 1) and a topic for inquiry (Principles 2 and 4). Thus, in a mentoring environment, curricular planning is a process of deep and far-reaching collaborative learning.

Prospect and retrospect: learning the student

Rick and I meet for the first time when he's ready to re-enroll in college to complete a bachelor's degree. He's already completed an associate's degree at a local two-year institution. He wants to transfer those credits and continue to concentrate his academic work on business studies. Nervously jiggling his left leg, he tells me that he's in his mid-thirties, married, has three kids, and wants to own a business.

"What kind of business?"

"A car wash. I managed several; now I want to own one, to provide a good life for my family and me. I want to get on with it."

Like most of my colleagues, I've seen all kinds of career holders and seekers walk into my office to plan their educations: accountants, social workers, ministers, managers, park rangers, bakers, ship captains, software developers, woodworkers, philosophers, pilots, child caretakers, firefighters, historians, state troopers, wrestling coaches, lawyers, poets, and even a professional skydiver. Rick is my first auto-wash entrepreneur.

"Have you learned a lot from managing small businesses?"

"I think so. And I've heard that at this college you can get credit for life experience learning."

"That's right. While you're planning your whole degree, you and I can look at your experiences, find the college-level learning there, and have it evaluated for credit. As you know, gaining credit for what you already know is part of what you can do here. In fact, this college has a specific course in which you do all that – our only required course – called Educational Planning."

"Sounds good. I need to get on with it."

"We can start right away. But, if you don't mind my asking, what's the rush?"

"Well, I'm kinda pressed for time." Rick's leg vibrates more rapidly as he turns to gaze out my office window into the gray late winter light.

"You want some of that American Dream, eh?" I ask with a professionally amiable smile.

"Yeah, I need to get things set up. I have MS."

Then I remember uncomfortably that Rick's application indicated he has financial support from the state's Office of Vocational Rehabilitation. And I remember that he'd dragged his left leg a bit, the shaking one, while walking into my office.

"Okay. Okay. We can do this," I try to calm both of us. "You can design your degree to suit your goals, and you'll get academic credit towards your degree for creating the design. You can think about Educational Planning as a full college course, a major learning project in itself. You'll figure out what you already know and what you need or want to learn, then put together a whole degree program plan that will have to be approved by the College. We can work on it together."

I am hesitant to say now anything more about Rick's disease – how that might affect the achievement of his goals – until and unless he signals that he is ready for this to become a topic of deeper exploration.

"Let's do it." He turns towards me from the window, his leg quiet for now.

During the following weeks, Rick, like most students thinking about planning their college studies for the first time, finds catalogs of other colleges offering majors related to his interest in business. And he interviews people working in the type of position he wants to have, in Rick's case, owners of car washes and other small businesses where labor is transient and managing includes intensive supervision. This is normal background research for the prospective part of educational planning. It provides information for one of the questions Rick needs to answer for himself: "What shall I learn that I don't already know or could usefully learn more about?" But this prospective orientation also highlights Rick's retrospective research question: "What have I learned already, in and outside of the classroom, that I can include in my program?" Looking at the descriptions of courses commonly required and listening to the advice of successful practitioners familiarizes Rick with the typical learning content of his field. He thereby also learns to describe the experiential learning both of us are sure he has but which he's never named.

Through such a process of planning, these prospective and retrospective views support and influence one another. Students decide what to value in their past learning, partly with regard for what they want or need to learn. They also decide what future learning to include in their curricular plans, seeing that "new" learning within the context of what they have already learned. Then, with the help of their mentor, they learn to integrate these two perspectives, creating an entire and coherent degree program plan.

Similarly, students learn to consider and synthesize contemporary practical and traditionally academic perspectives. For example, the course descriptions available in published college catalogs offer a useful guide to conventional academic expectations. However, sometimes those published offerings, having made their way through the deliberations of curriculum committees, lag behind innovations in a field.

For example, during a planning conversation with his mentor, another student, Joe, a steel production designer, casually mentioned that he had invented a promising new alloy made from production waste. It seemed that this alloy didn't even have a public name yet, though Joe was about to present a paper about it at a metallurgical conference. He was wondering if he could get some experiential learning credit for what he had done on the job and connect that learning to a set of studies he was beginning to imagine could form the core of his undergraduate degree. The mentor himself was (as Principle 4 encourages) learning from Joe's "lifeworld," and Joe was learning that what he had done and what he knew would be treated with respect and seriousness.

The practical or experiential perspective can also correct the condescension academics sometimes show towards the "real" world. Ruth, for example, had wanted to teach photography to poor grade-school children. She came to university after many years as a photojournalist and was committed to using her craft for the purpose of social change. The chair of the Education Department of the university she was then attending told her that while her goal was commendable, she should wait until after she'd attained the proper credentials. Though temporarily discouraged, Ruth didn't want to give up. She applied for and received a small grant from a local social service agency, created a community camera club, and taught kids to make and use the *camera obscura*, a pinhole and sheet of film inserted into the emptied cardboard cylinders in which a popular, inexpensive brand of dry oatmeal was sold. The knowledge she gained about resourceful teaching, program development, and about community action found its way into the experiential learning portion of the educational plan she and her mentor spent months crafting together.

The work of educational planning does not exist within a vacuum. Interviews with practitioners offer a window into currency, tricks of the trade, and sometimes unsettling wisdom about what the career to which a student is dedicated is really like. From the five or six car wash owners he interviewed, Rick discovered that hard as he had worked as a manager, he'd have to work even harder as an owner and should expect to wait at least several years before he saw much net profit for his efforts. He began to worry about reaching his career goals. He wondered if they were best for him. He reflected again about whether the plan he had begun to sketch out, even if he could attain it – and that was a question too – would really serve him well.

The mentor's role

In their regular face-to-face meetings, the mentor listened to Rick's interests and for clues to his educational needs. The mentor suggested how he might find relevant academic and occupational information and become better informed about his options. Complementing his ideas, the mentor also indicated areas of potential experiential learning and relevant future studies that could become a part of his undergraduate degree plan. And, importantly, the mentor asked Rick questions, which he hoped would help him look carefully at the contexts, both academic and professional, in which he hoped to thrive. He encouraged Rick to evaluate his research and his interests in light of the purposes (about which he became ever more explicit), which had brought him back to university in the first place.

Every two weeks, they discussed the information Rick had collected. He created his own lists, and he and his mentor used these as take-off points for discussions of possible topics for experiential learning and for future study. The latter didn't present any surprises. Rick and his mentor soon saw that his "concentration" (his undergraduate "major") would probably be quite similar to those of most business administration students. Why bother then asking Rick to discover what is only customary? The mentor might have given him a list of normal course requirements and array of typical electives. But those lists might have undercut a potentially powerful part of Rick's learning process. Through his research and reflection, through the questions that he asked himself and others and the problems he confronted, Rick actually succeeded in beginning to make the field, and thus his university degree, his own. He used his time to fashion his own intellectual place in a public context of knowledge and practice – a context in which he also constructed his own coherence and meaning. Moreover, as he moved along, Rick learned to test his dream against his own increasingly informed sense of the significant challenges to fulfilling it. For example, though Rick had managed the payroll and other local finances of a car wash, he learned that as an owner on probably a shoe-string budget, he'd have to become much more adept at the skills of accountancy and business math – for him, not at all a pleasing prospect.

The prospect darkened more when Rick looked at the problem of time. It would be years before he could earn enough to provide the sort of life he wants to enjoy with his family and that he wants his family to enjoy "later on." This "later" remains, for a couple of months, an unspoken topic in Rick's conversations with his mentor. The issues, however, are clear enough: How long will the MS allow Rick to work as a car wash owner? Will the stress of accelerated learning (both in school and after-wards on the job) also accelerate the disease? If so much of his limited time is to be fiercely concentrated on making his way to his ultimate goals – pride of ownership, prosperity, and, especially, savoring life with his family – will he risk those ends for the sake of the means?

And his mentor had his own concerns: by asking such questions, by wanting to acknowledge and respect Rick as a whole person, would he intrude on Rick's privacy? What boundaries should be maintained? (See Chapter 6, "The personal and the academic.") What is the appropriate role of the mentor? Can a faculty member, even in that mentor's most caring moments, ever presume to judge a student's ultimate purposes? To be sure, raising questions and encouraging the student to think with care about his/her plans, is central to this kind of collaborative educational planning process: "Why are you here?" the mentor asks. "What are you thinking about? What are your real interests? What are your educational purposes?" But by and large, mentors ask these kinds of questions because we expect students, over time, to clarify their answers for themselves. It is one of the fundamental assumptions of this inquiry that the faculty are not wise or knowledgeable enough to provide or preach such answers. The omnipresence of this provisionality is a sound, Socratic principle of education. As we earlier described in the first principle of mentoring, it is better to examine one's own claims, to know and to encourage others to do the same, than to presume one knows what is best, especially for another.

Mentors also need to accept that our students, adults who by and large already adeptly inhabit the lives they are here to enhance, do possess and will develop their own wisdom about ultimate ends. Rick's ambitions seemed a little crazy to his mentor, fraught, as they were with the great risk of self-defeat. Yet upon what authority can anyone pass judgment on Rick's hopes? The mentor was at least sure of this: the spirit that elevated Rick's learning should not be clouded – not by his ignorance nor by his mentor's.

Perhaps more than any other aspect of mentoring, collaborative planning brings into stark relief the question of what a mentor actually knows.

(See Chapter 7, "The mentor as learner," for a detailed discussion of what mentors learn and how they do so.) When so much educational autonomy and instructional responsibility are left to the student, when the expectation is that a student's curiosity will lead that student to what he/she needs to learn, what skills are mentors really practicing? We are indeed often working with students whose interests, questions, academic goals, and professional directions pull us well beyond the traditionally understood boundaries of disciplinary expertise. Thus, for faculty and for students, the process of planning encourages us to "stretch." As we noted earlier, mentors can not work alone. They learn to enlist other mentors to supply expertise they themselves lack. Students learn to ask clearer questions and to better articulate their interests. Both mentors and students gain valuable experience listening to each other and trying to understand ideas that are often alien. Such "experiential learning" gradually creates faculty generalists unabashedly curious about whatever our students want to learn. It encourages students to learn to teach themselves, to regard their questions as authoritative, to search for answers, and to regard those answers as worthy of serious reckoning.

This is Annette's third effort to complete a college degree. More than twenty-five years ago, she completed close to two years of university before thinking that she was, as she described to her mentor, "jumping through hoops" for reasons that were, at best, obscure to her. She needed money, wanted to find a life of her own, and knew she was drawn to singing and learning other languages. She also wanted to travel. Though in their early meetings Annette was obviously nervous and took every opportunity she could to question her academic competence and her "fit" in *any* university, her mentor was struck by what he perceived as gaps between Annette's low self-confidence and her obvious accomplishments.

"And then you started to teach people with second language needs."

"Yes," Annette matter-of-factly stated. "As you see, I took French and German at university so many years ago now, and the way anyone learns any language just intrigued me. A friend encouraged me to volunteer at a local library where they had a language and culture program for new immigrants. I started tutoring one student, then more, then I started supervising other tutors – I got hooked. I completed a certificate program in English as a Second Language. All of that was more than fifteen years ago. I've been teaching ever since."

"You've obviously learned a great deal from that training and work, and we should talk about what you already know. But I wonder about your plans: Have you done any thinking about what you imagine your degree will look like?"

"I need a degree. I have missed out on many jobs because even though I have good experience in the classroom, I have no university diploma. I want to get my degree as quickly as I can. I really don't care what my degree looks like."

"You really don't?"

"I need a degree."

Over the next three months, Annette and her mentor discussed what she has done as a teacher – what classroom strategies she used, how she planned her courses, and why she organized the courses as she did. Her mentor asked her to write about these things. While it was easy for her to describe what she does as a teacher, Annette only gradually became more adept at identifying the principles that informed her practice. Annette wrote many drafts of short essays whose goal was to describe what she knew. She also used this time of planning to gather information about current ideas in the field of language acquisition, an area which, Annette said, interested her a great deal.

Mentors *do* bring their own information and ideas to this collaborative planning process. Rick's mentor knows that it will be useful for him to talk with successful entrepreneurs, especially ones he already knew and others to whom they would refer him. And the mentor knows that he and Rick can trust the messages about the learning he needs to acquire – messages that are gathering implicitly in the information and advice he collects from those interviews, from the trade journals with which he is becoming more fully acquainted, and from academic catalogs. That is, the mentor is sure that Rick is gradually discovering the worklife and academic realities he will have to deal with in order to achieve his goal. Having learned something about Rick, the mentor also knows that he can rely on his rationality and on his ability to adjust means and ends reciprocally as he learns more about each. That is, Rick's mentor believes that Rick will use his learning, the learning he is acquiring through research and reflection, to shape a life he desires and an education suited to it.

What mentors know best is how to shape an inquiry, how to create an environment in which the mentor's and the student's learning grow symbiotically. For that nurturing to occur, mentors have to know at least this: They cannot presume to know that which they do not. And that includes not presuming to know with what meaning and value each student invests his or her education. Thus, above all, mentors must know how to take care to examine themselves.

"Your degree seems to be taking shape," Annette's mentor quite happily announces after they had been meeting for about three months and her experiential learning has been evaluated for a substantial number of college credits.

"I'm happy about the credits. I'm surprised. But I don't think I'm ready to make a decision about my degree."

"But don't you see that your past learning plus those new studies you have mentioned really form the foundation of a strong degree?"

"I'm not sure if I really can succeed in a linguistics study and I know I need one. I'm also not clear about other studies that I might want to do. I want more time to think about it."

"I think your degree will serve you well as it is," her mentor more anxiously responds. "Even if you choose to go on to graduate school, I'm impressed with the course of study you have put together."

"Graduate school is not something I think about."

How crisp is the distinction between the clarification and the *evaluation* of values? How valuable is the mentor's eagerness that Annette prepare for graduate school and that she commit now to the degree plan she has all but finished designing? How much authority should be given to Annette's insistence that she not concern herself about graduate school and that she take more time to think about her plan? The process of educational planning requires students to engage in prospective and retrospective research. It also requires that they, like their mentors, engage in critical *self-reflection*. Students must decide what learning – both past and future – to include in their degree programs. They decide according to their own purposes, but, inevitably, when they begin to decide reflectively, they also begin to examine those purposes. Annette's mentor has to honor the self-reflection in which she has thus far engaged.

Practical purposes and academic requirements

Rick and Annette, like most adult students, have returned to college for practical reasons. Rick wants a prosperous career and for that he needs the kind of practical knowledge typically offered in a business degree. Annette wants to be a viable applicant for jobs that demand at least an undergraduate degree. As Rick plans his degree program, for example, he reads college manuals and consults with his mentor to learn about the college's requirements for all bachelor degrees. By interviewing successful practitioners in his field, reading trade and professional journals, and examining business majors offered at other colleges, Rick learns what studies the variety of business degrees usually contain.

Some of these typical expectations are arbitrary: they are the historical accretions of institutions and professions. One wonders, for example, why universities so commonly require all business majors, whatever their goals, to take a year's worth of accounting courses; and why required courses in management principles will often emphasize the currently dominant academic and consultant discourse about managerial "philosophy," regardless of its tenuous relationship to actual practice or its demonstrable influence on business performance and cycles. And of course some typically required studies are probably useful but intensely distasteful or fearsome to the individual student. Sometimes crude but not unfounded stereotypes come into play: For example, many students, no matter what their field of interest, shrivel at the mention of math; and many computer-absorbed students are loath to improve their skills in mainstream written and spoken English.

Despite these challenges to rationality and desire with which Rick was becoming familiar, the pragmatism which brings so many adult students to university will afford them the prudence to manage whatever seems necessary to reach their goals. For example, if someone like Annette even wants to consider going on to graduate school in anything having to do with "language studies," and the department advises that successful applicants know some linguistics, then the prudent student will include it, no matter how disinclined she may be to such a topic. Rick knows, through prior college experience, that it will be difficult for him to learn the math associated with finance and investment studies. He has also learned, through his planning research, that those studies, including their quantitative dimension, will significantly help him become the successful businessperson he hopes to be.

Such requirements, and the practical student purposes that bring them to bear, can easily fill the greater part of an undergraduate degree program. Even so, curriculum development in the context of mentoring and collaboration needs to contain significant openings for individual invention. (Consider Principles 2 and 3, which call for curricular diversity based on individual student curiosity and for students to be regarded as autonomous collaborators in inquiry.) This is a virtue we faculty must vigilantly school ourselves to respect, and one that students themselves discover, sooner or later. It is part of the common learning in educational planning. (See below for some examples of this inventiveness and diversity.)

Nonetheless, it is rare that adult students, even with the opportunity to craft a program that draws their curiosity and responds to their pragmatic needs, create curricula that are completely unique or remarkably idiosyncratic. As described above, the list of studies on the business degree of a student like Rick will usually look quite like the studies found in the management or business administration degrees of other universities. In what sense, then, can it be said that students do design their own degree programs? It is this: during the process of educational planning, students are investigating both the commonly understood expectations associated with their individual purposes and the personal meanings and values associated with their purposes. Students learn to understand the rationale (however questionable) for the coherence and requirements of a discipline or profession; they also learn to understand what they care for and to what they are willing (or unwilling) to devote their learning. Then, they are in a position to decide for themselves what personal and public expectations to embrace. They are in a position to develop their own arguments to an academic institution for being exempted from some of those external expectations, and to take advantage of the loopholes often found in those requirements. Indeed, students can even create their own "concentration" titles, their own "majors," to describe precisely how their academic plans express their particular purposes, both academic and professional.

No doubt, the list of studies on a student's program, which is the tangible product of educational planning, may thus not appear to be very unusual. But the learning which gives rise to that list, the learning contained in the process of creating the plan, could not be more different from the list of curricular requirements many institutions prescribe. So much of commonly practiced higher education assumes (contrary to Principle 6) that the degreed "we," the faculty, possess the knowledge most worth having. It also assumes that, like medical doctors protecting public health, we are to prescribe and administer that knowledge to the less learned "others," as though we were to create healthily educated persons out of ones who are cognitively and contagiously impaired. By contrast, by reframing educational planning as a collaborative inquiry among mentors and students, mentors have to respect students' purposes and wonder about their own assumptions; and students, too, have to agree to engage in asking difficult questions and dealing with complex problems. The list of "courses" on Rick's and Annette's final degree programs might well look like many others. But that convergence only came about because of thoroughly informed decisions these students made about what learning would serve them best, decisions these students' mentors also participated in making, and which their colleagues who finally assess these degree plans will honor.

Unfolding purposes

But something more happens when students, even the most anxiously and strenuously practical-minded of them, are respected in this way. Other purposes, new ones, usually emerge during this process of reflection. That is, as students relax into trusting that their practical educational needs will be served, other interests and more meanings of learning unfold. More and more confidently and deliberately, students discover and present themselves as centers of widening circles of curiosity and aspiration: areas of intimacy and leisure, of purely intellectual achievement, of social status, civic commitment and spiritual quest. Mentors need to keep an eye out for the unfolding of those previously implicit purposes. At first with light questions and, perhaps later on, with suggestions for provocative reading, we encourage students to embrace this creation of a broadening self. And, we wait for them to be ready.

Over several months, Rick looked in ever-greater detail at the learning he will need to do for the career he believes he wants to have. He also became more occupied with wondering why. The "why" question called upon him to examine the sort of life he will be creating for himself and for his family.

Rick's mentor notices signs of this wonder: casual comments about the many hours a week, for many years, he realizes it will take him to build a business; about attending more closely to his medical condition; about starting off working in a large, well-established business so that he does not over-tax himself; about reviving former participation in the local volunteer fire department.

Rick and his mentor have been talking, not for the first time, about the intensity of the academic and work plan he was creating. Eventually, his mentor asks:

"What do you enjoy, for its own sake, aside from school and work? Do you want to make time for those pleasures while you are still earning your degree and building your business?"

"I like off-road bike riding. I meditate and read about Zen. I enjoy just being with my wife and kids, especially travelling around."

"Do you want to create opportunities to do those things while you are still a student and while you are learning the ropes of being a car wash owner?"

"I'd like to," he says.

As nervous as he, the mentor hesitantly asks, "Please tell me if it's none of my business, but may I ask you a more personal question?"

"Okay, go ahead."

"It's about your health. Will the study and work you plan to do, at the pace you plan to do it, affect your MS? Will they deplete or damage the time you want with your family and the other things? I'm sorry again if I am intruding . . ."

"It's OK. The answer is maybe, probably. But I want to get my degree and I need to provide for my family. I haven't worked in more than two years. I don't know." Rick looks down at his leg, which is now shaking.

"These are tough decisions. Big ones. I know they're not really my business or the college's. The faculty will approve any degree program you design so long as it meets the formal requirements we've discussed and the purposes you say you have. But do you want to look at those decisions, sort them out as you plan your degree?"

"Seems like a good idea. I probably even should. But how?"

"Well, part of your research could be to speak to your family and your doctor about these things. There is no need to tell me about those conversations – just the results that are relevant to your degree program design."

"Okay." Rick takes a deep breath. "I think I just might do that. It could be helpful to me. I never thought it could be part of this work."

"It can be. In fact, in addition to thinking and finding out more about your own situation, there are some interesting readings you might do. Juliet Schor's *The Overworked American* and William Greider's, *One World, Ready or Not* are examples of writings about leisure and entrepreneurship in a '24/7' world that I'd recommend."

More than a month passes. When Rick comes in next, he brings along a draft of a complete bachelor's degree program. It contains a large block of proposed experiential learning credit for "Supervisory and Small Business Management" and the customary advanced level studies for a business concentration. It also includes proposed studies in "Zen Philosophy," "Adaptive Trail Riding" and "Fire Investigation." Rick has read the two books his mentor had suggested. He has talked with his family, some friends, and his doctor. He has renewed his membership in the volunteer fire department and has discovered that if he trains to investigate a fire's causes, he can participate in this public service without straining his health. His wife and friends, though worried, want to support whatever decision he'll make. The doctor warns him that high-pressure activity might well accelerate the disease.

"I still want that degree and that car wash as soon as possible. But my doctor admitted that neither she nor anyone else knew exactly how fast a course my MS would take. I can go a little slower. Maybe instead of jumping into my own business right away, I'll get some more experience and earn some money helping out the owners I already know. And in the meantime, I'll have more time for my family, my self, and for the fire department. That'll be okay, for now."

Rick and his mentor polish his degree program and prepare it for formal college approval. The final program contains fewer business studies in the concentration than both Rick and his mentor had originally anticipated. Overall, the increased diversity of learning suits the multi-intentional life Rick has decided to lead (Principle 2, diversity of curriculum, and Four, learning from the lifeworld). The rationale essay he has written helps an outsider understand the student he was and the creative learner he is becoming. Such an accomplishment has taken time – time for research and planning, time for careful reflection, and time for emergence. Rick has completed the process nearly a year after he began. Mentors make suggestions about directions to pursue, and mentors help students assess their research and discoveries. But though mentors often guess what will emerge and sometimes wish for a particular outcome, we must wait for the unfoldings as they happen.

Life-long learning: revising the plan

The pace, rhythm, and continuity of these developments can vary widely among students. In fact, planning one's education can continue long after the formal planning is done, long after the student has achieved formal approval of a curriculum. This remarkable phenomenon, perhaps unsettling to those of us who like closure, occurs because something not at all surprising happens: once students have become successful independent learners, once they have experienced successful autonomy as students, and once they have learned to create their own educations and thus to learn about their own learning, they continue to do so. The self-examination continues. Our students learn to practice for themselves the first principle of mentoring. Thus, they become very sophisticated "life-long learners."

In the previous chapter, we saw Stella produce remarkable results from such reflection. The main purpose of her curriculum did not change; she still intended to pursue her business career. However, she dramatically and thoughtfully allowed a new purpose into her education, the study of Homer, something "soothing" to herself. Accordingly, nearly at the end of her undergraduate studies, she significantly altered the content of her curriculum.

Sometimes continuing, introspective educational planning does lead to a career change. Like Stella, Henry had formally completed his planning early on in his studies. A veteran corrections officer, he'd designed a program concentrating in sociology. Remarkably, he sought no experiential learning credit for his knowledge of corrections, nor did he plan any new studies on crime or penology. Expressing no particular post-graduation career ambitions at all, Henry told his mentor that he'd just "serve out" his "twenty-five" in corrections, retire, and then "do something else." During the many tutorial studies they did together, Henry wanted to understand the larger society, the moral and civic culture, which generated, depended upon and cozily ignored the brutal, contained environment in which he worked. He tried to embed and diffuse his daily experience of prison by studying the *Constitution* of the United States and exploring classical concepts of justice and honor. His inquiries brought him to consider the moral influence of families, to wondering how children learn virtue and civility. He wondered, as well, how he sustained his own. The more Henry followed what his mentor came to appreciate as an insistent, groping curiosity, the more Henry changed what he wanted to learn. Mentor and student discovered together that the bachelor's degree plan he'd originally designed was obsolete. Even so, Henry made no decision about a post-retirement career.

Gradually and informally, mentor and student changed the individual studies Henry had planned to do. Only when his final several studies and his final years of working as a corrections officer approached, did Henry decide what he wanted to do after he graduated and after he retired from the Department of Corrections. He decided to become a public school social studies teacher. He was convinced that this was the best way he could help kids not to wind up living or working in prison; the savage, hopeless place where he had spent the majority of his waking hours for so many years. Henry abruptly announced his decision to his mentor. Then, he threw himself into the intensive career research which students typically complete during their formal educational planning study. Henry learned how he could get a public school teaching certificate through a master's program and he learned the changes he'd have to make in his undergraduate program in order to qualify. He altered his degree plan accordingly, and then sought and received formal approval from the college for those significant curricular changes. Henry was accepted into a master's program just as he completed his final undergraduate studies. For him, planning his education lasted almost ten years. He and his mentor learned that "lifelong learning" can mean that one might change both the content and the purposes of an entire education.

From experiential to academic learning

Just as educational planning often continues after students design their programs, it often begins well *before* students formally begin the "course." Before coming to our college, Melanie and Wally had never attended or had very briefly attended a university. But they'd been busy, working and learning. Melanie, in her mid-twenties, was a parent and bookkeeper. And Wally, in his late forties, was a heavy construction worker, as well as a gadfly to the rural public school his children attended. Each of these adult students was an energetic learner. But, to all of them, the academy was a formidable if vague obstacle they figured they'd have to "get through" in order to "get on" with their lives. They all saw the university as alien territory.

Their mentor felt that he'd only be adding confusion to their wariness if these new students began their formal educations by dealing directly with such academic arcana as "concentrations," "liberal studies," "experiential vs. academic learning," and "credit hours." Of course as part of their orientation to the college, they learned about the requirement that they work with their mentor to design a course of study. Their mentor assured them that, when they felt ready, he'd help them design their own programs, including getting credit for the university-level learning that they had gained outside of any official academy. The mentor suggested that the upside to not having college credits to transfer was that they had plenty of time and room to explore and to become used to college. When each asked, somewhat anxiously, "What do I have to take?," the mentor replied, "What are you curious about?" "What do you want to learn?"

It emerged that each of the two had strong and quite specific intellectual passions. Moreover, none of those interests neatly fit the traditional course packages, which ostensibly introduce the academic disciplines. A generic "Introduction to College" course would have missed the quite different and individually intense curiosities of these students. So, with each of them, the mentor collaborated in designing a first independent study tutorial about her or his interests. Melanie loved Beethoven and was curious about his "life and times." And Wally was interested in citizens frustrated with bureaucrats and politicians. The students worked with their mentor to design a broad study on his or her individual theme.

Melanie made a list of her favorite pieces and picked out a recent Beethoven biography. Her mentor suggested a short book on music appreciation and the Durants' popular omnibus history of the late eighteenth and early nineteenth centuries. Wally read Orwell, Kafka, some selections from Weber and bell hooks, among others. And in the short essays he wrote, he also drew upon successful efforts he and one of his daughters had made to buck the local school administration. In this way, each student became used to university, to independent academic study, and to planning learning while actually doing it. After several of these experiences, both of them told their mentor, without prompting, when they were ready to do formal educational planning. They designed two-year degrees as platforms for eventual bachelor degrees. And, now successful with formal university-level learning, they found it much easier to identify, articulate, and be evaluated for their substantial "experiential learning." Indeed, each had more than enough potential experiential learning credits to even save some to include in the bachelor's degrees they'd designed.

For most matriculating students in a growing number of adult-friendly undergraduate programs, "getting credit for life experience," is a major attraction. In many institutions, like our own, prior learning assessment (PLA) or "credit by evaluation" occurs during the planning work. Making PLA part of degree program design rests on the assumption that learning takes on meaning, particularly as earned credits, only in relation to a context: to a degree program, an intellectual passion, a career goal – a life. "How much credit can I get for running a car wash?" Rick asked. Or, for teaching ESL classes (Annette), and for accounting skills and running a small accountancy office (Melanie)? Answering such questions depends upon the student and mentor exploring two more questions: "What do you believe you *know* from these experiences?" And, "How much does that knowledge matter to you?" Both questions imply and point to a context, often several layered contexts: to experience and plans, to domestic and social relations, to working for money and status, and to taking journeys of the soul.

Within each context, a mentor seeks to enter a dialogue with a student by asking similar questions: "What can you do now, what do you understand now that you could not do, did not understand before?" "Can you do as much as or even more than what other people with similar experiences do?" "How important is this knowledge in comparison to the other things you already know or want/need to learn?" Addressing these questions is often a long process. It requires that students learn to make subtle, often exquisite distinctions between "experience" and "knowledge," distinctions which we academics may neatly refer to but rarely examine rigorously. It requires that we, both students and faculty, look inside. Students and mentors learn to bring to consciousness material we surely but inchoately possess, and then to give it order and names. This kind of reflection is part of the collaborative process.

What is "learning"? Expanding the academy

Any project in educational planning, especially when students and mentors look back, trying to name the learning implicit in experience, stirs and disturbs our unexamined assumptions about what learning "really" is. We'd love to have a rule that sharply divides "learning" from "experience." What exactly is the learned part; what is the unlearned part of any experience, even an academic one? We'd love to know just exactly where in running a car wash, helping a recent immigrant learn English, raising children, constructing a building, or, for that matter, reading a book, the intellect listens and speaks, while the rest of us (whatever we might call that!) remains deaf and mute. The educational planning study asks us, both mentors and students, to resist this seduction of claiming that we really know the answer, that we can confidently make the distinction. Scraping at our comforting assumptions, the process asks us to explore this most fundamental question: What is learning?

We must begin somewhere, with something that, at least provisionally, looks like knowledge. So, mentors often ask students to make lists of what they think they've learned outside of school. At first, these lists usually fuse experience and learning: "I raised my children." "I built factories." And the topics can be very general: "I read books about American history." "I worked on community projects." Then, considering these taxonomies of their lives, students refine their topic-lists and write brief descriptions of the experiences and the learning suited to each item. "Raising children" might become "Maternal Skills and Thought Processes." "Building factories" might become "Industrial Construction Techniques." "Working on community projects" might become "Homeless Services." "Reading American history" might become "The American Civil War."

A portfolio containing these "learning descriptions" within an entire curricular or "degree program plan" becomes the student's effort to present and document what they know, as well as what they intend to learn. Many other universities in the United States with prominent adult education programs use "portfolios" as a means for students to document their prior learning and propose intended learning. (See Mandell and Michelson 1991, and a forthcoming new edition, for a review of programs and practices). At our college, these portfolios are given to appropriately expert college faculty and other professionals in our geographical areas. The written learning descriptions of experiential learning provide these evaluators with the preparatory memoranda for interviewing the students. It's on the basis of those interviews that the evaluators verify the students' knowledge-claims and make credit recommendations. The evaluators and the students, as well as the mentors who have overseen the entire process, all assess how much learning might be "in" the experiences. We do so by making connections with and understanding relationships between the individual experiential learning, what others have learned, and what's in the degree program this particular student is creating. All of us pass back and forth through the membranes separating "constructing" and "uncovering" knowledge. We straddle experience remembered and experience understood. It is no wonder that nearly every student who engages in this process, expecting to be "given credit for experience" proudly exclaims two things at the end: "I didn't realize I'd have to learn so much to do this," and, "I didn't know I knew so much." And, most often, the mentor's conclusions echo those of the student.

As with degree planning as a whole, the evaluation of any prior experiential learning never occurs in a vacuum. It occurs within contexts of institutional standards, received ideas, and customary expectations. Thus, as they do in planning future learning, students make use of standard course descriptions to identify, sort and name learning they've already achieved through experience. However, they need not be limited to those. Educational planning, including PLA, not only opens the academy to non-traditional students; it opens the academy to non-traditional learning.

For example, Ellen, a production manager for a high pressure "hi-tech" manufacturer, was concerned about the well-being of her production teams. She was troubled by the ethical tension between respecting her workers and demanding from them very high production quotas. Ellen and her mentor discussed this issue at length during their planning work. We provisionally understood that, within the broad topic of "business ethics." Ellen must have thought a lot about conflicts between the "family environment" the company claimed to provide and the grueling productivity it required. As her mentor interviewed her about her experiences, Ellen looked back at purchases she'd made of expensive machinery her teams used. She realized that an important criterion she used to choose among closely competitive products was "beauty" (as she called it) in both appearance and functional design. Her experiences convinced her that something like an "aesthetic standard" added both to the excellence of work and to the happiness of worklife. For Ellen, beauty was an immanent aspect of worklife itself, both entirely practical and deeply satisfying. For the experiential learning part of her curriculum plan, Ellen wrote a description of what she'd learned about providing a safe and pleasant work environment as a motivating factor for workers. Then, taking a more contemplative approach to the same experience, she and her mentor also designed a future tutorial study on "Aesthetics and Ethics in Worklife." This would complete her degree.

Conflict: authority imposed, authority shared

Discovery and creation occur at the margins between familiar and unfamiliar. Those are also tense places, where liberation and oppression are experienced. When students and mentors plan well, we visit those liminal places. The visit is an elaborate and delicate experience, but when that experience is apprehended, it too becomes part of the learning that is achieved. Further, students and mentors often discover that they learn in quite different topographies and that they have very different notions of "real" learning. These differences, potent with conflict, can become occasions for mentor and student to inquire farther. They push the collaboration.

When tensions rise over these differences in liminal places, who should wield authority? How do we balance the "authority and uncertainty" that is at the heart of our first principle? The *student's* expectations of what should be counted as real learning? The *mentor's*? The layers of questioning and conflict can be even more complex than that. At the individual level, both student and mentor can each be separately conflicted. Students might defiantly desire to receive academic credit for almost anything they've done or wish to do, and at the same time deeply fear that they really know nothing. Faculty might pride themselves on their commitment to critical inquiry, yet, confronted with their own uncertainties and with demanding students, find comforting clarity in customary academic expectations. And any institution, especially as universities are confronted with "unusual" students and unpredictable situations, can be driven from exploration by the seductive politics of "accountable standards" and "productivity." As these pressures mount beneath the terrain elaborately fractured between the desire to learn and the desire to be certain, the resolving release can often only be found in the "waiting" we have sought to describe earlier; that is, in literally slowing down the time devoted to educational planning. In our planning work we wait in order to become clearer – carefully and caringly. Even so, sometimes, after waiting, we impose our authority; and sometimes, we become energetic advocates to, and on behalf of, our students.

Lonnie, for example, worked for twenty years in low-level, often part time, human service jobs. (We have discussed her already in the previous chapter, "Waiting as learning.") She now wants to get as much credit as possible – a lot – and as quickly as possible. To her, this seems simple. It is what has drawn her to our adult-friendly program. To her, it is a kind of cashing in on her years of dedicated, poorly paid, and little honored service to others. But to her mentor, it is problematic because Lonnie seems to be a very unreflective student, unable and unwilling, during the time set aside for planning, to do the demanding work of identifying, ordering, and describing the learning she may have acquired through her experiences. Mentor and student expectations clash.

Moreover, Lonnie's mentor is not at all sure how or when to help her learn to do what he is certain she must, and what she's equally certain she need not do. Her mentor strongly urges – eventually, insists – that she wait until she becomes more adept, through her other studies, at doing the sort of advanced-level learning, the careful analysis, reflection, and writing, that putting together her portfolio of prior learning necessarily requires. Finally but suspiciously, Lonnie agrees. After a time, the expectations of both student and mentor change somewhat. Lonnie reluctantly becomes more practiced with more thoughtful questioning, analysis, and exposition. And her mentor becomes more certain, as he now listens to her talk and reads what she's written about her human services experiences, that she has acquired substantial learning and that she can successfully articulate that learning. Did Lonnie know these things in the first place, as she had believed? Was her mentor too impatient with her demands? Or, did she become a stronger student, more capable of meeting the expectations, which her mentor had been, from the start, so certain were correct? Thinking about the tensions and the outcome months later, the mentor still doesn't know. Lonnie completes the process of having her experiential learning evaluated. The evaluators award her substantial credit, though not as much as she expected. The curriculum she had planned is formally approved, though not as easily as she had hoped. Lonnie's relations with her mentor remain tense enough that they both decide it would be better if she work with other mentors. Their decision to part company expresses an incompletely resolved conflict, but, it is a collaborative decision.

Sometimes, however, this distribution of initial expectations about what and how much a student has learned is reversed: The mentor believes there's much more to be uncovered than the student does. Rina, in her early fifties and a recent *summa cum laude* graduate of a local two-year technical college, announces that she wants to become an English teacher. She'd frequently tutored weaker writing students while earning her own degree, and she was certain she'd finally found her calling. But Rina is not sure she can do it, fearing she's just too old. Rina's mentor suggests that as part of the planning process she learn about the current public school and college teaching shortages. Skeptically, she agrees and discovers a vacuum so strong and persistent that even New York State – infamous for its rigid teacher education machinery – is working on alternative, more flexible methods of teacher certification. Further, Rina's mentor encourages her to consider applying for some substantial credit for what she already knows. She's even *more* skeptical about that, although experiential learning credits will get her all the more quickly to a bachelor's degree and to a teaching career. Exhilarated by the experience and prospect of "the higher learning," Rina sees the academy as an august place to fulfill her long-postponed dreams. In fact, at first, experiential learning strikes her as "not quite the real thing" and as something irrelevant to the academic career she does so desire. Eventually, Rina's mentor asks her:

"What have you been doing instead of going to school?"

"Just keeping house, managing the farm, and, you know, raising kids. Four of them. They've all gone to college now. I've loved raising my kids."

After more conversation, the mentor inquires: "Are there any similarities between nurturing children and teaching?"

Rina thinks about this question for several weeks. She returns eager to write an experiential learning description on "Parenting and Teaching."

"I didn't know *that* was learning. I thought it was just something I did."

Rina's learning description eventually becomes a fine, searching essay on the similarities and differences between parental and academic nurturing. No doubt, slow, leisurely time, with room for talk, questioning, and clarification, can allow a student to discover that she already knew what she believed she had yet to learn.

When collaborative planning takes students and mentors beyond academic custom, the results can be controversial and politically significant. Then, we are especially challenged to critically inspect our intellectual routines. For example, it is common and easy for students to seek credit for their prior experiential learning in the business world. These students are mostly men. It is much less common for adult students to seek credit for their learning experiences in the domestic world. These students are mostly women. The academically recognized skills and information collected under "strategic planning" or "supervisory management" are, from habit, easy to see, name, and evaluate. Not so for "maternal thinking and practice" or "household management." But, can we say with the same intellectual rigor we faculty demand of students, that the cognitive demands of raising children and managing a home are any less than those of supervising employees or leading a business? In Chapter 7, "The mentor as learner," we discuss Beth, whose extensive parenting and child-care experiences challenge her own and her mentor's routine beliefs about what academic learning "really" is. Both the mentor and Beth have to reflect very carefully on their expectations, a process requiring time and calm. The outcome, in this instance, is that Beth successfully seeks academic credit for her "domestic management" learning and the mentor successfully advocates on her behalf to his colleagues who are suspicious that such a topic could be considered university-level learning at all.

Educational planning often gives students confidence in what they have done and what they know. It often confronts the faculty with our own ignorance and our own vulnerabilities. Every time mentors honestly do educational planning, a Delphic voice, like Socrates's, reminds of our embeddedness in our own assumptions and calls us to know ourselves better (Principle 1).

Institutional pressures, as suggested above, can sometimes significantly stress the leisure both students and mentors need for such reflection and the curricular creativity which often emerges from it. Sometimes, contexts of inexorable academic expectation can be pernicious to learning itself. The cultural and economic politics of education in universities across the State of New York and in the US as a whole, have squeezed the vital freedoms of curriculum planning. New York State amply manifests national cravings for certainty and stability in a changing, multiplicitous world where, as Marx long ago observed, "all that's solid melts into air." In response to these fears of difference and change, institutions of higher education have sometimes paradoxically chosen to disinvest in public higher education and, at the same time, to demand from the university system "higher" standards, more efficiency, and a greater yield of more skilled, productive and responsible citizens. It is thus not surprising that college administrators (sometimes supported by the faculty) and university trustees have devised and imposed new sets of requirements.

In the name of intellectual rigor and democratic citizenship, the faculty (including those at our college), are now required to provide closely monitored and testable doses of a range of "general education" studies. It is doubtful that most students will remember much of these things after they've passed the required tests. But what memorable lessons will the trustees and faculty have modeled for the diverse citizens of democratic societies? That a privileged few will use their power to make "the others" become comfortingly like themselves? That higher degrees and the higher status they purchase perforce contain a higher wisdom? Where, under this regime, will there be room for inquiry and creation? When will students and their mentors have time to explore together and to thoughtfully examine what they assume they know and need to learn? Chances for wonder, for admitting ignorance, and for learning together will have been lost.

What mentors learn from educational planning

Collaborative educational planning provides a rich context for practicing the principles of mentoring. For example, when people follow their curiosity in designing their curricula to support both their educational and life goals, they learn and plan well (Principle 2, diversity of curriculum). And, when their curiosity is nurtured, it expands indefinitely, beyond "getting credits" required for a career. Thus honored, curiosity not only achieves those necessary practical goals; it also transcends them, embracing questions about the meaning of personal and civic life, and even more (Principles 4, learning from the lifeworld, and 6, the knowledge most worth having). Stella discovers Homer; Wally, De Tocqueville. Rick wants to run a car wash; and he wants to think about *sartori* and nature, perhaps while tracing a bike trail or the cause of a fire. While she manages production quotas, Ellen thinks about improving the beauty and civility of her workplace. When students like these discover that the state or some uncompromising educational authority has prescribed for them small injections of this science or that math, this history or that language, what will happen to the beauty and happiness of their intellectual lives? Perhaps following the example of higher education policy-makers, they will plan their learning with exactly the cynical and intellectually shallow acquisitiveness too commonly attributed to "adult" students.

However, such students may be less dispirited, feckless, and complicit than faculty have been in immunizing themselves against arrogant prescriptions. During educational planning mentors can discover how extraordinarily adept our students can be at managing and comprehending the stunning complexities of their lives. Students can learn how to transform the clamor of their multitudinous experiences into diverse, coherent, and liberating educations. They are experts at finding freedom and creating expanding selves amidst the seemingly intractable constrictions of their obligations and circumstances. And, these students inspire their mentors to do the same.

When adult students return to or begin university study, they commit an intrinsically revolutionary act. Consciously or not, they have decided to overturn their routines. They do so at an age when things are supposed to be "settled." And even when they seem merely prudent and practical, driven by force of circumstance and convention, they are also choosing to challenge the suppositions of their families or partners, their colleagues and bosses. Even more deeply, they are questioning the habitual views they have had of themselves. This churning critique bursts into view during curricular planning. Marriages and workplaces become objects of contemplation and overtly political territories. Even so methodical and practical a matter as learning "self-directed academic time management" becomes, for people with lives already filled with affiliations, commitments, and myriad demands, a passionate struggle to create the freedom to savor reading, writing, and inquiry.

So often, students begin to plan by fearfully wondering what they have really learned and have yet to learn. They frequently emerge confident that their learning experiences matter and that they can learn whatever it is to which their curiosity leads them. They become able to question the seemingly unquestionable. Mentors who nurture and bear witness to these passages are awed. And, if we are lucky and shrewd enough to be inspired as well, we wonder, "If they can do it, why can't I?" In collaborative planning, we mentors often learn profound lessons for our own lifeworlds. (See Chapter 7, "The mentor as learner.") We saw Rick, for example, feeling the power of his wasting illness and considering how to respond and to make his way in the world. Gradually, he turns his attention to discovering what he loves most of all, at any risk. This is the risk we as mentors have to take. Should we, should any educator, really do any less?

As we and our students engage in these reciprocally stimulating relationships, important questions appropriate connection and boundary between what is personal and what is academic. This unsettled border is the topic of our next chapter.

Chapter 6

The personal and the academic

Dialogue as cognitive love

When Sully got to the top he went inside and let the door swing shut behind him, then came back out again. "Don't forget to feed the dog," he called.

Peter had forgotten all about Rasputin, who was presumably still chained to the kitchen cabinet in the Bowdon Street house. "It's not going to be easy being you, is it?" he called back.

Sully raised his hands out to his sides, shoulder level, as if he were about to burst into song. "Don't expect too much of yourself in the beginning," he advised. "I couldn't do everything at first either."

Richard Russo, *Nobody's Fool* (1994: 439)

So I'm telling you now that everyone should honor Love, even as I myself honor love-matters, thoroughly devoting myself to them and calling upon others to do likewise. Now and always, as much as I can, I glorify the power and pluck of the Erotic.

Plato, *Symposium* (212b–c)

Mentors invite adult students to bring their lives into their learning. From them, as our examples have illustrated, information, questions, and themes emerge which make the academic learning process collaborative and which enhance the significance of the academic content. Further, the distinctive intimacy of the mentor-student relationship all but inevitably means that students will confide to their mentors "personal" concerns – information, feelings, preoccupations, and problems from their private, familial, social, civic, and work lives. Nonetheless, the context of our collaborative work is academic and professional. What then is the appropriate relationship of the personal to the academic? What is the appropriate etiquette of this intimacy between mentor and student? What are the proper boundaries within which we should work?

But there are further questions: What is this "intimacy" and what sort of learning does it engender?

We believe that this intimacy is Socratic or "cognitive love," which engenders the love of truth. Socrates describes himself as a "midwife"

(*Theaetetus*: 149–151e) and as a "lover" (*Symposium*: 212). He claims to help bring to birth, not his own, but someone else's intellectual child. And he offers himself, not as a partner in physical sexuality, but in the love of the beautiful itself, in seeking the good of the soul. Mentors, too, offer to join with their students in coming ever closer to learning what is true, just, and beautiful. In this chapter, we examine closely the special nature of this cognitive love.

Entering the world of the student: intimacies and boundaries

In these dialogical encounters, mentor and student come dangerously close to a psychotherapeutic or even more inappropriately intimate relationship. We allow and even encourage our students to tell us what matters to them most; and then we listen, even if the content seems very personal. Are we not also thereby encouraging or seducing our students to believe that we can "cure" them of their distress or otherwise make their lives happy?

Apart from the fact that we lack the professional skills, we should not become too involved in our student's lives for other reasons. Absorbing academic learning into psychotherapeutic learning or "growth" would also shrink the social, economic, political, and cultural dimensions of human life into strictly personal terms. The autonomy and value of those dimensions of human experience would be denatured (cf. Rieff, *The Triumph of the Therapeutic* 1990), particularly the integrity and strength of our civic or public domains (cf. Sennett, *The Fall of Public Man* 1977). Mentors seek to touch the personal in order to help students reach from there to broader terrains of association, learning, and meaning. Perhaps even more important, students do not enter university or into dialogical learning to receive psychotherapy, parenting, friendship or romantic love. Whatever their unconscious motives and projects may be, they are here to learn whatever they actually say they are curious to know and for the purposes they articulate. The dialogical contract is based on a reciprocal understanding that these contents will be treated seriously and respectfully, and that they will be invested with cognitive authority. Mentors who distract themselves or their students from this commitment are thus violating the most basic commitment of learning, which is to truthfulness (Principle 1).

Nonetheless, we do invite students to "know themselves." What kind of caring or "therapy" (whose root meaning is "care") is this dialogical and introspective learning? In this section, we offer a number of examples to show how this question arises in different ways. Then, in the next section we return to each example to show how mentors try to answer that question.

Louis

Louis is a community and human service worker who has gained a great deal of expertise in the area of public housing. Although he has advised many community groups and gained a good deal of status as a result of his successful negotiations with landlords in his New York City Dominican community, as much as he tried, Louis has never held a full-time job. The demands of two part-time jobs (and sometimes a third on the weekends) have clearly strained his family life and significantly limited the time he has been able to devote to his college studies. No doubt, his lack of a college degree adds another burden to his already complex life.

There are moments in which Louis's responses to his mentor's simple greeting, "How are things going?" suggest that Louis's life is about to unravel. Louis is usually quiet about the details, but over the year since they have met every other week, his mentor has learned to sense the tensions. Even more, in their tutorial sessions the mentor has tried to find ways to offer Louis an opportunity to talk about the problems he and his wife are having with their two teenage sons, his response to his wife's feelings about her dead-end jobs, and Louis's frustrations with his own employment situation and overall quality of life. His mentor believes that attention to this experience could deepen Louis's academic learning.

In fact, when Louis inquired about whether he could study something about "family life in contemporary America," his mentor thought the topic would provide an effective vehicle to link "the academic" and "the personal." Louis could examine a significant social institution and, through his scholarly reading, he could also begin to find some personally useful distance from the immediacy of his own highly charged family situation. Both Louis and his mentor were pleased with the learning contract they were developing together.

But the mentor quickly saw that the student/mentor conversations were often tricky. Once the formal learning context granted legitimacy to the expression of complaints, feelings, and conflicts Louis had never mentioned before, it was hard for the mentor to pull Louis away, both in his writings and in mentor-student discussions, from rather vivid descriptions of his everyday life. And, while clearly relevant to the topics and issues of this tutorial, and while the mentor admitted to himself that he was, indeed, seeing good academic results of Louis's greater comfort in this learning environment, the mentor also worried that he was not equipped to adequately respond to what Louis was presenting to him. The future of marriage; race, class, and family life; the family and part-time work, and "why poor mothers stay single," had opened the way to a range of complex and powerful personal concerns. Instead of offering a richer and more relevant way into the questions and considerations that have absorbed scholars in the field, mentor and student found themselves in uncomfortable terrain where what was important was clear, but what could be held onto as academically meaningful was much more problematic.

Elena

Elena resumed her college studies after completing a traditional two year degree in liberal arts and nursing. A gifted singer, songwriter, and musician, she hoped to design a bachelor's degree that would help her become a music therapist, an alternative health care practice in which she already had considerable supervised experience. Inspiring all of Elena's health care, musical, and academic efforts was a deep religious piety. Her faith rested on a very precise and all-encompassing fundamentalist Christian theology. She believed that the Bible was the literal and absolute truth, in every word, and, further that only one version of the text was sacred, the "word of God." Elena's scientific and secular health care training comfortably co-existed, for her, with her beliefs in divinely wrought creation. She also believed that her musical talents were a divine gift and could be used to comfort and even cure people afflicted with grave physical illnesses. She regarded her vocation, her "call" to music therapy as a ministry. Moreover, although Elena expressed a gentle sadness and hope for people who did not believe what she did, her theology was sufficiently strict and absolute that she was sure that people who did not have her particular faith would be damned.

Aware of the curricular flexibility of the college and its claim to serve the individual learning purposes of each student, Elena intended her academic education in every detail to serve her ministry. She thus freely spoke of her faith to her mentor. But as an agnostic, inconstantly loyal Jew, he shared almost none of Elena's beliefs. He was troubled by her theological and moral absolutism. Although Elena was not seeking a state or professional license for her vocation (for that she would have to complete graduate training at a different university), he also wondered and worried what it would mean if his secular college should seem to underwrite a particular theology and a health care practice guided by it. On the other hand, Elena's gentle and open nature (consistent with her wish and duty to share her faith with anyone she encountered) moved her to discuss her beliefs clearly and without anxious insistence. And the mentor's willingness to explore what he did not understand and what he knew for sure he did not know, enabled him to listen carefully and to confide to Elena his own doubts and worries. Both of them wanted to find a way to make Elena's academic learning move effectively and harmoniously among her faith, her scientific training, and the dialogical learning in which she was now engaged.

George

As much as Elena wanted to suffuse every aspect of her life with her faith, George was determined, as his mentor discovered, to keep his personal life as separate as he could from work and school. His commitments to his job and to his academic learning, though earnest, were guided by a deep cynicism about institutions, a belief that they simply used people for the benefit of those who controlled them, and, borne of that cynicism, a pragmatic determination to do what he could to use those institutions to serve the prosperity of his home and family life. George worked as hard and learned as much as he had to in order to gain the advancements which served his goals of better positions (especially ones in which he'd be freer of supervision) and higher pay. George wanted an academic degree that would help him obtain those benefits as quickly and smoothly as possible.

His mentor sought to interest George in becoming more reflective about his learning and in exploring the bases of his cynical practicality. The mentor expressed this urge in the several studies he and George did together: Educational Planning, Organizational Behavior, and Business Ethics. But George was not interested. He did not care to individualize his program or the studies in it except in so far as they would help him finish his degree quickly and would satisfy the bosses at work who approved the funding for his education. For example, he discovered that online, "pre-packaged" or "template" courses often required less intellectually intense participation than in-person tutorials. He chose to do these whenever suitable ones were offered, and he did well enough to receive positive evaluations. For the in-person tutorials he did do with his mentor, he wanted to be told in advance exactly what and how much he would have to read and write. George resisted his mentor's encouragement to use his work experiences as case studies for Organizational Behavior and Business Ethics. Instead, George wanted to stick to the texts, do as little "extra" research and reading as possible, and maintain the separation between his academic and work lives.

George's mentor was disturbed by these resistances and separations. Not only was he sure that George was more than academically capable enough to reach this more profound intellectual level, he was bothered that George seemed uninterested in truth, justice, and beauty – values the mentor believed to be the fundamental and inherent topics implicit in any freely undertaken academic study. George, in other words, seemed to be a "case" which contradicted the very principles and promise of mentoring itself.

Marie

Marie (whom we discussed in Chapter 4, "Waiting as learning") was in love with dialogue, and her mentor fell in love with her love of it. She passionately wanted to understand more profoundly and to create lives – her own, her family's, and her associates' – ever more just and beautiful.

The intellectual intimacy and freedom of mentored education suited her perfectly and enlivened all her faculties. Her mentor could not help but be attracted to and inspired by such a student. Neither of them were surprised to encounter "boundary issues."

It was partially practical concerns that brought Marie to this college. Though happily married, she was the primary caretaker of the three of her four children who still lived at home. Though she worked part time to supplement the family income, Marie suffered from a chronic and enervating disease. Because of her busy family life and her poor health, she needed to proceed slowly and somewhat irregularly with her studies. And of course she hoped that she could pursue and complete a university degree that would enable her to gain more lucrative and satisfying part-time employment than she was now qualified for.

Important as those practical concerns were, it was primarily a spiritual and psychological boundary problem that pre-occupied Marie, and she hoped to use her studies to solve it. Like Elena, Marie was a deeply religious person. But her faith had little to do with dogma. Rather, since childhood she had had a very intense relationship with God, a presence whose separateness she experienced as very definite and as powerfully loving and prescient. Through this agency, Marie seemed to unerringly sense what was troubling other people, often simply by listening to the quality of their voices or by physically touching them. Of course, her fellow congregants in her church, her friends, relatives, and co-workers depended on her. They sought her insights and her advice; they were drawn to the benevolence which, her mentor could also see, so naturally emanated from her.

But Marie dispensed her inspired gifts at increasingly great cost. As she grew older and as her health became more fragile, Marie was gnawed and constricted by the neediness of others. And thus her special intimacy with this uncanny spiritual or divine presence became oppressive and even dangerously debilitating. But how could she ignore it? By no means a credulous person, Marie was deeply pious and learned in her faith. In genuine humility, she recognized similarities in her gifted experiences to the painful vocations of such tortured Old Testament prophets as Jeremiah and of course to the terrific suffering and ultimate sacrifice of Christ. Marie had no desire to be a martyr; she wanted to live a happy, fully human life. Yet how could she do so without denying the spiritual intimacy at the very heart of the faith which gave her life (and many others') so much meaning? She wanted her academic education to help her answer this question. She wanted to learn how to find or construct a boundary between a worldly life gently suffused with spirituality and one painfully, even damagingly overwhelmed by spiritual demands.

The mentor was completely fascinated by Marie's search, for indeed it resonated so deeply with his own efforts to make separations, while sustaining the coherence, between the personal and professional aspects of his life. He believed, though he never said, that Marie felt this attractive resonance as well. How, then, could each so love the inquiry and not fail to feel love for the inquirer? It was thus uncomfortably ironic that in collaborating on a study about resolving boundary problems, Marie and her mentor created a boundary problem for themselves.

The questions framing the study became even more urgent and, like a therapeutic transference and counter-transference, became essential to "work through." A strong piety defined and animated Marie's inquiry: her love of God and of her family, her strong sense of obligation to her spiritual gifts. The mentor's questions, now both personal and academic as well, even though they stemmed from a very different and deeply held set of philosophical commitments, were not so dissimilar: Was not the true object of this "love inquiry" not the other inquirer, but rather understanding a truth about the meaning of dialogical commitments? Was not the good of this collaboration one that would do justice to its true object and to the other commitments of the inquirers? And would not the happiness Marie and her mentor hoped to enhance by solving the "boundary problems" in their separate lives be served if they could beautifully shape this academic relationship, a shape properly bounded by their efforts to seek truth and do justice? Such questions, more or less softly, influence every student-mentor relationship: The quality of their inquiry – its truth, its justice, its beauty – will speak to the quality of the inquirers' lives.

The "therapy" of academic mentoring: transforming personal confidence into intellectual discourse

Louis

Louis's mentor wanted him to know how important it was that he was finding connections between his academic study and his everyday life. But he also wanted to communicate to him that sometimes his understandable preoccupation with family problems undercut his ability to carefully focus on examples different from his own experiences and to find themes and arguments embedded in those particulars. While the mentor worried that speaking directly with Louis about this concern could push him away, he also hoped that the discussion would help the two of them think together about the boundaries of this study. He wanted Louis to become aware of the assumptions he, Louis, was making in filtering his academic work so much through his personal worries.

But the mentor hesitated. He wanted Louis to understand the kind of conversation that he hoped would guide the study. He wanted Louis to see it in practice. The mentor thus used their face-to-face tutorials as opportunities to focus directly on the readings Louis was doing. He asked Louis about assumptions an author was making and value judgments that informed a specific argument. Together, they tried to interpret passages from texts and evaluate what an author was presenting. Here, Louis did have an opportunity to link his own experiences with the ideas he was examining, but it was not unusual for the mentor to have to quietly insist that he try to "stick to the texts." Still, Louis was beginning to cultivate some detachment from the material he was reading; he did not respond to it as "personally" as he had.

Indeed, during a period of a few months in which the mentor and student met every two or three weeks, there were many moments of wonderful attention. Louis was able to show what a careful reader he was becoming. But the complexities of his life, even if they did not completely dominate their time together, were taking a toll. Before the close of the study period, Louis began to cancel appointments and finally left a phone message asking the mentor to send his comments on Louis's most recent essay to a friend's address. A few weeks later, mentor and student spoke. He had left home, Louis explained, but was still thinking about his college work. Though burdened with a second rent, tuition for his son (who had transferred to a parochial school) and the consequent necessity of a third part-time job, Louis still hoped to find time to complete this learning contract. Louis's mentor offered sympathy and support. He also assured him that he would accept his final papers well beyond their official due date. There would still be time for Louis to fulfill his academic obligations. But the demands of Louis's life took over; the work was never completed.

Elena

Elena presented educational purposes and a worldview disturbing to her mentor. In psychotherapeutic terms, it might be said that he experienced a "negative counter-transference" to her desires. How then could he work helpfully with her? What did the mentor need to learn?

Accompanying the mentor's conversations with the student was an internal dialogue with himself, one that emerged during and after each of his meetings with Elena:

> *What, exactly, is problematic for you about Elena? That she is so assertive about her faith, a faith that does not accept you?*

> Yes, but also that she wants to make her remaining college studies serve this faith, her ministry. She wants to use this secular institution and education to give some kind of authorization to her religion.

> *But you've said many things, here. What do you mean by them? Is she really trying to convert you? Does she treat you disrespectfully?*

> No. In fact, she's very friendly and open. I mean that she tells me about her faith, but I don't feel that she's trying to persuade me of

anything except to take her seriously. She knows I'm a Jew and that I'm not very religious. This doesn't seem to bother her.

Then what's the problem?

Well even so, I'm bothered by our huge differences. Aren't they getting in the way? And I'm worried that she'll do a degree that she'll use as a kind of license, as though we were a religious seminary.

But why must your differences get in the way of learning? Does she demand authorization of some kind to ignore evidence and reason and get academic credit for her beliefs?

No, I think not. I mean, I don't really know that her religious beliefs are false, though she believes mine are. I suppose that if I challenge her, I would be claiming I do know "the mind of God," when I'm not even sure there is one. Also, for sure, I don't know enough about music therapy to assess it. She knows that she has to get professional training in that elsewhere.

So, then, how exactly does Elena's religion influence her academic degree?

Her faith guides her interests; she relies on it to choose what she wants to learn and what experiential learning to seek credit for.

You have business and other students whose academic choices are guided by their interest in achieving worldly success. You don't seem to be very bothered by that, even though you make much of fundamental values – truth, justice, beauty. Surely, Elena is interested in those very ideas, even though you and she seem to have very different beliefs about them. Also, you have students who want to be teachers or counselors, and you never seem to question their motives at all, not even privately. Is Elena competition of some kind? She's probably thought about fundamentals as much as you have.

Sometime later, after more conversations between Elena and the mentor, his internal dialogue continued:

I do ask my students to think and write about fundamental ideas, but I don't give them credit or withhold it because of their conclusions. I mean, if they agree or don't agree with mine. I do try to be careful about that. Those topics do come up all the time, and we do have differences of opinion.

Then do you ignore or not take seriously their opinions about what's true, or right or attractive? I thought you insist that it's the work on those ideas which are the deepest purposes of learning.

No, I don't ignore them. We talk about those things. But, I am careful to say that I won't evaluate their learning for the content of their conclusions but how they get to them, how thoroughly they gather information, how aware they are of different points of view, how carefully and clearly they reason their way to the conclusions they come to.

Then can't you work with Elena in the same way? You said that she's very open and comfortable in talking about her ideas and that she doesn't turn away or become combative when you share your own with her.

That's true. She's interested in dialogue, at least in the sense of exchanging views. Maybe that's why we can speak so easily with one another. We've kind of learned about one another's views, including where we disagree.

Then, does she want to get credit simply for what you'd call her conclusions, for the actual tenets of her faith? Does she want credit just for "The Truth," as she sees it, for the truth of "religious dogma," as you regard it?

Not exactly. No. We've talked about this, quite a bit. But she does want credit for the knowledge she already has of "pastoral counseling," and for "creationism." Also, she wants to devote a major part of her new learning to writing a "spiritual autobiography" and also to writing a little book of biblically-based advice, hopeful advice, for parents who have "prodigal" children. How can those activities become secular academic learning?

You're always referring to Socrates. Remember how the Meno *ends? 'Til the last part of the dialogue, it seems like Socrates and Meno have certainly learned that "virtue is knowledge," that it's something that can be learned. But in the very last part, they seem to discover, equally for certain, that virtue is acquired by good fortune or as a gift from the gods – a position perhaps not so far from Elena's.*

Okay, okay. But what's your point?

Well there are two of them, really. First, everything we read in Plato about Socrates suggests that he believes that virtue is knowledge.

Doesn't this then fly in the face of what seems to be the conclusion of the Meno? Doesn't Socrates just send Meno off with the advice that he continue talking with people about what he's persuaded is true, which at this moment is that virtue is not teachable but comes by grace?

Yeah . . . but, I don't think that's exactly the point. Socrates and Meno, in this dialogue at any rate, don't really know, one way or another, that virtue is a kind of teachable knowledge or comes by grace, because they haven't really learned enough yet about what virtue is. Socrates stresses that point over and over again during his conversation with Meno.

Exactly. Then isn't Socrates being true to the understanding that's come from the dialogue itself? In their collaborative inquiry – something else you're always talking about – they've discovered that they don't really know yet whether or not virtue is knowledge. They've discovered their own ignorance, as you also like to say.

Yes, I get it now. He doesn't really send Meno off to "preach" that virtue comes by grace, not learning, but to continue thinking and conversing, starting from where the two of them have left off. And, for sure, Elena does believe that virtue, or as she'd put it, "salvation," comes from grace, that it's up to God and human faith in Him. It's not part of my job to try to persuade her otherwise; also, I don't know that I know so much more about these things than she does. So, I should just keep the dialogue open, kind of like having "faith" that both of us will understand more as we go along.

Yes. Now you're understanding something.

But what's your other point? You said there's another one. Also, remember, Elena wants credit for what she's already sure she knows. And she wants to earn new credit for learning more about how to write about and persuade others of what she believes.

Well, let's say Augustine showed up at your college, a learned fellow for sure, who had had the best of both "pagan" and Christian education of his time. But he's shrewd enough in how the world works now to know that if he wants to get people to pay attention to what he has to say that he'd do well to get a college degree.

Oh come on!

Humor me; play along. After all, he knew something about how the world, the earthly world works. Let's just pretend he'd want to "get credentialed." And he wants to get credit for having already written this huge spiritual autobiography, which he's calling...

The Confessions. All right. And then he also wants to earn more credits for another project, not finished. He wants to write an even bigger book about the possibility of hope and redemption in a corrupt world, *The City of God*, is his working title, right?

You're beginning to understand. Good. So, would you tell Augustine that he can't do that at your college? Would you tell him that there's no "academic" learning there?

Don't be silly. Of course not. But I don't think Elena is in the same league as Augustine.

How would you know? And maybe she's not. So, think about Meno again. Do you think he hasn't learned anything, understood anything by the end of the dialogue, however inconclusive, that he didn't understand before?

Uh, well, he seems to have learned to be more careful in thinking through what he believes, in working out and stating his reasons. Yes, he has. And, he's learned to tolerate the pain and numbness of the sting of the torpedo fish. He is discovering that he wasn't as clear or correct in his ideas as he thought he was.

And how do you know that?

He hangs in there. He's willing to stay in the dialogue. Anytus, who shows up near the end, isn't. As soon as Socrates seems to be questioning the virtue of prominent people famous for their wisdom, Anytus not only gets upset, he leaves, with the not very subtle threat to prosecute Socrates, a threat he's going to make good on. But still, I don't think that Elena is the scholar Augustine was.

But surely your college doesn't just give credit for intellectual masterworks. Isn't it "the process," "the journey," that you keep talking about?

Yes. That's right.

And can't you have some faith in Elena, that she will continue to learn, that she will keep trying to understand her faith, her revelations, or whatever? Haven't you yourself said that she is eager and open to discuss these things?

Yes.

Then spend some time thinking about this, and talk about your thoughts with Elena. She does with you, after all. Maybe the two of you aren't so radically different. What's the learning in the faith-practices she's already achieved? What learning can she achieve for the projects she wants to do?

And so Elena and her mentor continued to converse. Eventually, she did seek and receive academic credit for her prior study of "creationism" and for her experientially acquired "counseling skills." The evaluator for the former was a biologist. She recommended credit not for "the truth" of creationism but for Elena's very thorough understanding of the debate between creationists and Darwinists, of the scientific and theological assumptions at the basis of that controversy. Similarly, the clinical psychologist and pastoral counselor who evaluated Elena's counseling skills did not recommend credit for the possible spiritual or divine origin of her talent, but rather for her practical understanding of techniques any counselor, secular or pastoral, should have: active listening, reflective questioning, empathetic interpreting etc.

And for the new projects Elena wanted to work on as part of completing her undergraduate studies, the spiritual autobiography, and the handbook of hopeful guidance, Elena and her mentor agreed to work on these as projects in written composition. They focused on clarity, on vividness and organization; they talked about the selection and careful interpretation of the biblical passages Elena intended to use, and about the tone and diction of the writing so that it would reach the people Elena hoped to help. They did not speak that often of their different worldviews, except to acknowledge and respect their presence in the work they were doing together. When Elena completed her degree and spoke at her graduation, she thanked her mentor for "showing me new perspectives on life." The mentor was a little surprised. Of course he had hoped that through their association Elena would not exactly change her beliefs but soften them a little, make room for the idea that a "non-believer" such as himself might have to offer some genuinely good will and truthful understandings of fundamental things. But, for the most part, the mentor was grateful that Elena had provoked his own self-examination. Thanks to their collaboration, he thought he would now respond much more carefully and caringly to people with beliefs drastically different from his own.

George

George wants to complete a degree as easily and quickly as possible. Though friendly, he makes it clear during nearly every conversation with his mentor that he's not interested in becoming very engaged with his studies, nor with the opportunity to individualize them except in so far as that would serve the efficiency with which he completes them. Several times, the mentor makes him aware of the possibilities and intellectual promise of deeper engagement, but George politely and firmly declines. On the principles of respecting George's autonomy and his curiosity, the mentor agrees and makes sure that George understands the basic requirements of the college for graduation with a degree in marketing. Though somewhat disappointed and also very curious about George's lack of interest, the mentor decides to wait and see what will emerge from their respectful and business-like relationship.

For the most part, George takes online, "off the shelf" courses. These are often well designed equivalents of large classroom-based courses: the readings are current and offer the generally accepted main topics and issues in the field; the teachers who evaluate the students' assignments are expert with the content and patient with the students. George takes these courses because, as he says, they suit his schedule, he doesn't have to do "extra" work, and he knows from the usually generic assignments and the responses he receives "what the teacher wants." They enable him to complete credits efficiently. However, during in-person tutorials on organizational behavior and business ethics, which the mentor and George do together, he becomes more revealing. These studies are largely based, at George's request, on standard textbooks and case studies found in them. However, George does agree to substitute for a few of those case studies, some of the experiences he's had at his own workplace.

In his essays and his conversations about them with his mentor, George expresses a surprising combination of cynicism and idealism. It seems that George tries to keep the same distance from his business life as he does from his academic work. He does what is expected of him, including what is expected to achieve raises and promotions. He is shrewd, calculating, and acidly analytical about organizational culture and the integrity of his colleagues and superiors. He enjoys reading the harshest criticisms of work managed solely for the sake of profit and power, and he scoffs at calls and programs for reform. The recent burst of the "dot.com" bubble and news of multi-billion dollar accounting shenanigans don't surprise him at all. Nonetheless, as George gradually and very hesitantly reveals, he quietly and as invisibly as possible refuses to participate in what he calls, "the corruption." He says to power what he believes power wants to hear; he obeys orders. But, within the limits of his control, beneath the notice of his bosses, he handles his customers honestly and he does not try to get the better of his colleagues.

Inevitably, George makes compromises. He knows and begins to speak freely of this. The rationalization he offers is a fascinating twist on "going along to get along." George deliberately cultivates a dissociation from his work life, as well as from the institutional schooling he sees as entirely beholden to the business world. More and more, he begins to talk about his personal or "real" life: a vibrant marriage and his wife's sociable, extended family (he is estranged from his own divorced and apparently not very loving parents), his house and garden, his friends. George's life within this domestic world could not be more different, by his account, from his work. The mentor is being given a fuller and more intimate view of a man's life.

At home, he is happy and at leisure, nor much involved in domestic efficiencies. Each spring and summer, for example, George plants a garden and works on a landscaping project. Living in a place of harsh winters and clayey, damp soil liable to heave and crack from freezing and thawing, George, unlike his neighbors, nevertheless plants flowers to look at, not vegetables to can, and he makes elaborate rock gardens which, each spring, he laboriously re-constructs or invents anew. He happily lavishes hours, nights, and days on these projects; he will even take time off from work and school to absorb himself in them.

Moreover, these projects require in-depth and sophisticated learning: landscape design, horticulture, soil composition, skills with tools both powerful and delicate. During one of our conversations, which had been initially about organizational planning, George described the research, the calculations, and drawings he'd done in preparation for a small fish pond he intended to build that coming spring. He spoke for example of calculating the depth of the pond basin and the fresh water supply he'd create so that the fish – carefully selected for both their cold temperature, low-light endurance and the colors they'd display from beneath the surface in the warm weather   would survive beneath the winter's ice. This was learning which George thoroughly loved. The mentor suggested that he might want to seek academic credit for some this experiential learning, hoping (shrewdly, as he imagined) that this would not only broaden George's academic education but also appeal to his desire to acquire credits toward the end of his degree so much the sooner. George gently and firmly declined. He wanted to maintain the moral, aesthetic, and intellectual separation between the spheres of his life.

Like Wemmick, in Dickens's *Great Expectations*, George has for himself a piece of property, where he is "own engineer ... own carpenter ... own plumber ... and own gardener" (1987: 196). To George, his home really is his "Castle." (Wemmick actually paints his small cottage to look like a castle, complete with battlements protected by a real miniature cannon and a drawbridge.) This is where he can be with whom and what he loves. George's landscaping and severely enforced intellectual dissociations protect his private life from the office just as Wemmick's Castle does his:

> No; the office is one thing, and private life another. When I go into the office, I leave the Castle behind me, and when I come into the Castle, I leave the office behind me.
>
> (ibid.: 197)

George deftly used the freedom afforded him by this college, just as he used the pragmatic cynicism he cultivated about his workplace, to protect from those environments his beloved "real" life.

Although it was not his own way, the mentor learned to respect George's particular kind of privacy. At first, he tolerated it, because of the injustice of using his authority to force a resistant student to include his personal thoughts and experiences within his academic education. This allowed George to be more forthcoming about how and why he separated the spheres of his life. He knew that he would not be judged and badgered for the distinctions and distances he'd fashioned, or for the cynicism and superficiality with which he managed his work and academic studies. And once the mentor began to understand the attitudes George gradually shared and explained, he began to appreciate the somewhat sad but thoughtfully wrought beauty of George's world. He'd created a mosaic from the pieces of his life. The pieces did not touch, but they formed a coherent picture. It was a picture truthful to what George understood as the intractable conditions governing the lives of people strenuously trying both to succeed and to preserve their integrity. To lead a prosperous and satisfying domestic life, George had to acquire a certain level of status and monetary reward by working in organizations which practiced no respect for the aesthetic and family values he loved. Seeing "school" as largely an instrumental extension of that workplace (especially since his employer funded his college education), George cultivated the same protective distance from the academy as he did from his job. He was not about to let himself be absorbed by either. Understanding George's decisions, the mentor achieved a kind of wonder at his student's achievement. And he became appreciatively curious about the compromises and distances other working adult students fashion to manage their lives in a harsh world (cf. Lasch 1995). George's confidences inspired curiosity. The mentor received them as a gift; and he learned to respect the particular privacy intrinsic to it, the separation between the academic learning George needed to finish and the intellectually active but private life he loved.

Marie

From the outset, Marie's studies were about her efforts to create boundaries and distances – from her church, from her illness, from people who sapped her strength – so that she could find work and live piously and lovingly without being destroyed. She was explicit about these purposes. She and her mentor first created a study about psychological and spiritual boundaries so that she could articulate this project and examine its meanings. Later, they did a study of Old Testament prophets, so that she could contemplate the contrast between the suffering lives they often led with the life – still a life of faith – she hoped to create for herself.

Marie liked to write poems and small essays. These were meditative pieces, sometimes remarkable for their vivid images and graceful lines. Her mentor suggested that she collect her work for evaluation as experiential learning and asked if she might like to devote some of her academic studies to writing. The evaluator, a poet and creative writing teacher, confirmed Marie's skill and promise, and thus encouraged her to develop this talent with further study. Marie did a study of short stories, writing her own and reading some classics, including some from Joyce's *Dubliners*. She was inspired to take an online course on Irish drama and to do a tutorial with her mentor on *Ulysses*. For her final project in the latter, she wrote an account of her long evening's experience attending the reading of the novel which the local Joyce Club did each year at a local pub on Bloomsday. Marie turned her experience into episodes, each depicting encounters and conversations she observed or participated in during the long, increasingly boisterous celebration. She ended the tale with a somewhat inebriated late night walk with her husband along the shore of the lake near which they lived. The literal contents of the episodes were her own, but the themes were some of those she shared with Joyce: epiphanies of yearning and loss, of vulnerable expansions and protective contractions of self, of struggling to making a place in the wide world and of recovering both stability and passion within the protective boundaries of home. Marie wrote each episode in a different style, each a stunningly dead-on imitation selected from Joyce's repertoire.

Marie was becoming a writer. Moreover, her experience of online learning gave her the idea that she might like to teach writing in this way. The distance learning technology and the growing academic market for it might allow her to work part-time and from home, thus preserving her physical health. And the mediacy of this educational method would allow her to keep her distance from the material and desires her creative writing students might present. She could protect her psychological health, even while she shared her extraordinary gifts. By the time Marie had finished her undergraduate degree, she had published a short story and a poem, and she had been accepted into a graduate program in creative writing, one which emphasized online and distance learning. And what of Marie and her mentor?

Transformation and succor are inspiring and alluring. The mentor was attracted by Marie's gifts, as was everyone who encountered her. He was also enchanted, filled with wonder and yearning. Here was a contemplative, creative person, complexly constricted, obligated, and absorbed by a powerful spiritual, physical, and domestic life, who was discovering a way to express herself and work in a wider world, yet preserve both her obligations and her integrity. And the mentor sensed that Marie responded in kind to the nurture he happily offered, a nurture inspired and enhanced by the example of her quest.

They did not overtly discuss this volatile reciprocity. Had their work been psychotherapy, explicitly "working through" the transference and counter-transference would have been an essential topic. But not here. The mentor-student relationship is a different kind of intimacy and work. However personal its sources and consequences, the "manifest content" of the academic material and methods take precedence. Thus, to make private feelings an overt focus of the dialogue would have obscured the truth of its purpose, spoiled the beauty of its process, and corrupted the ethics of the relationship. Moreover, because in the peculiar intimacy between mentor-student, the personal and the academic can never be absolutely severed (not even, for example, in a case like George's), the mentor was sure (and he believed Marie was also sure) that beneath the "merely" academic content of their conversations, he and Marie were creating exactly the boundaries both of them understood to be right.

The academic dialogue indirectly transformed their latent personal relationship into something workable and entirely proper. Each contributed something from his or her own experience to solving the problem. The mentor knew that, simply for the sake of enriching the breadth of Marie's education, it was essential for her to work with a variety of faculty. Thus, although they did some studies together, he arranged for her to work with colleagues and adjunct tutors on her studies of writing, literature, philosophy, and psychology. And Marie, once she had discovered the satisfactions and convenience of distance learning, proposed that she and her mentor conduct some of their conversations by email. This mediated dialogue afforded her "social distance" (Coulter and Herman 1994a). It gave her the leisure and solitude to contemplate and construct her responses to the mentor's expectant questions and eager suggestions, an enthusiasm she sometimes experienced in their in-person discussions to be, as she called it, "prodding." In this delicate, indirect way, they figured out how to do their common work; they achieved an appropriately bounded and distanced intimacy.

The intelligence of the erotic

At the outset of this book, we argued that what distinguishes the mentor-student relationship from that of professor and students is "care." The mentor cares for the particular learning of each individual student. In our discussions of principle and practice, we have examined the cognitive truthfulness and goodness of caring. And now we must consider its aesthetic dimension. How do the affective and personal constituents of the relationship serve the beautiful? This cognitive journey toward the truth, as Diotima instructs Socrates, "Is the love of the engendering and the birthing in beauty" (Plato, *Symposium*: 206e). The offspring of this cognitive love is human access to the entire realm of epistemic and moral truth, "the beauty of every kind of knowledge" (ibid.: 210c). How, then, shall we understand these erotics, these "love matters," which are neither sexual romance, personal friendship, psychotherapy, the business-like striving for worldly success, nor the attachment of scholars to their subjects – this love which nonetheless shares something with all those passionate efforts? Such an understanding would offer yet another way to think about "the personal and the academic" in their complex interconnections.

Since the mentor serves primarily to nurture the student's learning, the topics of their dialogues emerge from the curiosity, the learning purposes, of each individual student (Principle 2, diversity of curriculum). These topics are as diverse as the students, and thus, practically infinite in their variety. Even so, the learning is framed, more or less explicitly, by the most general topics, which, as we have argued and illustrated throughout this book, are fundamental, universally human concerns: What is true? What is just? What is beautiful? What is it to thrive and be happy? The questions are abstract, but curiosity about them, the cognitive care or love for them is not. Students are asking, from their individual lives, "What is true, good, beautiful, happiness, for me?" Thus mentors ask, more or less explicitly, in their care for the learning of each individual student, "What do you desire to learn that will help you understand what is true, good, beautiful, and offers you happiness?" This question governs the mentor's love.

But can such a love be selfless, genuinely devoted to the interests of the individual "other"? And, if it can be, would not mentors be merely serving a kind of solipsism, each student's idiosyncratic view of the world, a view governed entirely by personal feelings, attitudes, and desires? What becomes of "the academic," the kind of learning to which the mentor is professionally committed and which, after all, each student is seeking a public recognition, a certification, a degree, for achieving? Academic institutions, moreover, are responsible in turn an even larger world of institutions. The "funding streams" that flow from governments, businesses, non-profits, philanthropic organizations, and "the market" also shape which disciplines and topics universities offer and require their students to learn. In what risks do mentors involve their students by inviting them into a "cognitive love" heedless of those currents? Yet, what beautiful discourse disappears when too much attention is paid there? If we linger, as T.S. Eliot's Prufrock realizes, too much with "sea girls" in "the chambers of sea," we can drown in the practical human exigences we've ignored (Eliot 1971: 7). But, if we also ignore such beautiful visions, our lives become the thin, insubstantial chatter of "afternoon teas" and we devote our minds merely "to prepare a face to meet the faces that you meet" (4).

When we mentors ask students to tell us about themselves, their curiosities, and their goals, any kind of personal information and feeling is likely to emerge. We hear about their desires and despairs, their work and family lives, their intimate histories. Sometimes this material emerges in a flood of confidences. Sometimes they barely emerge at all, or only after months of talk and study. Louis talks about his family troubles; Elena wants to share her faith and ministry; Marie worries about the oppressive gifts her god has given her and the intrusiveness of her associates who feel the succor those gifts can give them. Even George, who wants his learning to be as business-like as possible, shares his protective cynicism as a precious personal confidence. These confidences easily pull mentor and student toward psychotherapy or some kind of personally intimate relationship; they pull us away from what both parties have taken for granted as academic dialogue. How then does the conversation hold true to its purpose, retaining even in its proper intellectual focus the personal resonance that gives the learning meaning for the student?

Of course mentors clearly assert the boundaries. We listen to our students' stories and confidences, but we remind them, as straightforwardly as necessary, of the business to be done. We are friendly, but we do not offer friendship. We are empathetic, but we do not offer psychotherapy. We listen to and respect personal confessions, but we do not offer absolution. Rather, we do offer to help students name and explore the ideas present in what they disclose to us. This opens the prospect of integrating the personal and the academic, and of midwiving the labor by which the idiosyncratic is born into an intellectual community. How does this occur?

As mentors listen to their students, we learn that every articulation of even the rawest emotion contains cognitive claims about the self and the world. In his book on Freud's understanding of "meaning," Jonathan Lear argues that emotions and symptoms not only encode private and idiosyncratic history. Once unconscious content is represented by words and taken into discourse, emotions then become "an orientation to the world" (Lear 1990: 49, 88–89 and elsewhere). They represent beliefs about what is true and false, good and bad, lovable and hateful. Considering Freud's claim that "sexuality" or "libidinal investment" so pervades us that it determines what we learn to recognize, attend to or avoid in the world, Lear pushes the epistemology of feeling even farther: "It is a condition of there being a world that it be lovable by beings like us" (ibid.: 143).

Of course human beings are not so powerfully solipsistic that they can live, except perhaps in infancy or psychosis, on the assumption that existence occurs only according to their desires. However:

> That the world only be lov*able* frees the world's existence from any causal dependence on our actually loving (or hating) it. The world does not exist because it is actually loved – or invested with libido – but it is a condition of there being a world that it be lovable by beings like us. This is more than a psychological condition of there being a world *for us*. There is no content to the idea of a world that is not a possible world for us. And a world that is not lovable (by beings like us) is not a possible world.
>
> (ibid.: 142)

To put this in terms of academic learning rather than psychoanalytic therapy, we should say that our feelings, even our most private ones, contain beliefs about what is true of the world and that our curiosity, our *desire* to learn is driven by our wish to love and to be loved. This is how we make the world real.

Further, Martha Nussbaum's philosophical examinations of emotion offer a path to understanding how this epistemology of affect might support a mentoring approach to learning. She starts with the ancient Stoic Chrysippus's odd claim that passions, all passions, are literally nothing more than "false judgment or false belief" about what is valuable in the world, the falseness being the corollary to the basic Stoic principle that nothing in the external world, not even one's biological life, is worthy of attachment (Nussbaum 1994: 336 ff.). But if we choose to live in this world, if we choose seek and savor love, we shall form and value attachments. Further, since that to which we are attached (things, persons, images) are necessarily external to or "other than" us, they are inherently beyond our immediate understanding, beyond our absolute control and possession. Knowledge requires indefinitely prolonged learning; love requires vulnerability, curiosity, the individualized desire to learn, thus risks an encounter, as Meno discovers, with our ignorance and helplessness. And wonder, we might say, is the pleasure of risking this cognitive love.

Nussbaum rejects the Stoic effort to "extirpate" emotions and thus to achieve *apatheia*, emotionlessness (Nussbaum 2001: 301). Her reasons are epistemic, ethical, and political. Without the valuing or love of the world our emotions imply, we could not care for or be cared for by others (ibid.: 335–342). The world is valuable because we live in it with others. Moreover, the emotions do give us information about what we desire or fear, about our attachments in the world. In this, the Stoic analysis was correct; it's their evaluation that is wrong. Nussbaum updates the Stoics' epistemology of emotion. She supplements their descriptions with current psychological and neurological research, as well as with discussions of modern Western literature and music. And, in a fine and moving application of the ancient Greek injunction, "know thyself," she uses everything she learned to understand the grief she experiences upon the death of her mother. Nussbaum concludes that emotions are in fact sufficiently constituted by judgments (more or less unconscious and implicit) – beliefs about our attachments to what we do not control, about what we value or love beyond ourselves in this life (ibid.: 19–88).

Mentors and students discover that emotions disclose our risky love for and vulnerable cognitions of the world. Thus, applying Nussbaum's analysis to understanding the mentor-student relationship and the appropriate content of their academic dialogue, we might say this: In the personal confidences mentor and student share, in the passion-laden expressions of worry and need, there are to be discovered not just idiosyncratic attitudes or psychotherapeutic material, but also the foundations of curiosity. Every personal confidence is at least implicitly a judgment about the "lovability" of the world; it is an implicit and intensely valued question that hopefully, as well as frighteningly, reaches beyond the isolated self. The midwifery of mentoring is to help bring forth into dialogue those judgments and those questions.

To take a simple example: George confides to his mentor that he wants to learn as little as he needs, as quickly as he can to finish his degree. The mentor might respond disparagingly to George's apparent anti-intellectualism. But, keeping his feelings to himself, as a "good professional" should, he might simply let George go his way, making sure only that George does meet the minimal requirements for a degree. Perhaps the mentor will also hope that George will encounter a topic or a teacher who will inspire him to a deeper engagement with his academic studies. If he were a psychotherapist, he might wonder why George has such difficulty forming trusting attachments in his workplace, what private fears compel him to invest so little in his schooling when he has the opportunity to make of his learning something much more meaningful than the instrument and credential his bosses expect.

Although he does not push George to explain his attitudes more than he desires, the mentor does express his curiosity. He wants to understand George's attitudes, his views about work, learning, and being at home in the world. The mentor thus naturally models the very curiosity he hopes George will adopt. Gradually, in during their discussions of organizational behavior and ethics, George reciprocates. In explaining the separations he's made between the domains of his experience, George, even if he does not change his decisions, expands his learning about himself. And in so doing, he also helps the mentor learn. The mentor acquires a much deeper and more sympathetic understanding of how people protect their life-worlds, their autonomous selves from organizations (whether businesses or universities) which would otherwise dissolve and use them as tools profit and power. The mentor begins to understand that their *desire* and *pleasure* in secreting and dissociating themselves protects their capacity to give and receive respect and love, while they continue to earn their way in the world. He begins to understand that these emotional reactions are not blind and foolish impulses at all, but represent rational and honorable judgments.

As the discussion of George's studies shows, he does go beyond the textbook in offering material from his experiences for case studies. He thereby can articulate the principles of his worldview. But the mentor is sure that it will do little good to require George to critically examine those principles, just as he does not try to challenge Elena's theology. Again, he lets George go his way.

Nonetheless, George has borne something new into his academic intellectual life. In explaining his attitudes to another, to an "official," who neither ignores nor disparages them, but takes them as serious ideas, George has had to learn to understand what he himself habitually thinks. He has made his values available for self-examination. Whether or not he chooses to pursue that project, perhaps while he muses during some late winter night of planning his garden for the coming spring, the mentor will never know. But the mentor will be better prepared and more understanding of other students like George. Perhaps his responses, both deliberated and "emotional," will be finer, gentler, more compassionate, and more usefully encouraging.

In the cognitive love the mentor offers to and evokes in students, important academic learning occurs about diverse practical matters. But both mentor and student also learn to understand more than they had about truthfulness and justice. Because the cognitive love they experience is genuinely *for* "the other" – each offering and waiting for disclosure – their desire is truthful and it is just. Moreover, in the delight they experience through a shared inquiry that seeks a better life and coherently embraces the diversity of the unknown, mentor and student discover beauty.

Cognitive love means not only that mentors help their students learn, but learn with and from them as well. Just as parents often learn to become better parents because they are inspired by love of their children, so mentors learn their art from their students. This is the topic of our next chapter.

Chapter 7

The mentor as learner

Habits of work

> I am willing to die many times over, if these things are true... I think that would not be unpleasant. And the greatest pleasure would be to pass my time in examining and investigating the people there, as I do those here, to find out who among them is wise and who thinks he is when he is not.
>
> Plato, *Apology* (41a–b)

Socrates is eager to pass his time in eternity by investigating who is wise and who only seems so, in order that he might better understand what wisdom really is. The mentor is also at least a "lifelong" learner. But so all are good professors and instructors of any kind. As scholars, they become more and more expert in the contents of their fields. As teachers, they learn to be more eloquent and deft in transmitting what they know to their students, including the "know-how" of being active and increasingly independent learners.

What then distinguishes the sense in which a mentor is a learner? It is that we concentrate on learning *from*, *with*, and *for the sake* of our students, each one, individually. And, in the practices of helping our students develop the freedom and responsibility of scholars, we are acting as scholars as well. That is, we devote our intellectual abilities to creating dialogical learning with our students. From these inquiries, important discoveries will emerge for and about ourselves and our students, which beforehand we had not known. Mentors, as well as students, experience wonder.

In this chapter, we illustrate how mentors learn to do their work through experiential learning: We learn the work of mentoring by doing it with our students. Then, we begin to consider the sort of polity, the governing context, which enables students and mentors to be dialogical learners with each other.

What mentors learn

What, then, have mentors learned, which enables them to do their work well? We have described "cognitive love" and we have referred to the art of Socratic "midwifery." But is there not some kind of knowledge or intelligible expertise, which informs this disposition and manner of acting? The most famous of Socratic paradoxes is his claim to know nothing except that he does not know anything (the corollary to which is that he only asks questions and teaches nothing at all). The knowledge Socrates insists he and all human beings utterly lack is the sort of knowledge the gods have: absolute, permanent, and complete. Human beings seek to know in this sense, but, if we are wise, we understand that we do not achieve such perfect cognition. We are perpetual learners, who know that every moment of knowing is incomplete and provisional. We are wonderers and seekers, not omniscient and complacent consciousnesses. Thus, in this book, we have offered and applied a set of principles which define what it means to be a knower, a nurturer of learning, in this liminal restless zone between absolute ignorance and perfect omniscience. These principles, we might say, are what mentors need to learn and continue to learn through their work.

But the principles are abstractions. Although they ultimately govern mentoring, they are remote from the exquisitely dense particularity of practice in the moment. Mediating between the silent equanimity of principle and the noisy rush of practice, however, stands a relatively stable but improvisationally adapted set of "habits." These are what mentors learn how to do.

How do mentors learn? By and large the same way our students do, through experience. We act within an organization; it has a formal and informal culture, a documented history and oral traditions. We see and hear what our colleagues do. We note distinctions and conflicts between pronouncements and practices, as well as which behaviors, both subtle and obvious, are punished or rewarded. From this mixture of factors and values, some purely pragmatic or systemic and others inspired with the sort of lifeworld the institution claims to represent, we acquire habits, routines of behavior which, through repetition, become skillfully deployed.

However, we are also members of a university. Intrinsically, it is or ought to be a community of learning. To be entirely consistent with the kind of institution ours claims to be, we should be regarding our own behaviors, our own habits, as topics for examination (Principle 1). This does not differentiate us from any other human organization. Every institution in order to thrive must "learn" about what it is doing, in order to determine if it is really doing what it claims. And every institution must continue to understand what it means by "quality" or "good," if it is to do well whatever it happens to be doing. But the very reason for a university to exist is neither profit nor power but to foster learning. For us and for our institution, "the good" is always and primarily about learning itself.

When we are learning about what we routinely do, we are simply doing for ourselves what we help our students do when we ask them to recognize and articulate their experiential learning. Thus, our discussion of "habits"

in this chapter is an effort to take the common actions of mentoring as topics of learning.

Habits and principles of mentoring, not "techniques"

Habits may be very simple behaviors or combinations of them, such as being silent and waiting for a student to say something. But, as concrete phenomena, they often have multiple determinants and motivations. Thus, a single habit may be informed and governed by more than one abstract principle. In the following sections, we therefore present a series of mentoring habits and point to the principles at work in their construction.

But there is a necessary fuzziness in our categories. "Habits" are customs of self-presentation governed by a deliberate desire and purpose to enter into a certain kind of relationship with students, what we have called "cognitive love." They are not little formulas or methods for acting upon students so that they learn something we have determined they ought. Our habits are not techniques; their application is not mechanics. A technique or method sees the entity worked upon as entirely malleable material to be transformed into something entirely determined by the concepts applied to it – as an object. Instead, we try to see our students, as well as what they are learning, as subjects independent of complete comprehension. We do not try to "grasp" them, but to encourage them to uncover or reveal themselves to us, an indefinitely incomplete process. In doing so, we are not acting as detached and authoritative technicians of teaching; rather, we too reveal ourselves as subjects trying to learn. We are, as we shall claim at the conclusion of this chapter, entering into a certain kind of community, a polity of inquiry.

Most of the habits below have been discussed or at least mentioned in prior chapters. Here, we are offering them as the behaviors of a "learner." Mentors practice the very behaviors they seek to help their students develop as well. As learners in our mentoring, we are practicing, as we've said, a kind of scholarship. That is, we try to discover how to help our students participate in the freedoms and responsibilities of an intellectual community. We try to govern and improve our habits according to the principles of mentoring, and in this effort, we continue to learn what those principles mean in practice.

Self-reflection

This is the most fundamental of all the habits of mentoring. To become aware of the limits of one's understanding (Principle 1), and thus to realize that one should learn something new, one must be looking at and asking oneself what one is doing. Every mentor must acquire a watchful "little spirit" within, the *daimonion* of Socrates. We can take this presence as lit-

erally or as metaphorically as we please. We can regard it as something
like the eye and voice of an inner divinity inspiring us, or as a metaphor of
a distinctly active aspect of entirely human consciousness. Either way, this
spirit is a palpable presence in our work, sometimes quietly vibrating in
the background of our consciousness and sometimes loudly questioning. It
offers us self-recognition. Now with a riveting shock, other times with a
gentle shudder or *frisson*, it asks, "What are you doing? Look."

Some of us learned to look by doing literally that. Two colleagues,
Xenia Coulter and Sylvain Nagler proposed that a small group of mentors
videotape actual conversations with students and then meet regularly to
watch and discuss the tapes (Coulter *et al.* 1992, 1993, 1994b–c). Our discussions were guided by two simple questions: "What are you doing?"
"Are you doing what we have all claimed 'mentoring' to be?" This project,
which lasted several years, is a normal part of the training discipline of
therapists and counselors, but had never before been practiced by the
faculty in our college.

Marty, me, and my "little voice"

Mentors in our group had often claimed that it was more important, nearly
always, to ask students questions rather than to lecture to them, and that
those questions be "opening" rather than "leading."

I make a tape of an early conversation with Marty. I ask him to participate because, although he is a new student, we are long-time acquaintances,
comfortable with one another, and he is used to operating a video camera
and being on tape himself. Also, I think he will be a good student with
whom I might illustrate the important skill of asking open questions
because his area of professional experience and academic interest, audio-
visual production, is relatively unfamiliar to me. I am sure that I will be
asking him a lot of questions so that I can understand what I need to do,
including which expert colleagues I shall have to call upon, in order to help
Marty identify and complete the learning for his bachelor's degree.

What I see (and what I know my colleagues are seeing) on the hour-
long tape shocks and embarrasses me. Again and again, I see myself
asking inauthentic or disingenuous questions. I set them up with seemingly
modest comments, which allude suggestively to my own supposedly vast
and deep (but actually narrow and thin) knowledge of "film," of documen-
taries, and of television production. I ask questions which, instead of
encouraging Marty to speak openly of his own large and varied practical
experience, direct his attention to readings and ideas I'm familiar with
about the "cultural" and "philosophical" significance of audio-visual
technology in the "age of rapid information." My questions are long;
Marty's responses are brief. Thinking during the conversation that I was
making common ground for collaboration with him, I see on the tape that
I am reducing him to respectful silence.

I've never forgotten that tape, or, to be honest, the many more like it I saw. My colleagues were aware of my embarrassment (as I was of theirs when they experienced, as all of us did, similar moments). Instead of criticizing one another (perhaps because none of us was in a position to "cast the first stone," and certainly because we were all professional friends who cared for each other), we learned to ask, seeing such moments: "What were you thinking at the time?" "How does your act differ from your intent, or what you believed your intent was?" "Why does the difference matter?" "What, seeing what you have seen, might you try to do instead?" So it went on, for hours and months of conversation among ourselves. I grew used to learning that, often, what I believed or hoped I was doing with a student was not what I was doing at all.

I could see that my on-tape behavior was slowly changing. I began to ask questions more frequently that were really questions, and not occasions to show off. Of course all of us participating in this project knew that we might be learning to "behave" well or perform for the camera, whose presence we were always aware of. No doubt this was happening. But so was something else. We began to realize, each in his or her own way, that we were becoming habitually "self-conscious" even in the absence of the camera. This self-consciousness, I found, was not inhibiting; it did not disrupt my thoughts or take my attention away from the student. It was not that kind of self-consciousness. Rather, in some way I can not really explain, it joined with the flow of the dialogue. At first this "little voice" took the awkward character of a small child's shrewdly pragmatic conscience: "Would you be doing this if you believed you would get caught on videotape?" But even before the voice became more principled, more intrinsically motivated, it enhanced my consciousness of what I was doing. At the same time I was absorbed in listening and responding to a student, I was also listening to and for myself. It was as though the dialogue had acquired another collaborator.

Learning the value of distance

Nearing the end of her undergraduate studies in social work, Rianne has become interested in how and why people comply with oppressive, even clearly malevolent social systems. It seemed to her, for example, that so few slave rebellions occurred in the United States and, similarly, that so many "ordinary" Germans accepted the Nazi regime, and so few Jews resisted deportation to concentration camps or, once there and unequivocally informed about their fates, tried to escape or attack their murderous oppressors. She wondered why. A creative and successful independent student, Rianne planned this study herself, including an excellent bibliography (Principle 3).

She knew that her curiosity about the topic was connected to her social work studies of counseling and family dynamics (Principle 6). Her prior readings, internships, and personal experiences had made her wonder why, so often, therapy patients seemed to passively accept changing domestic arrangements, friendships, and workplaces, which they knew made them miserable. To be sure, Rianne knew all too well about objective or external risks. She knew that it was sometimes simply dangerous for people to change. But why didn't people change when those risks weren't apparently very large at all? Or, for that matter, why did some people brave even the gravest dangers? Why was it so difficult and complicated to be free? Rianne hoped that a social and historical exploration of complicity and rebellion in the face of genocide and slavery would give her some additional insight into these fundamental problems.

Rianne's mentor, who had worked directly with her on several prior studies, knew her to be academically very competent, a careful reader, thorough researcher, and clear writer. However, he'd been struck a number of times by a dissonance between the good quality of the essays Rianne wrote and the hesitant, ambiguous, and even confused way she responded to his questions when they met to discuss what she'd written. He knew Rianne well enough to know that she was not a shy person and that the essays she presented were entirely her own work. Their relationship was, moreover, collaborative enough so that the mentor believed he could ask Rianne, without being intrusive, as he had done several times, about this dissonance between her writing and her speaking about it (Principles 3, 4, and 5). Rianne acknowledged the problem but didn't understand it either.

Then, during this final study, called "Oppression and Complicity," Rianne herself raised the issue. She and her mentor were talking about an essay she'd written on Daniel Goldhagen's recently published *Hitler's Willing Executioners*. The mentor felt typically frustrated and puzzled by Rianne's hazy answers to his questions about her essay; this time, unknowingly, he let some of this feeling show. To which Rianne responded:

"Your questions bother me."

"Why? Am I unclear?"

"No. I think I understand them, but when I see you sitting there, expecting me to answer, looking at me, I become anxious and distracted. It's hard to think about what you're asking."

"I'm sorry. I do get frustrated sometimes. You write such clear essays, but then I have a hard time understanding what you say about them. We've talked about this difference before. I am sorry to be impatient; I will try to do better."

"No, I want to try doing something else. What if we have our conversations by email?"

"By email? Even though you live and work so near the office here?"

"Yes. That's my point. I want some distance. I feel crowded here. If we conversed by email, I'd feel freer to think about your questions. It wouldn't matter to me if you were impatient or not because I wouldn't see it or hear it and I could take my time and pay attention to what you were actually asking about."

The mentor told Rianne that her proposal might be a good one, but he wanted to think about it overnight. She agreed and he said that he would email her the next day with his response.

During his contemplations, he began to understand several things about his behavior (Principle 1). He'd usually and automatically associated "dialogue" with the physical presence of the participants; and he'd also assumed that it was his responsibility to suit the manner of his self-presentation, his professional "role" or "character" of the moment, to the needs, as he understood them, of his students (Principle 4). These assumptions now became clear to him; that is, he now recognized, in his self-reflection, these beliefs *as* unexamined assumptions.

Does dialogue really require physical, immediate presence?

I need to know what my students really believe.

But what if they don't know yet, what if they need some time to discover what they really think? You've had conversations, dialogues, with other students, by phone and email. You've done entire courses online. You've worked with many students who can't come to your office because they live too far away or their schedules are too busy. Do you think they were giving you inauthentic responses?

No. That's true. Whenever I've suspected a student is borrowing words or ideas, which isn't too often, I can tell from what they write. I usually learn their own style pretty fast; it's not very hard to tell what isn't theirs. Phone, email, in-person, I guess it doesn't matter much. But I learn so much more, so much easier when we are actually together and I believe the students do too.

Why would presence necessarily be easier for the student? I know that you try to be friendly, patient, caring, and attentive. But still, you're the Professor, the mentor. Don't you think that can be distracting or even intimidating? When you were in graduate school, weren't you submissive to authority, even when your professors no longer much expected you to be? Maybe it was enough for you that they were still officially your professors.

Yes. Yes. But I try *not* to act like "the Professor." Anyhow, isn't it my responsibility to be whatever sort of person my students need me to be so that they can learn?

Perhaps it is. But then how do you know if you've succeeded? Are you the sole judge? If what you're claiming to do with students is really a dialogue, really a collaborative inquiry – a phrase you like to use – then aren't they important participants in helping you learn if you are really behaving helpfully? Maybe responsibility and helping others be intellectually free is more complicated than you think. Maybe you could learn something from what Rianne is studying.

So this internal conversation went on. Later that day, the mentor emailed Rianne: "I think your idea is a good one. Let's try discussing your essay by email. As long as it seems to work okay, both to you and to me, we'll continue this way through the end of the study." They emailed back and forth, each often within minutes of the other. Rianne did fine. She made clear, thoughtful, and obviously authentic responses to the mentor's questions about her essays. In this somewhat odd way, the mentor learned to "wait," using the very mediacy or lack of full presence afforded by email, to construct with Rianne a "distance" that gave her time and space to concentrate on discovering and then articulating what she really believed. (We explore this idea further in the next chapter, "Authenticity and artifice.")

Learning the student

Principle 4 requires mentors to learn their students. This includes not just what students want their academic learning to be, but also enough about who they are, their purposes and conditions of their lives so that we can accommodate, as best we can, *how* they learn, as well as *what* they learn. Sometimes, the mentors' learning means getting an idea from a student about a helpful change to make in the planned learning activities. And sometimes, as our first example will illustrate, "learning the student" means that mentors discover limits to what they can do for and expect from the student.

Martina: learning the limitations of cultural expectations

Martina recently immigrated to the United States from the Ukraine. There, she had been in business and had completed an academic degree in "commerce." However, after she and her family had arrived, a local agency serving new migrants placed Martina and her husband in a "medical laboratory assistant" training program. There were readily available and reasonably paying job opportunities in this field. Martina's success would not depend upon her being fluent in colloquial English or with American business practices. Bright and ambitious, Martina took to her new vocation and enrolled in university in order to complete a degree in biological laboratory technology, an achievement which would afford her significant increases in pay and status.

While doing degree program planning with her, Martina's mentor also learned that her written and oral English were quite limited and that Martina was uncomfortably aware of her lack of fluency. Supposing that her intelligence and ambition would motivate her to eagerly improve her English language skills (Principle 2), he proposed that they work on these together, even within the context of their curriculum planning study. Here, the mentor thought, was a good opportunity to get to know the student, and both to gain and build her confidence in an area in which she was obviously uncomfortable. Martina agreed to the mentor's proposal. Trying to help Martina make some other academic connections, the mentor did some research for books and articles on biology and medical biology written for the general reader (for example, by Stephen Jay Gould). He sought advice in making these selections from colleagues with academic expertise in biology and the history of science; and he asked colleagues particularly skilled in teaching English composition, if they would serve as ancillary tutors for Martina. She agreed to these proposals as well.

However, as their work proceeded, the mentor realized that Martina was not making very much progress with her English. Her writing and speaking improved somewhat, but only a little and very slowly. Although clearly a disciplined and energetic person, Martina seemed only fitfully to use a dictionary and otherwise practice her English language skills. From the mentor's view, each time they met, they were starting over. Moreover, he learned that Martina had not contacted any of the composition mentors and not participated in any of the writing or speaking workshops they offered for groups of similar, English-as-a-second language students. Because Martina had been occasionally shy, the mentor made sure that she would have easy and welcoming access to the help his colleagues could provide. Why didn't she seek this help? Why was Martina's English improving so slowly and unreliably?

The mentor was puzzled. He directly but gently raised his questions with Martina. Her answers seemed vague, even evasive. He also asked colleagues with whom Martina had begun doing conventional studies in biology, how she was doing. They reported that she was doing "okay," well enough to get by, although one colleague said that Martina's written work sometimes contained too much unacknowledged, "borrowed" content and language. The mentor began to suspect or speculate that some complicated cultural dynamics were at play. He knew directly from Martina that she was scared of the academic and linguistic challenges she'd taken on. But he began to believe, from what Martina had told him about her life as a student and commercial person in the Ukraine, that she was even more scared of being "found out," of being "other" or "less than" what teachers and bosses expected her to be. She had learned to conceal her deviations and deficiencies enough so that she could "get by." This is just what she seemed to be doing here, in this university in the U.S., even though her mentor and his colleagues had repeatedly tried to make it clear to her that she wouldn't be academically "punished" for her weaknesses or other-ness, and that she would be rewarded for honestly working at what needed to be improved (Principle 5).

The mentor tried many approaches, even as he tried to be careful not to be attached to his little "theory," his potential stereotype of Martina as a product of the authoritarian culture from which she'd come (Principles 1 and 4). Martina did not ignore these suggestions, nor did she exactly resist them. Rather, she described the demands of a job, a home, a marriage, and parenting. She insisted that she was doing as much as she could and that she was managing to do "well enough" in her studies (a claimed confirmed by the mentor's colleagues). The mentor continued to believe that it was too bad that Martina didn't take more advantage of the learning opportunities offered her. He continued to hope that she would significantly improve her English in the safer environment of an accommodating university, and to practice some of the freedom afforded by her new culture.

Still, the mentor wondered if he also wasn't expecting too much, if he wasn't perhaps trying to exceed the practical and proper limits on what he could and should do "for" Martina and what she was responsible for doing for herself (Principle 3). Perhaps, he wondered, the freedom afforded by his own culture, which normally expects people to be openly assertive and ambitious for themselves, was actually inhibiting her. He even wondered if Martina wasn't ironically exercising her new freedom. He suspected that Martina had quietly chosen to excel in her workplace (where her English was no problem) and to be just good enough in her academic studies to get by. She wanted her mentor to respect the important consequences of this choice for her life – consequences only she was free to judge. Hadn't she been telling him, trying, in effect, to teach him exactly that? He learned to appreciate the intricacies of Martina's cultural lifeworld, as well as the limitations which his own could impose (Principle 4).

Beth: the academic discovery of "personal" knowledge

While Martina's mentor had learned to trust the student, Beth's mentor learned a new topic of experiential learning (new at least to him) by persistently collaborating with her. (We've already introduced Beth in Chapter 5, "Curriculum as collaborative planning.") Beth was planning a degree in the management of not-for-profit organizations. She'd already worked for some years administering the budget of a village government and was planning to open, with a friend, a childcare center. Beth loved taking care of and raising her own children; she and her friend had also offered state-approved childcare services for others out of their own homes. In addition, Beth had some academic background in both business and childhood education studies. She seemed to love organization and management as much as she did direct care. Her mentor asked her one day:

> "Isn't it very complicated and stressful to be running your own household and raising your own kids while at the same time and in the same place providing care for other people's children?"

She answered that it seemed a "natural" thing to do, although it was indeed more complicated than managing the business affairs of the village. So I asked:

> "Why is it *more* complicated?"

> "Well, you have to pay attention to more different kinds of things – food, money, schedules, health, recreation, and so on. Also, at my regular work, for the village, I can put things off; and you can bargain and negotiate with adults, the village employees, more easily, I think, than you can with children. Especially when it comes to safety or meals, you can't really wait long or tell small kids to look after themselves. Sometimes I feel like I have to be paying attention to and doing everything all at once. It's juggling."

The mentor, who had no children, was interested. He asked, "Did they teach you about managing all these things, juggling, in the childhood education courses you took at your former college?"

> "No. This is just something you just do as a parent. How can you learn that from a textbook?"

> "But haven't you met parents who are overwhelmed, who can't manage all those different tasks? Didn't you get better at it as time went on?"

> "That's true, I guess. It seemed like that the more kids I had around, my own and others', the easier it became."

> "So maybe you learned something about managing itself by running a household full of kids. Maybe you learned something that you didn't learn in those classes and you didn't even learn by managing village business."

"Are you saying I could get college credit for that? It's important to me, especially since I want to manage a daycare center. But I never thought that I was really *learning* something."

"I'm not sure." And indeed, the mentor didn't know.

"Domestic management?" the mentor asked himself. What would his colleagues or other universities think? Would such learning be dismissed, as faculty sometimes joked about "basket-weaving" when they criticized how all kinds of non-academic subjects crept into course offerings and cheapened "real" university-level learning? On the other hand, people got credit all the time at many colleges for learning elementary skills, like playing the piano or beginning conversational Spanish. For that matter, what was so non-academic about "basket-weaving"? More to the point, business students quite normally did academic internships in management practices; they didn't just focus on "theories" or "philosophies" of management. Didn't "domestic management" require as much skill? Were there some gender politics and stereotypes at work in the mentor's own hesitation? (After all, not always, but most of the time, to his observation, it was men who sought academic credit for their managerial skills.) Indeed, if Beth knew what she was talking about, maybe it was even more sophisticated and complicated than managing a business (Principle 1).

The mentor asked Beth if she could write an essay in which she compared the skills and knowledge she needed to administer the affairs of the village with those she needed to manage a household with children (Principles 4 and 6). The mentor also asked her to pay particular attention to the ways in which domestic management seemed to differ from "regular" management. She agreed, hesitantly, to try. Perhaps she still doubted that her skills as a household manager were "real" learning.

Two weeks later, Beth presented an essay on "Domestic and Business Management." It was clearly and neatly subdivided into a comparative discussion of diverse skills: communication, supervision, discipline, planning and scheduling, delegating responsibilities, conflict resolution, and budgeting – all of them skills to be found under those or similar labels in even advanced management books. Moreover, under "prioritizing," Beth included a brief discussion of "juggling," of what it was like to have to manage a number of very different tasks more or less simultaneously (e.g. making a hot meal, checking on a crying baby, stopping a fight between two other children) because it just wasn't safe or otherwise responsible to let something go. He showed the essay to a colleague whose academic specialty and experiential background was business management and who, he knew, had raised several children on her own. His colleague was skeptical at first; but she took time to think and to talk with Beth. Eventually, she prepared a detailed and substantial recommendation for college-level learning in "Domestic and Business Management." Afterwards, Beth's mentor habitually asked students who were also parents, both women and men, what they knew about domestic management and "juggling." Years later, the mentor discovered that "juggling' had made its way into management literature. But now, no longer confined to the home (and, perhaps no longer considered a "feminine" virtue) juggling was called "multi-tasking."

Improvising

"Learning the student" offers discomfiting and enlivening surprises. Mentors of course can not know what they are, but we gradually learn to hold ourselves in readiness for them, and to change our expectations and suddenly add to our own learning accordingly.

Mentors and students plan individual studies and entire curricula. But, as students continue to learn, they also continue to examine the meaning of their plans and to assess what they have regarded as important (Principle 1). With new discoveries, unanticipated openings appear from which new lines of inquiry emanate. And sometimes these seem to the student and mentor so valuable and evocative that they will modify their original plans (Principles 2 and 3). Mentors are thus adept at improvising and helping their students do so as well. We and our students learn to improvise upon almost any learning plan, activity, resource, and outcome. We've offered examples in prior chapters of revising curricular plans and of making use of experiential learning resources which happen to appear. Here, we offer an example of a mentor and student learning to improvise new content and new purposes for a study already underway.

Howard enjoyed reading poetry and novels. Not having done very much academic study of literature, he wanted to put some formal order to and expand the great deal of reading he had done by means of an academic study of "world literature." With some suggestions from his mentor, Howard created a reading list. It was very long and the number of credits he intended to devote to this study were few. Mentor and student thus decided that they would at first just plunge into a few of the classics from the list, which seemed most appealing (Principle 2). The reason didn't matter; coherence would emerge in the dialogue (Principle 6). Howard and his mentor would reflect on their conversations about these works in order to see which themes they talked about the most (Principle 1) and then focus on one or more of these themes to select the remainder of the readings they would do (Principle 2). They began with Salinger's *Catcher in the Rye* and a modern verse translation of Homer's *Odyssey*.

Early on in their conversations about these works, Howard spoke more and more of his fascination with style. He loved Holden Caulfield's cutting, lean, and precise slang, but also Homer's elaborate and vivid similes. "I'm interested in diversity of style," Howard said during his second conversation with his mentor. This became the cue for selecting the remaining works. The mentor suggested that for the sake of coherence and intimacy with language, they confine the rest of the readings to works written originally in English. Howard agreed to this idea and to putting off a study of "world literature" for a later time. The mentor then re-titled the learning contract to "Classics of English Style in Novels and Poetry." (He also included in the contract a note to explain the presence of the *Odyssey*.) The final list included works by Shakespeare, Blake, Keats, Jane Austen, Dickens, Mark Twain, James Joyce, Virginia Woolf, T.S. Eliot, Toni Morrison, and Marilynne Robinson (a writer by no means so well known as the others but whom both Howard and his mentor highly esteemed).

The study was proceeding happily until Howard's attention began to be overwhelmed by conflicts between his work and personal lives. He and his mentor began to worry that he might not be able to continue with the literature. At their scheduled appointments, Howard would appear distracted and distraught. Randomly, he would begin to talk about his non-academic concerns. The mentor decided to take a risk. He asked Howard if he saw any connections between what he was reading and what was happening within him (Principles 4 and 6). He also asked if Howard might like to re-focus the literature study on those connections. But in making this offer, the mentor also warned Howard that they would have to be careful to sustain the academic focus of the study. Despite the personal resonances, they would have to be vigilant about not letting the study be absorbed by confessions or transformed into an occasion for counseling.

Howard thought about these proposals for a long time. He and his mentor had several more conversations about them. Eventually, Howard identified a theme, "personal authenticity," to integrate many of the readings (e.g. the Homer and Salinger; Dickens, *Great Expectations*; Eliot, "The Hollow Men"; Woolf, *Mrs Dalloway*; Bellow, *Humboldt's Gift*; Morrison's *Beloved*; Marilynne Robinson, *Housekeeping*). The mentor once again amended the learning contract, now retitled again as "Literature and Discovering Personal Authenticity."

The goals of Howard's project now became identifying similarities between the experiences of the characters he encountered and his own, and developing his understanding of the ways in which the former might yield insights into himself. Further, in making these connections, Howard would have to distance himself enough from his own experiences in order to apprehend the aesthetic integrity of the characters he read about. This plan worked. Howard wrote a number of brief essays, well balanced between analytical detachment and appropriately veiled confession. He wrote and spoke about characters trying to find their true places in the world. He also used what he had already learned about style to examine relationships between language and characters as they search to become themselves, to find their "authentic voices." Although long after the projected end date, Howard successfully completed the study. The mentor could report in the contract evaluation that Howard had closely read much literature and that he could sensitively enter into the worlds its authors had created while at the same time use what he found there to understand important things about his own. Both mentor and student had learned to be bold in taking improvisational risks.

Seeing the student as a teacher; seeing the teacher as a student

Mentors often work beyond the expertise afforded them by their formal education. This occurs as a matter of principle – following the student's curiosity and making connections meaningful to the student (Principles 2, 4, and 6). And it occurs as a matter of circumstance. We often work closely with whoever comes in the office door; their professional and educational interests may well not fall within our own fields. Mentors thus often sail against the winds of modern professionalism and scholarship, although we use them, depend upon them in fact, to tack and turn. We make our way with our ability to cross boundaries of disciplines and specialties. We therefore have to be constantly vigilant about the distinction between intellectually nurturing transgressions and intellectually irresponsible travesties (Principle 1). We try to maintain this vigilance by being widely curious "lifelong learners" ourselves, and by making use of every resource we encounter, especially the learning of our own students. As the examples below illustrate, we learn from our students about fields of work unfamiliar to us; we learn from their own academic reading and research; and we learn from their experiences a richness and depth which extends beyond our own reading.

Sarah: learning the student's worklife

Sarah worked in a steel mill, as a skilled laborer on the production line. Due to injuries and also conflicts with some colleagues and supervisors who did not take well (during the early 1980s) to a woman steelworker, she wanted to get out. She knew a college degree would help. Her mentor had never been in a steel mill; Sarah gave him a tour. He didn't directly know the operational systems or the production methods of this or, for that matter, other kinds of factories. In his sociological and political studies, he'd of course read about "systems of production," but Sarah (and, later, many other students from other workplaces) showed him how a factory actually operates. An assertive student, who wanted to acquire substantial credit for her experiential learning, Sarah, in effect, became a teacher. In describing her experiences, she eagerly explained, for example, how steel is made, molded, cut, sold, and distributed. And she urgently discussed how power, money, gender, racial, and personality conflicts and alliances give full life to a sophisticated formal organization which officially barely recognizes the presence of those phenomena.

The more the mentor learned about steel mills – listening to Sarah, talking with colleagues who could evaluate her learning about production, and doing some reading recommended by both – the more clearly he was able to understand her particular workplace as both a carefully designed system and as a spontaneous human community (Principle 4). In addition, the more the mentor listened, the better he could understand Sarah's desire to leave a workplace, despite her considerable efforts, she despaired of changing. It therefore didn't seem a stretch for him or for her when he recommended that she read some Shakespeare, particularly plays dealing with ambition and with abuses of power (e.g. *Richard II, The Merchant of Venice*). One day, he said to Sarah on a hunch, after reading an essay she'd written in defense of Shylock entitled, in her direct and pungent way, "Shylock Got the Shaft": "Sarah, maybe you ought to become a lawyer." Which is exactly what she did, more than fifteen years later. When she entered law school, she reminded her mentor (who had forgotten) of his hunch.

From experiences such as these, the mentor learned to become enthusiastically curious about his student's experiences, especially in spheres of life and work unfamiliar to him: childcare, foster care and adoption, human service and health care management, manufacturing and finance, construction, human resource development, counseling, community sports and improvement projects, sales and marketing, information technology, the ministry, political fundraising and campaigning, medical technology and nursing, advertising and filmmaking, aircraft maintenance and piloting, firefighting and police work, arson and narcotics investigation, the operations of prisons and the lives of prisoners, art and music therapy, banking, substance abuse treatment, and the care (both institutional and community-based) of the mentally ill, dance, coaching, and physical education, services for the poor and the battered – the list will not end.

In none of these subjects would the mentor become an "expert"; he could not offer lecture-courses or write scholarly articles about them. Nonetheless, he's acquired a useful familiarity with these jobs, professions, disciplines, and other fields of learning. He knows (especially after working with at least several and often many students in each) how they operate, their policies and problems; he's familiar with how people work, thrive (or fail to) within them. He understands much of their vocabularies, leading ideas, and the skills they require. Above all, the mentor understands how these spheres of experience are complete, if sometimes insular, cultures. They are environments where people spend often more than half of their waking hours; and they encounter there nearly every aspect of human social experience. Finding themselves immersed among diverse personalities, organizational politics, ripples of macro- and micro-economics, layers of local and large history, natural phenomena and their scientific manipulation, people try to grasp what is true, struggle to do the right thing, and to endure or protest injustice. They also seek out the beauty and try to avoid the ugliness in their working lives. They might savor the hum of people and machines in symphonic flow, or flee the boring clatter into reverie, offering to the workplace only the functional awareness of an automaton. As though in exchange for the intellectual nurture mentors provide, our students share with us these instructive glimpses into their lives. We learn how resilient and full any human experience can be in even the most alienating environments.

Tom: learning the limits of current knowledge

Sometimes a student's current experiences become invaluable resources for an academic study. These experiences usually, though not always or necessarily, come from the student's worklife. They not only serve to illustrate what's written in books and articles or render academic ideas personally meaningful. They can also serve as sources of information and ideas not otherwise available. The student's worklife becomes, in effect, a kind of text for both student and mentor. As mentors, we make it our habit to study this living text, just as we habitually learn about the occupations or professions students have pursued by listening to and reading their descriptions of prior experiential learning.

Tom was a veteran fire-fighter in a small city. In addition to performing the usual on-the-scene duties, he'd also become a skilled manager of emergency environments. He understood crowd and automobile traffic control; he knew when and how to evacuate people living around a fire scene, and when and how to secure normal services (gas, electricity, telephone), and bring in specialized emergency help (e.g. chemical hazard personnel). Because of his intimate knowledge of the city, he understood how all the city and other public services fit together and interacted. Thus, when the "Y2K" or "Millennium Bug" threat appeared, it was natural that Tom become one of the people responsible for monitoring the condition of all local services which might be called upon during a police and/or fire emergency.

Tom had already done studies with mentors expert in emergency and disaster management. But as the millennial turn approached, he wanted to do a study on the social psychology of a technological crisis. He was fascinated by the discoveries people were making, seemingly everyday, both experts and "ordinary" citizens, about how the seemingly simplest and most taken-for-granted components of life depended on PCs and dedicated chips: phones, food, water, and so on. Every basic and humble necessity had become an "information system," and each part of larger and interdependent systems. He and his mentor were also uneasily amused that no one quite knew what to expect or exactly what to do if one small but essential part (the digital calendar) simultaneously failed in each of these systems.

For Tom, this ignorance and this complexity presented an urgent prospect for which he had direct practical responsibilities. And Tom's mentor was as grimly attentive as anyone else to the possible practical effects of computer systems crashing all over the city and far beyond. But alongside this survival curiosity, Tom and his mentor were fascinated by the intricacy of human communities at once local and global. How could they begin to comprehend this spectacle even while it was developing?

The mentor could recommend, in addition to the multitude of articles and position papers about "Y2K," appropriate readings about techno-logical dependency and modern culture: for example, Beniger, *The Control Revolution* and Zuboff, *In the Age of the Smart Machine*. He expected that Tom would find these good sources for organizing his imme-diate concerns (Principles 2 and 4), and for making connections to some of his prior learning in sociology and psychology (Principle 6). The mentor also expected that Tom would be able to use his current experiences in emergency management as meaningful case studies to understand and apply the general ideas he was reading about (Principle 4). And, in fact, these things happened.

What the mentor did not expect was how valuable this study would become for both himself and Tom because he and the other members of his emergency management team were figuring out how to cope with a possible situation no one had ever quite confronted before. It was enough of an awful wonderment to consider that a design limitation in the calen-dars of ubiquitous computer chips might reverberate throughout the technology-suffused social systems on which those communities depend. But added to that was the irony (which Tom and his mentor felt with uneasy amusement) that in those rapid months leading up to a single click of clocks around the globe the unintended and unpredictable con-sequences of immense human sophistication might be hastening us all back to a state of nature, unknown and uncontrollable.

Nothing could happen, everything and anything could happen; there were too many contingencies to plan for, including unimagined contingen-cies. It was, as Tom quite precisely said, "weird." Understanding this weirdness became a focal point of the study, even after the new year arrived and nothing at all seemed to happen. Tom observed that within a short time, it seemed that people were acting as though the impending crisis had never occurred. Tom explored how his team came together, a little culture part of larger expert and governmental cultures, in which everyone was trying to share with and learn from everyone else vast amounts of technical and practical information – information which might or might not be useful if any number of things did or did not occur. They formed layered, concentric societies around possibly insufficient hypotheses about contingencies. They lived a kind of provisional exist-ence, and, in the event (or non-event), they seemed to shake it off like a bad dream. There was nothing quite like this in the books or articles; but Tom, from his experiences and observations, could supply the "real world" information for this study. He had become an expert source and a necessary collaborator.

The mentor had had many students whose experiences had taught them things which couldn't be learned very well from books – refined skills, sensitivity to and appreciation of vital subtleties, meanings of abstract ideas, and high ideals in everyday living. But the very oddness or singularity of Tom's experience, preparing for an unknown which so many people around the world knew about, made the mentor look for something else in his students-as-collaborators: that they might be sources of understanding things which no one else, not just the mentor, might have yet learned to understand. To be sure, it was the unusual drama of Tom's experience, which stimulated this wonder in the mentor. However, from this wonder grew more. He now looked with wider eyes at his students' experiences, even "ordinary" ones, asking himself if there might be learnings folded in there, which perhaps even no one else had yet named. Mentors learn that they can often "stretch" themselves in this way. But the question lingers, "How far is too far?"

Theodore: "stretching" too far

Through collaborating as Tom and his mentor did, we can stretch ourselves very far into learning something quite unfamiliar. But how far is too far? Our failures help us learn when to set limits and seek help.

Working on a degree in public policy and health care administration, Theodore became fascinated by the connections between politics, class, ethnicity, and medical technology. He was concerned, for example, about the availability of public funds for medical research and services addressing health care problems (such as asthma) particular, if not unique, to the children of the African American urban poor. He'd learned from his reading that pharmaceutical companies were disinclined to develop new products for small markets, especially when the potential customers were not prosperous, and publicly funded health care did not reimburse "exotic" treatments. Theodore wanted to develop an in-depth understanding of this public-private political economy. His mentor thought he could help. Although not a specialist in the public policy or economics of health care, he believed he could use his familiarity with politics, economics, and policy to sufficiently supplement Theodore's more tightly focused research.

The study began well enough. Theodore and his mentor developed a list of current articles and monographs, some of which they read together. But they soon discovered that they were getting into very technical material, the understanding of which presupposed statistical skills, and knowledge of both medical biology and the micro-economics of heath care, which they both lacked. The mentor became aware that his ignorance was too great. He could see that even when he asked himself and Theodore apparently useful questions, they would have to spend so much time and take so many steps to answer them – often unsteadily – that their progress was too slow with respect to what Theodore really wanted to learn. No doubt, they would have done well had their time been unlimited. But Theodore's effort and ability were defined by the larger lifeworld concerns which had brought him to this study (Principle 4). For the technical questions (essential, if not ultimate) which were absorbing so much labor and time, Theodore needed instruction and guidance from experts.

Fortunately, Theodore and his mentor realized the vastness and depth of the waters in which they were attempting to swim quite early on in the study (Principle 1). Both embarrassed and relieved, the mentor proposed to Theodore that they call in some help and revise the original plan of study. Also relieved, Theodore agreed. The mentor located colleagues knowledgeable in both health care economics and econometrics. The study was revised; it actually became two studies: one on economic statistics, and the other on policy. Although Theodore had to modify his expectation that he would be able to proceed swiftly to the in-depth understanding he sought, he was able to use what he'd already begun to learn. The mentor did the same. He too had learned much more about statistics and health care policy, knowledge he made use of in subsequent years. More important, he learned about vigilance and "stretching." He understood more now that when a student embarks on a study which involves heretofore unpracticed skills and technical language, these are signs to heed. The mentor's ability to be a nurturing generalist depends upon the subject-specific expertise of others.

Shifting and integrating institutional roles

Academic mentors usually begin their work in higher education as teachers and scholars. Upon becoming mentors, they find themselves also directly providing to their students administrative, clerical, counseling, and other non-academic services. We shift roles, sometimes occupying several at once. All of them, however, are directed by the educational effort of nurturing the student's learning. Interestingly, the variety and cohesion of our professional experience mirror our students' lives. We shift roles in response to students' need to manage their usually complex lives so that they can continue their educations (Principle 4). Stimulated – sometimes prodded – by our students, we have to learn new roles and to integrate them coherently within our students' and our own learning.

By the time she returned to university in middle age, Paulina had become the acting director of human services in her county. She'd begun working in public human services as an accountant, and then gradually learned and moved into different direct service and administrative roles. As her career widened and advanced, she acquired experiential learning about human services in nearly all its aspects, but never had time to complete the degree she'd begun many years before. However, once she became acting director, she was required to complete a bachelor's degree within a year in order to keep the job. Thus, when Paulina resumed her education, she had to be a full-time student. She thus had to quickly recover and develop the academic skills she once had (Principles 4 and 6). As her mentor, I discovered that I too had to work fast in order to respond to Paulina's pressing schedule. And, because Paulina could not usually meet with or otherwise communicate directly with me except after her normal working day (this was in the pre-email era), I found myself doing in the evening the clerical, billing, and other administrative work for Paulina that during the daytime I would normally delegate. It was a busy, rushed time for both of us. Used to operating in more leisure and working at more intellectual pursuits, I wondered, quite often, what I was doing.

Paulina and I met for nearly two hours one evening. We'd each already had long busy days. We talked about her essay on Henry James's *The Portrait of a Lady* – Paulina had never really read any literature. It's not an easy novel; but it seemed like a good choice for someone trying to find her freedom and duty in a life of complicated and conflicting commitments. Paulina was making her way slowly but enjoys the novel. We needed to discuss her academic writing too. It's rusty; she's used to writing memos, policies, and reports to people who already know exactly what she's talking about. There was also a billing problem to straighten out. Then I left a phone message for a colleague who'd agreed to evaluate Paulina's experiential learning in the financial administration of human services but from whom she hadn't yet received a response.

Time is pressing. Paulina is used to stress and to juggling many tasks, but not quite like this. For that matter, neither am I. She's worried about finishing this degree on time, about neglecting her other work and her family life (her children are grown, but she's very close to them and to her grandchildren). I'm worried too. We talk about this and about stress management. I try to be honest and helpful, but I don't know if she can make it and I'm not sure what to say about my own uncertainty. I reminded myself that I need to get advice from a colleague who's a more experienced counselor than I am. Maybe I should suggest to Paulina that she seek some professional help – but that would be yet one more set of appointments to add to her schedule. Which reminds me, I have to find someone who can do a study with Paulina on counseling. She already knows a lot from her experiences, now some years back, doing client intake and case management. That ought to help her grasp counseling theories and methods quickly. I hope. Also, she seems to be doing fine, last time I checked, on the American social history study she's working on with Judy, my colleague.

I'm trying to make sense of all the tasks I'm doing with and for Paulina, and to evaluate my commitments:

Why are you doing all this?

Uh, I'm not entirely sure. I've sort of fallen into it. I want to help Paulina. I admire her and the work she's done. I think she deserves to keep the position she's in.

Really? Is it so much up to you? Are you trying to save her? Trying to help her as you are, doing all these things at once, are you being as efficient and responsible as you could be?

Maybe I've taken on too much. Maybe trying to do the right thing for someone else I'm actually assuming I'm "bigger" or "wiser" than I really am. It's hard to tell, now that I'm in the thick of it. But I am asking other people, like Judy, to help, and Paulina is certainly taking on her share of academic work and responsibility. I'm sure we could have been more efficient if we'd really appreciated what was coming from her job. But we didn't, and here we are. Anyhow, Paulina is making good progress. And, you know what? So am I.

What progress is that, yours I mean?

I'm learning about my limits and learning to expand them. Some are practical skills: I'm learning to manage a lot of different kinds of tasks, to jump around usefully, and not just burrow in on one thing. I didn't get into this mentoring work to become a clerk or an administrator or a counselor – especially all at once. But I'm learning to juggle, partly by watching and listening to Paulina. I'm sure I'll be more cautious and restrained in the future, but I'll also be more skilled when it seems like I have to get involved in all this again with another student. And there's something else, maybe more important: Strangely, despite all the stress, we're having a good time. She says so too. I guess I'd call it fun.

Fun?

Yeah. Maybe that's not the right word. When we get busy, we just roll or flow along. It feels like everything is operating; everything we ever knew about, including how to learn fast, is in action. It's an adrenaline rush.

Hmmm. That's nice.

I know, I know. I've got to be careful, for my sake and for hers. But I've also got to be careful to remember this experience. Now I'm really understanding what it's like to be an adult student. Even if I never do so many different things all at once again, I will appreciate better that my students' lives are quite often not so different from Paulina's. They are deeply serious about their academic learning, but they have so many other equally or more serious responsibilities too. It's so important that everyone in this college pay attention to that and that we be as flexible and accommodating as possible, especially when so little else in our students' lives so seldom is.

Admirable thoughts. I see you're busy and excited. So, get back to work. But remember what you said. I'll be around to remind you.

Paulina graduated on time, just. And, she kept her job. The mentor also kept his.

Judging and not judging

Principle 5 requires that mentors evaluate students' learning developmentally. It also requires that they enable students to participate genuinely in their own evaluations, according to goals to which both mentor and student have agreed. These requirements entail that we cultivate a variety of perspectives on making or not making judgments.

Corinne: never shame; look for new beginnings

Corinne had never done well in math courses, at least not since an algebra teacher had humiliated her in a high school classroom and her guidance counselor had advised her to avoid university and become a secretary. Nonetheless, Corinne went to a traditional university and struggled through two math courses, having to repeat each one. She left university without completing a bachelor's degree and made a very successful career as a counselor and teacher of incarcerated adolescents. It was very rough work, sometimes physically so. Corinne was very good at it, but after some twenty years, she knew that she had to find a position less damaging to her mental and physical health. This meant moving up, and that meant completing a bachelor's degree.

When Corinne first met with her mentor, she seemed tired, anxious, eager, and determined. When she discovered shortly thereafter that an administratively or clinically oriented degree in human services normally meant acquiring some statistical and empirical research skills (Principles 2 and 6), she nearly left. Her mentor listened to her frustration and fear, and suggested that she might postpone these quantitative studies until she had successfully studied other topics and developed more confidence in her academic skills and her ability to learn new things.

The mentor was familiar with the intensity of Corinne's feelings. Many students feared and loathed math. But he was struck by her *shame* that she had not learned math, and by her certainty that she was "not good enough" *ever* to do so. Although a psychologically aware person who knew that she had been taught and counseled poorly (even cruelly), Corinne nonetheless believed that she was a moral failure for not having completed a bachelor's degree when she "should have" and that, as though in punishment for this original sin, she could not complete one now because of the math requirement. She judged herself as cruelly as her teacher and counselor had done so many years before, and she did so with the same false conclusion (Principle 1): that not doing well in an academic subject necessarily means an intractable cognitive deficit. Further, her feeling of shame implied another (false) belief about herself, that she was somehow morally unqualified to achieve her goal. (See the discussion of the cognitive aspect of emotions in Chapter 6, "The personal and the academic.")

For more than a year and half, off and on, Corinne and her mentor discussed this problem. She also sought help from friends and from a therapist. Eventually, Corinne separated the false conclusions she had drawn from her prior academic record (Principles 1 and 5). She and her mentor designed a "quantitative skills" study built entirely around empirical questions which had for a long time fascinated her at her current job and which were relevant to her hope of a achieving a more managerial and staff-development position (Principle 2): "What is the relationship, if any, between worker stress levels and absenteeism? If the one contributed to other, what could be done to decrease both problems?"

Over some six months, Corinne worked with her mentor and one of his colleagues on this question. She learned to understand its quantitative and social science meanings. She learned enough statistics and research methods to understand other people's research on her own or closely related questions. And, as a final project, she designed and implemented empirical research on her own workplace. Corinne was relieved and proud. She did not become very proficient with math, but she learned as much as she needed to meet the professional expectations to which she had committed herself (Principle 5). The mentor learned to become far more sensitive than he had been to the complex predicaments of learning. He learned to remind himself that students embarking on new learning and seeking a fresh start can be burdened with old but still punishing myths of deficient aptitude and shame.

Talia: judge how much, and how little, a student really needs to learn

Talia is a successful playwright who believes that she can not write, at least not academically. She struggles to write a clear and thorough exposition of the impressive research she has done for a new play about a young woman taking over her aging father's small business. And, both she and her mentor struggle collaboratively to address the writing problems they have identified together (Principle 3). A good part of this joint learning is about discovering exactly what the problem is. Talia knows the words and the grammar. Her ability to collect information is remarkable. And she deploys that information in her playwriting with both scholarly precision and powerfully dramatic effect. But she has difficulty writing discursively, syllogistically, with translating a dramatic image or revealing moment in a play's dialogue into the clean, straight lines of exposition and argument.

As they proceed, the mentor begins to wonder about something else: How much is enough? How proficient an expository writer does Talia (who does not intend to become a scholar or a journalist) really need to become? Doesn't the quality of her academic writing already exceed that of the "typical" student who has passed composition courses and completes more than acceptable essays for advanced undergraduate courses in a "typical" field such as psychology, history, business or non-literary arts (Principles 5 and 6)? Has Talia expected too much of her own academic writing because of the excellence of her playwriting? Has the mentor failed to offer some realistic signposts, which might guide and appropriately moderate the demanding expectations she has set for herself?

When they at last decide to end the study they've been doing, which has combined her research-work with her efforts to improve her expository composition (Principles 2, 4, and 6), Talia's mentor asks her to write an assessment of how much she's improved her writing (Principle 5). It reads in part:

> How did I do? Why can't I leave that for my mentor to judge? Because according to his theory of teaching, the assessment and in fact the responsibility for the course itself is to be directed and redirected to the student. This does burden the student with more work, more responsibility. It also guarantees – to the extent anything can be guaranteed and of course nothing can – that the student will be active, not passive, and engaged, not disengaged, and will undertake an academic journey designed by the person who is the greatest expert in that student's interests: the student herself. With the student's interests engaged, there is a greater likelihood that the student will both persevere and learn something. And, as directed by the student, it is more likely that her style of learning (however unconscious) will be engaged, which will assure her a greater chance for success.

Talia's statement is often clear and fluent. Both mentor and student know that she can learn much more and that she's already come a very long way. Her efforts to become a better expository writer will no doubt continue, but she has successfully completed this study. And her mentor will continue to learn to be more attentive to how much and how little it is necessary to expect from his students.

Connecting to the world

A current runs throughout all the habits and principles we've discussed. Everywhere, there are connections: between the inner voice and every diverse presentation of self in the academy, at work, and in every other sphere of social and personal life; between lifeworlds and systems; between theory and practice; between learning, teaching, advising, counseling and managing; and among all the academic disciplines. "Connecting" is a theme of all our habits and it is a kind of habit itself.

Thanks to their colleagues and to students such as Marty, mentors learn to connect to their internal, questioning voices. Rianne, achieving a certain social distance from her mentor, learns to reach him with her full cognitive capacities; while Martina and Talia reach a fair compact between their abilities, their goals, interests, what others expect of them and what they expect of themselves. In connecting her domestic and work lives, Beth and her mentor discover unexpected depth in her experiential learning. Howard, improvising his learning while he learns, turns an originally idyllic study of literature into a powerful exploration of the relationship between fictional and all too real personal experiences.

Through Sarah, Tom, and countless others, windows are opened for mentors on worlds of work they had barely known. Each of these students creates academic studies and entire curricula both feeding and fed by their working lives and aspirations. Adventurous and forgiving students such as Theodore help their mentors become better collaborators, both with students and faculty colleagues. Paulina and other students whose pressured lives make extraordinarily complicated demands on their learning challenge mentors to diversify their own roles and to integrate the ensuing complexity. We realize and learn to appreciate that many of our students have to do exactly the same. Corinne and Talia, while learning to effectively integrate their aspirations, interests, true abilities, and academic expectations, help their mentors do the same. Further, their mentors learn to apply this integrative skill to detecting and undoing false or damaging connections, such as between a poor academic "performance" and intellectual potential or, worse, moral shame. In these ways, mentors learn to help make nurturing learning communities with their students.

By creating and discovering "connections," mentors-as-learners practice a scholarship of engagement. We and our students learn to see that all kinds of boundaries and separations – authoritative pronouncements, unexamined rules, and passively received ideas – can be crossed and (re)unions made. In mentoring, the world is a wonderment that waits for continuous and unbounded comprehension. But, equal to our sometimes tired sense of incompletion, we encounter everywhere intimations of inspiring coherence, which continuously draw us on. Our habits are ways of trying to love whatever and whomever we are called upon to understand.

Creating polity

We hope that our readers will have already noted that this "community of inquiry" is also a political community. In the service of autonomy and collaboration (Principle 3), power, authority, resources (e.g. books, time, labor), and information are distributed and deployed. The unquestionably practical consideration of how these elements are used, who gets to decide, and by what criteria are also political questions. They are necessarily related to a vision of a "just" state of educational affairs. In the world view of mentoring, an educationally just community is one in which all participants grow increasingly free and reciprocally communicative according to their diverse capacities and purposes. The student-mentor relationship, the dialogical relationship, is a tiny state continuously growing toward the equality of its citizens, toward democracy. Moreover, this democratic dyadic association can expand into larger groups (see Chapter 4, "Waiting as learning," for an example) and can also be sought in a traditional classroom (Shor 1996).

This little polity is formally governed. Every student-mentor learning project is represented by a written learning contract. Like other kinds of contracts, these specify purposes, activities, as well as methods and criteria of evaluation, all of which are reciprocally binding upon the contracting parties and upon the completion of which "payment" is made in the form of academic credit for learning achieved.

As with any particular contract considered legitimate in democratic society, there is an implicit constitution. The contract must serve the just and reasonable interests of all the participants, including the students; and it must be within their reasonable capacity to fulfill. The contract must be freely, non-coercively, entered into. Its meaning and consequences must be equally disclosed to and well understood by everyone involved (including the right of the participants to make consensual amendments in response to unanticipated discoveries). Even when a mentor recommends that a student do something as "ordinary" or "generic" as taking a prepackaged course in a classroom or via the Web, that particular mode of educational delivery should suit the student's way and ability of learning at the time (e.g. the desire to participate in a group or the need to receive closely supervised and supported instruction). The learning contract should also accommodate the student's schedule and other resources (e.g. computer equipment, money for books). And these conditions must be fully known and seem manageable to the student. Further, learning contracts must contain activities and openings which help and allow students to thrive, that is, expand the autonomy and content of their learning within and even beyond the formally defined limits of the contract.

Without attention to these safeguards of individualization, studies become standardized. Standardization is often a necessary (but still not sufficient) condition of quality in factories. However, in learning, standardization is not necessary at all, unless there is some good reason for every-one to learn the same thing in the same way. Otherwise, expertise and authority are hoarded by the faculty. And students are taught dependency and passive obedience. Their problems are regarded as evidence of deviance and deficits, as moral, pathological, and/or innate incapacities to behave as full, responsible, and free persons. But even a classroom of young children can be seen as a polity of persons developing their free-doms and responsibilities, and their social, moral, affective, imaginative, and intellectual abilities exceeding the anticipatory stereotypes ascribed to them (Paley 1992). Every legitimate learning contract thus enacts the ori-ginal "social contract" of the learning community. This is the small "state" of which mentors and students are citizens.

In fact, this polity is not really so tiny after all. Through the connecting which mentors and students practice, they bring into their dialogue many domains of experience. Their dialogues both reflect and influence those domains. Mentor and student do their intellectual work within a large aca-demic organization, which necessarily allows and disallows certain actions and upon which mentors are dependent for their jobs and students for the legitimation of their learning. The academy, in turn, reflects and acts upon many other intellectual, economic, social, and of course political institu-tions. But the intellectual work of mentors and students affects the charac-ter of the academy within which they do that work. In turn, mentors and students also influence the lifeworlds and systems beyond the academy, where they are also agents.

And there is yet another sense in which this little association is "large." As we described in our very first chapter, mentors and students inherently and often explicitly take up the universal themes of human curiosity: How shall we live? What is truth, justice, beauty, happiness? As we argued in that chapter and try to demonstrate throughout this book, dialogue itself is essentially democratic, and it immanently bears within itself experiences of truthfulness, justice, beauty, and happiness.

Once the dialogue is opened and makes deliberate connections to any and all of these contexts, it becomes inexhaustibly fertile with meanings. Moreover, the justice mentor and student seek to create between them-selves becomes a model, a potential "little voice" for examining the justice of every other domain in which they act. Students and mentors-as-learners become politicians. Through dialogue, they learn the habits of citizenship in a large and multi-dimensional world. One of the dimensions of our world now is virtual reality. Perhaps more than any other recent phenome-non it challenges us to learn and choose how we shall live with power and what kinds of global citizens we shall be – the topic of our next chapter.

Chapter 8

Authenticity and artifice
Mentoring in virtual reality

I'm Nobody! Who are you?
Are you – Nobody – Too?
Then there's a pair of us!
Don't tell! they'd advertise – you know!
Emily Dickinson, "I'm Nobody! Who are you?" (1960)

In virtual reality, we can go to anyone, anywhere, anytime, and at rapidly diminishing cost. We can acquire almost any piece of information on any topic, and use it as we choose. Thus, we can transcend nearly all the limits which inhibit learning: of space, time, status, and situation. In virtual reality, we have a means of communication with which we can potentially solve all the problems we discussed of access to and within the academy. The technology of virtual education gives us the freedom to escape all the impediments of history and nature. It seems the perfect medium for mentoring.

But virtual reality also allows us the freedom to represent ourselves however we please and to use the information we acquire for almost any purpose, including making others believe we have learned what in fact we do not know. Is authentically dialogical community therefore possible in virtual reality? Mentoring depends so much on the participants to inquiry saying what they really believe. How is it possible to follow the path of dialogue into the digital realm, where it is so easy to make up anything, even an entire identity?

These are crucial issues in academic learning conducted in virtual reality. The tensions they create within the academy are an extraordinarily clear manifestation of the abiding and often conflicting human desires to know what is real, to make the world pleasing to ourselves, to have faith in what we are told, and to make others have faith in what we tell them. Virtual reality perfectly confronts us, in academic and all other contexts of dialogue, with our troubled efforts to embrace both authenticity and artifice.

Freedom, control, and the problem of authentic learning

Virtual reality offers all but limitless freedoms of access and communication. However, the very composition or substance of this digital medium presents a nearly equal freedom for manipulation. The material of all our perceptions of sight, sound, depth, motion, and even taste, touch, and smell can be transformed into digital information; so can the products of all our past and current understandings. Virtual reality seeks to immerse us entirely in an undetectable fabrication (Heim 1998). This information, both sensorial and conceptual, is accessible to anyone with a connection to the Web. And, within the digital medium, it can be borrowed, reorganized, and transformed by anyone and presented to anyone as a credible and impenetrable simulacrum of whatever "truth" the one wishes the other to believe. Thus, if the only access students and teachers have to each other is through virtual reality, it becomes very difficult to check the authenticity of the communications and the validity of the claims they make about themselves or what they seem to know. Simply, it is difficult to know what is really being learned and who the learner really is. Knowledge and truth recede behind seemingly endless veils of make-believe.

This freedom necessarily shows an obverse face: control. Within virtual reality, I can make whatever I please; but so can anyone else who interacts with me there. Whatever I offer of what I've made can be translated, evaluated, and re-made by whoever receives my offering. I can present myself however I choose; I can also be re-presented however "they" choose. The authoritative reality or truth that exists between "me" and "them" will be determined by whoever has the most control – the most access to information and the most virtuosity at manipulating it. The bewildering expanse of freedom in virtual reality easily becomes, if any party to communication there chooses, an intense contest for control.

It is easy to see this contest at work in distance or "electronically mediated" learning. To the extent that universities and professors see themselves as conservators, transmitters, and arbiters of knowledge rather than as collaborative participants in dialogue, so will they seek to shape the endlessly malleable material of virtual reality into ever more perfect forms that reproduce and enhance that control. It is thus no accident that Web courses so often come in complete packages and modules, or that the "interactivity" those items offer is so often densely channeled with minutely designed assignments, and with closely monitored, prescribed discussions, and of course protected with access codes and identity checks.

To be sure, students are not helpless mice in this contest with academic traps. They are often as experienced with the Web or even more so than their (usually older) teachers. Students learn how to find whatever and whoever material they need to borrow and successfully re-present as their own learning. Virtual but inauthentic learning is commonplace, profitable, and, so far, legally protected (Fritz 10 March 1999; Rao 20 April 1999). Anyone can access essays for sale on many websites (such as "Evil House of Cheat," "schoolsucks," and "Essaytown"); and, no doubt, students more easily and cheaply can barter for the work of their associates, especially those who are skilled at hacking into teachers' archives of correct responses to assignments.

Not surprisingly, in answer to these artifices, the academy offers an equally proliferating array of software that scans for plagiarism. (See, for example, the Pennsylvania State University Website providing information on the detection and prevention of plagiarism, "http://tlt.its. psu.edu/suggestions/cyberplag"; and the plagiarism detection service, "turnitin.com.") These devices continue to become more powerful and intrusive. In the United States, the new Office of Homeland Security now possesses software that can record every "mouseclick" of anyone online (Greenway 4 February 2003). No doubt, universities will acquire their own versions of this software and use it to scan their students' web-searching. But better mousetraps always produce better mice. So goes the game. It is not a new game at all; virtual reality merely opens the field and makes education-as-control into a caricature of itself. When this contest is so easily and temptingly joined, the question for mentors is how to make authentic learning possible.

Control and freedom – the tension between these qualities always tightens with every technological advance, whenever we extend the repertoire of artifice with which we remake what is given us in nature. This dialectical presence is particularly clear in the history of the Internet and World Wide Web. They were created collaboratively by the United States Department of Defense and a consortium of universities (Tobin 2001). Virtual reality thus emerged from an institution which exists to exert power and from an institution which exists to expand learning. This hybrid environment – now so teeming with commercial and sociable, as well as government and academic activities – offers a fertile ecology for the constant struggles between free expression and invaded privacy, between unrestricted access to markets and information and corporate or governmental control. The battles are confusing because embattled interest groups do not neatly line up with a philosophical commitment to freedom or to control. For example, one person's free expression invades another's privacy; one corporation's demand for unrestricted market access stimulates another to call for government regulation. These inconsistencies of course occur in "normal" reality as well. But they bubble more effervescently in virtual reality because that medium offers so little resistance to change. Indeed, this malleability points towards the fundamental source for the strife and confusion in virtual reality.

These are struggles to create freely and to impose order on entirely artificial ground. More than any other human invention – more than all other tools and useful products, more than any art object or culture, even more than the manufactured environments where we live and work and play – virtual reality is a thorough and all encompassing artifice. It is the product of abstract and immensely comprehensive mathematical ideas applied to the apparently limitless and infinitely pliable material of digital information. Virtual reality is a place where we seem to have transcended nature and achieved a perfect simulacrum of omnipotence; everyone can become, in both theological and information-age parlance, an "avatar." But in a reality where everything seems possible, it becomes nearly impossible to determine what is authentic. Virtual reality easily moves us all to both visceral anxiety and philosophical confusion about what "really" exists. Thus, as all the heightened attention currently given in universities to academic cheating and honesty demonstrates, even the most pragmatic student or teacher immanently experiences this existential uncertainty. For all learning, as we have discussed throughout this book, presupposes that truth exists, that there is really something for human beings to know.

The virtues of mentoring in virtual reality

Mentoring does not resolve the immanent existential anxiety virtual reality imposes. However, mentoring does explicitly engage both the wonder and the fear in our existence. It directly addresses the human project of revealing and sustaining a purposeful, autonomous identity in association with others. It does so by embracing the disturbing and invigorating capacities of human beings to act freely and to control their environment. Mentors seek authenticity by trying to let go of authoritatively controlling what students shall learn. Instead, we offer and accept trust – trust that the "mere" ideas through which we and our collaborators in inquiry present ourselves to each other are "the real thing." Virtual reality is thus simply yet another context – albeit an exceptionally clear and pliable one – where encounters between freedom and control play out.

In our explication of how mentoring maintains the integrity of dialogue in virtual reality, we will take advantage of the neglected side of the ambiguous meaning of "virtual." This word derives from the Latin *virtus*, which, like its Greek counterpart, *aretê*, means both "strength" (or "excellence") and "goodness" (Lewis and Short 1966: 1997; Liddell and Scott 1968: 238). A virtue can thus be a skill or power, something useful and of instrumental value, such as the virtue of cleverness; it can also be an end-in-itself, such as justice.

In the modern world, the differences in these meanings are strong and the consequences of those differences, tremendous. A world where virtue means only power and learning can only be pragmatic is one in which virtues as ends-in-themselves (truthfulness, justice, beauty) are merely subjective and irrational, unknowable, and beyond the reach of rational inquiry (MacIntyre 1981: 11–12; and see also our second chapter, "The principles of mentoring and the philosophy of dialogue"). This is a world dominated by systems and fantasies, where the lifeworld is replaced with merely manipulable material and manipulating desires. People and all other ends-in-themselves become subjected to force. And force, as Simone Weil said of the characters in Homer's *Iliad*, turns a person into a "thing" ("The *Iliad,* or The Poem of Force" 1986: 163).

Educators realize they are in such a world every time they encounter students who seem to care for learning only as a means of career advancement, who respond to questions with only a "What are you looking for?" and who respond to criticisms with only a "Everything's just a matter of opinion and everyone is entitled to their own." But students experience the same world when their teachers dismiss their curiosity and opinions as irrelevant, when their professors seem to care much more for grants and publications and status than for teaching, and when universities market themselves as merely a convenient means of getting on with one's career and run their courses as though they were mass production lines.

The evolution of such a merely instrumental and systemic world is, as we have said, easy to see in the digital domain. Within virtual education, this de-naturing of fundamental values is especially obvious in the obsession with academic cheating and in the language used by sellers of both plagiarism and anti-plagiarism services.

For an example of the former, one can go to the current website of "Essaytown.com" (10 January 2003). Here is how material is offered for sale:

> If you've run out of time, or have more work than you can handle, we can help. Thousands of quality college essays, research papers, and book reports are available for only $25.99 each. Just send us your exact requirements, and we will email a term paper, essay, or research paper on almost any topic within a few short hours.
>
> We offer over 50,000 premium college essay, MLA style research papers, APA style term papers, and book reports. Our professionals also write unique, Ph.D.-level dissertations, master level theses, and research proposals in all styles, including Chicago, Harvard, and Turabian. Since 1997, we have helped students worldwide by providing the best, lowest-price service on the internet for all educational levels.

No doubt, most faculty and also students who do not or would not use this service are outraged, *morally* outraged. After all, this is the selling of fraud, a species of lying, through which the purchasers can credibly present learning not their own as if it were. One's outrage is perhaps especially strong because the language of the advert does not allude or refer to *any* moral standard at all. It is cheerily and unselfconsciously *a*moral. The material is offered as a perfectly practical way to solve a purely practical problem: Pressed for time? Effectively manage the task by delegating it All one needs to do is make the decision to invest one's resources – to pay the cost. It's a smart, even admirably efficient way to produce completed work.

Academics respond in kind, by trying to control and punish cheating. We turn to Web services of our own for help. And, once again, the language reveals a culture without intrinsic virtues. Consider "turnitin.com" (23 January 2003). It advertises itself as "the world's leading plagiarism prevention *system* [emphasis added]." It "deters" plagiarism, and it offers to "protect against collusion," including "pre-emptive plagiarism education." This is the language of control, of suspicion, and of war. Should we not be as morally outraged as we are by plagiarism, that intellectual integrity has come down merely to domination?

But what, then, is exactly wrong? That is, with reference to what, to what ideas or principles, can one claim that there is a violation of virtue here? After all, from a student perspective, *if* truth is a commodity, what's wrong with buying or selling it, and what's wrong with trying to control it? If knowledge is simply a matter of credible construction, how one can say that the students who present their possession as knowledge in fact do not "know" what they claim? All that matters is the success of their efforts to convince the teacher that they have created a compelling impression of learning. What matters is influence (MacIntyre 1981: 12). Beyond that, in a relativistic world, there is no "real" learning or truth to be known.

From the academy's perspective, *if* intellectual integrity means nothing more than controlling, with software scans or some other prevention "system," what teachers accept as genuine or reject as fake also has nothing to do with truth at all. This is a regime in which power alone matters. We can hardly be disturbed that teachers behave like wartime commanders. Catching students becomes merely a practical or tactical problem. And business-like students, of course, should recognize that, after all, every investment carries a risk.

If moral questions are not rationally resolvable, if moral discourse is impossible, then problems of evaluation, questions of honesty and integrity, are only settled with money or other means through which power is exercised. The only available answer to the question of what is wrong with "cheating" or "domination" within such a world is: "I don't like it, and I shall use whatever means I can to change things to suit myself."

Mentors try to let go of this struggle for power by tending to the neglected meaning of "virtue." We do so by trying to engage in dialogue. Relativistic assertions often appear in those conversations. We often hear that everything is a matter of opinion, one is as good or true as another, and that learning is valuable only as a means to success. But because we know that such assertions are fundamentally self-contradictory, we continue to ask students what they mean and why they believe they are correct. (See Chapter 2 and Principle 1.) We assume, in what might be called "good faith," that everyone really does want to know more than how to protect and aggrandize themselves in the struggle for power. We assume that we and our students deeply fear a world reduced to such brutality, and that we all long to re-discover and receive nurture from our lifeworlds (Principle 4). We assume that evaluative judgments are legitimate and indeed necessary topics for rational inquiry (Principle 5). We assume that we can learn more and more about what is true, good, and beautiful – though not finally all there is to learn. We have tried to show that reasoning about these matters in dialogical inquiry is profoundly meaningful and not merely a camouflage for manipulative artifice. (See Chapter 2, and Chapter 7, "The personal and the academic.") In effect, at the heart of mentoring is our understanding that the "virtuous" or good life is something we can all learn to live, something that in fact we experience, through the very process of seriously seeking to understand it.

Virtual reality, as we've suggested, makes so clear the futility of devoting oneself to the struggle for power because it tends to make accessible equal information and equal powers of manipulating it to all the participants. No one can "win," at least not for very long. Why then bother to dissimulate, when instead one can seek the deeper and more abiding gratification of truthfulness by choosing authenticity and trust in the authenticity of others? Ironically, this is a very *practical* choice! Learning in virtual reality places everyone in something very similar to what Rawls calls in *A Theory of Justice*, "the original position" (1971: 118–194). That is, we are all equally free to use whatever powers or capabilities we have as we choose, but we must assume that everyone else will do the same and that we are not guaranteed any advantages. The "smart" decision for all the participants is therefore to assume and to agree that everyone will accord everyone else the same respect and the same freedoms. Truthfulness is necessary for everyone because dissimulation is dangerous and ultimately futile. This is the beginning of justice. Learning in virtual reality thus gives mentors and students a wonderfully clear opportunity to (re)discover the fundamental and intrinsic virtues.

The trust and authenticity mentors offer and hope to receive amounts then to simply this: We ask students to tell us what they really believe and we offer the same. We promise to take what they say seriously, including that they take themselves seriously enough to explore the implications of their own ideas and questions; and we ask them to expect the same of us. Such faith may seem fragile, but especially in virtual reality, no other kind of strength or virtue can be as reliable or enduring.

We shall illustrate and further analyze these ideas with two examples from our mentoring experience. Both are studies conducted entirely online (with the exception of some brief phone conversations). In the first, although acceptable academic learning appears to occur, the mentor's effort to create a dialogical community fails. In the second, the mentor becomes used to the student's "virtual" presence, is convinced of the student's authentic engagement in learning, and their dialogue is successful.

Ancient Greece and a post-modern *polis*

I receive by email a request from a colleague to teach a Web-course on Classical Greece which my university offers. The course is a package: the books are already selected and ordered; the assignments, each specifically keyed to the readings, are already designed and organized into detailed modules. I know the material well (the subject has been an abiding interest). I know the readings are excellent and very nicely representative. Some are key primary text selections from the great playwrights, historians, and philosophers of the period; and there are modern scholarly writings on the history, society, and arts (including excellent visual reproductions) of Greece in the classical period. Were I a student in this course, the materials would fascinate me and the assignments would inspire my learning.

But I am not expected to be a student now; I'm supposed to "deliver" the course. Nor do I know very much about the students I have. I'm told that ten have registered for the course, which begins very soon. I can perhaps modify the assignments as the students and I become familiar with each other. When I receive the enrollment list, I see that all of the students are geographically dispersed. We shall have to communicate entirely by email and snail mail, although I am hoping that we might arrange some phone or online conferences.

As a mentor, I am eager to learn why each student has signed up for this course. In my first messages, I introduce myself, I distribute a list of email addresses so that the students can communicate with each other, and I ask them to tell me and each other what they particularly want to learn in this study and how that relates to their other studies and interests. The replies, most of which are sent only to me, are not encouraging: nearly every student says that he or she was "told" to take this course, because it would fulfill an elective liberal art requirement and because it was being offered at a convenient time during the academic year. None expresses any specific interest in the subject, and nearly all have questions only about when the first assignments are due and about my expectations for the amount of reading and writing that will be necessary.

I'm unable to significantly enrich communications within the group. Indeed, so far as I can tell, there barely is a group. It's more an aggregate of individuals. The students do not seem to use the collective mail-list. However, some, I suspect, are in communication with others, since the style and content of their responses to the assignments are suspiciously similar. On the other hand, the assignment modules are both generic and tight enough that the range of "correct" responses is small and easy enough to grasp for anyone who has done the reading. Several times, I suggest (whereas some Web-course teachers require) that everyone commit to contributing to online discussions about particular topics and questions. These discussions quickly become both too perfunctory and too large for me to follow closely. I let them die out.

With several students, I do engage in individual email exchanges and even a few brief phone conversations. These tend to focus on practical administrative matters (such as how much work needs to be completed within how much time). Even over time, few students seem to become engaged with the course content, with me or, so far as I can tell, with each other. I'm able to learn little about what genuinely interests them. When I offer to personalize the assignments according to individual interests, no one takes up the opportunity.

On the whole, the quality of the work the students turn in for each of the module assignments is not bad. Most of the students seem to understand what is required of them, although I often have lingering doubts about whether I'm receiving non-plagiarized work. A little ashamed, I find that I easily become bored reading the brief essays I receive. I wonder if the students are also bored.

The final assignment requires a longer essay, a term paper. The course guide gives a long list of potential topics from which students might pick. I email everyone to ask that each person develop his or her own proposal, modifying a topic on the list or offering something entirely different, so long as it will clearly address the course content. I ask that the proposals contain some description of why the person wants to work on the particular topic. Few proposals stray from the "approved" list, and nearly every statement of interest is brief and formulaic:

> "I think *Oedipus the King* was really interesting and I don't think he was treated fairly."

> "The Peloponnesian War seems like such a waste. I want to know why the Athenians made so many mistakes and lost."

> "I can see that Socrates was annoying, but why did they have to put him to death? I don't understand why he went along with them when he could have escaped."

These and all the other proposals have potential. I ask the students for a little more information about their curiosity and how they plan to pursue it:

> "What do you think was unfair about Oedipus's fate? Do you want to think about how your idea of 'fair' is similar to and/or different from the Greek ideas of 'justice' you've read about?"

"What do you think was 'wasted' in the Peloponnesian War? Do you want to explore how the two sides could have avoided or stopped the fighting? Are you interested in how this conflict relates to others you've read about in this course or to conflicts you see around you today?"

"Do you want to look into Socrates's reasons for rejecting the court's offer of a compromise and his friend's offer to escape? Are you interested in the politics and law surrounding his trial?"

But mostly in reply I receive variations on, "I don't know; I just think it's interesting. Are you saying I should be answering all your questions? How long does this essay have to be; how many sources must I use?" Their questions are all so practical, so focused on finding the most efficient way to finish the course and move on. I believe that I'm completely missing these students and that if I continue to question them, I'll only further stimulate their resistance rather than their curiosity. Unaccustomed to such failures of connection, I'm frustrated. I think of the "waste" of the Peloponnesian War and how, once both sides absorbed themselves in the struggle, they couldn't stop fighting until, although Athens lost, both were morally and materially exhausted. Why couldn't or wouldn't the students think about this? Why wasn't I better at helping them do so?

Most of the final essays are quite late; everyone is busy and most ask for extra time. Except in a few instances, the quality of the work is acceptable but generic and uninspired. I remembered an American history class I took in high school in which the teacher expected us to provide rote answers to questions derived from his lectures and the textbook, such as: "List and discuss the four causes of the Civil War." Anyone who bothered to pay some attention could pass; anyone who was good at memorizing could receive a superior grade. Though I was interested in American history, I was bored, and now I wonder if the teacher was too. My students in Classical Greece didn't feel to me like real people and I imagine that they perceived me to be merely a taskmaster.

When the course began, I had eager fantasies of stimulating something like the Athenian agora, a public, civic place in virtual reality where ideas would be energetically explored and debated. I imagined a *polis* of dialogue, in which the students would experience something of the open passionate and intellectual engagement which makes the classical era in ancient Greece something so valuable to re-discover and think about today. Instead, I felt like Odysseus encountering the shades of the dead in the underworld, who blow about like dry, falling leaves. Those insubstantial beings were hungry to be alive; my students just seemed to want to finish the course as easily as I would allow. Odysseus fled the Underworld as quickly as he could. And I too wanted to get this course over with. I was shaken by this encounter with insubstantial learning in a world which seemed as though it had been designed by a post-modern theorist, in which no abiding values or realities existed except appearances shaped and shifted with power alone.

At that time, I was relatively new to distance learning in virtual reality. Perhaps the students were too, or perhaps they were completely accustomed to regard education (especially learning which they did not consider useful) as being told what to "take," what information to acquire, and what to reproduce. I want to do better.

Brother Cal, metaphysics, and a chicken-farm

Many months after the decline and fall of the Classical Greece course, I receive another request to do an online study with a student unknown to me. His name is Calvin Smith. He wants to do a study in philosophy, metaphysics. He's not matriculated in my university, but had found our Website and emailed one of our Web-course specialists with his request, which was then passed on to me. I accept, but I am wary. I now frequently work with students at a distance (online, by phone, by mail). I put much effort at the very beginning in getting to know the students and their purposes, and in encouraging them to ask questions of me and (when there is a group) to get to know each other. In-person contact helps, but it is not necessary. The key, I believe, is that we "learn" each other – that we make authentic connections – through the very process of collaboratively designing the study according to the students' purposes, interests, and abilities (Principles 2, 3, and 4). This didn't happen with the Classical Greece course. It began too quickly, the pre-designed content was too rigid, the students were too uninterested, and I was not sufficiently imaginative to reach them. I rarely use "course packages" now, unless the material and learning activities truly respond the students' curiosity. And even then, we often modify the modules to make them more suitable and interesting. I take time and care that students understand this freedom.

Calvin Smith and I exchange several emails before formally beginning the academic study. I learn that he is a Trappist monk, living in a monastery in Arkansas. Knowing little of his world or his religious order – which I'd supposed to be much too austere for email and for Web-surfing – I learn that he is thinking of someday attending graduate school in theology (hence his interest in learning the Western metaphysical tradition) and that he prefers to be addressed as "Brother Cal." When he's not in prayer or doing liturgical service, he works as the assistant manager of the monastery's chicken farm.

Brother Cal already has a general familiarity with the history of Western philosophy. He now wants to work closely with primary texts from the metaphysical tradition: the Greeks and Scholastics; Descartes, Spinoza, and Leibniz; the early modern critics, Hume and Kant; the positivist and post-modern deconstructors of all claims about fundamental and abstract realities; the reclaiming of ontology in Heidegger; and hints of its revival in the hermeneutics and "communicative action" of Gadamer and Habermas. Brother Cal is particularly interested in Aristotle, Aquinas, Spinoza, and how their ideas might serve an understanding of and faith in God in a post-modern world. He wants to explore the question of "immanence" – how an abiding fundamental or ultimate reality might necessarily suffuse and determine our ordinary experience.

It's a very ambitious project. Although Brother Cal's interests are genuine and compelling, I fear that the plan we've made might be just too much work to complete within a single study. I write to him to tell him so and to suggest that we might want to divide the study into smaller pieces. That suits him fine. But he also tells me that he's not very concerned about the time or about finishing. Yes, someday he would like to go on to graduate school, but his primary commitments are to God, his faith, and to the worldly and spiritual devotions of his monastic order. To my surprise, he suggests that we speak by phone to make sure that we "understand each other and the plan." I am even more surprised when he opens the call he's got permission to make to me from Arkansas by saying, "This will be a helluva study" in a rich and melodious West Indian accent. Smiling to myself, I agree and tell him that I am sure our work together will succeed.

We begin to make our way leisurely through Parmenides and Heraclitus, Plato and Aristotle, exchanging emailed comments and questions about the reading. He is precise and clear. Though committed by faith to the idea that existence is larger and more stable than material appearances and subjective, intellectual constructions, Brother Cal seems fully aware of the conceptual and logical difficulties of apprehending an absolute reality. Moreover, he understands far more intimately and urgently than I do, that in his faith the humility of the human condition makes God at once necessary and mysterious. How then or in what sense can one say that one somehow "knows" the existence of this Being that is also necessarily incomprehensible? This question appears repeatedly and in different forms in our virtual conversations.

Brother Cal seems both utterly fascinated yet untroubled by the question. The tone of his emails is serene and effervescent, even jolly, like the sound of his voice on the phone. When I ask him if his work on these philosophical difficulties influences his faith (I'm hesitant to ask if he's become troubled or doubtful), he knows exactly what I'm thinking. "Oh, I'm not worried at all," he replies. (I imagine him laughingly saying something like "Oh no, mon, not at all. Don' you go be worryin' yourself now.") Then, he emails me:

> This is not work. It's worship. We devote our lives trying to become closer to God. This is my way. Finishing the road is not important; it's not even relevant. It's like praying. An 'answered' prayer is not that you eventually get something you ask for; it's in the sincerity of the

praying itself. That is closeness to God; that's 'immanence.' These philosophical studies help me understand this, and I feel that closeness right there while I'm trying to understand. If Being is immanent, it's everywhere, even in this schooling, don't you think?

For Brother Cal, dialogue, which occurred between us and within himself, was not a contest at all. Rather, it immanently realized such virtues as generous attention, openness to new ideas, acceptance of other voices, and service to something "higher." In dialogue itself, Brother Cal lived a spiritual life (Ferrer 2002).

As our study proceeded, Brother Cal began to have more trouble dealing with the 20,000 chickens on the monastery farm than he did understanding the immanence of Being. The manager of the poultry operation fell ill. Brother Cal had to take over. Eventually, he told me that he would have to interrupt his academic efforts indefinitely. I expressed regret that he could not finish the study but reminded him that he could resume and complete the work when he was ready. In turn, he reminded me that it wasn't "work" and that, although he looked forward to returning, he was happy to have had the opportunity to begin this study and that he would pursue his "intellectual devotions" as best he could on his own "but always with God."

I will miss Brother Cal – his earnest, happy inquiry; his faith; his monastery and, of course, his chickens. He re-inspired me to think that human beings can do just fine with reality, virtual or otherwise, because its truths are always immanent for us through wonder.

The virtual lifeworld, absent and present

Virtual reality did not cause the failure of the Classical Greece course; it just made the non-engagement of the mentor and students easy. By the same token, virtual reality was a necessary but not sufficient condition of the strong engagement which occurred between the same mentor and Brother Cal. Without virtual reality, it is unlikely the two of them would ever have connected. In fact, we might say that the existence of virtual reality is not *intrinsically* problematic at all; it's merely an important aspect of reality which human beings have created by understanding, imagination, and artifice from what is "given," from the data, of nature – namely, the electrical and mathematical properties of the material universe. But virtual reality, like every other medium of experience, does necessarily *pose* an existential problem for human beings: How shall we choose to live with each other? And the question becomes all the more urgent, the more we depend upon virtual reality for any interaction – whether commercial or philosophical – which requires even some small and reliably truthful or authentic presentation of self.

What failed to emerge in the Classical Greece course did indeed appear so powerfully in the philosophy study: the lifeworld. In the former, the students apparently regarded the learning activities simply as a series of obstacles to their instrumental goals (finishing the course, fulfilling a liberal arts requirement, completing a degree). They did not bring into discussion any of their genuine curiosity, any of their fundamental concerns. They did not make themselves present except as shrewd operators or functionaries in a system. And, apparently in the students' perception, the mentor also failed to present himself any more fully and authentically as an inhabitant of a lifeworld.

But in the second example, Brother Cal barely seemed to care at all about instrumental matters; he cared for them primarily to the extent that they could be shaped (in good part, thanks to the flexibility of both the mentor's college and virtual reality itself) to serve his devotional inquiries, which, for him, were ends-in-themselves – the very heart of his lifeworld. Indeed, Brother Cal seemed almost amused that his mentor cared so much that they had to indefinitely interrupt the study so soon after they'd begun and that the monk's goal of entering graduate school would remain remote.

The mentor will likely remember nothing of the individual students who took the Classical Greece course, except that each, indistinguishably from the others, wanted to get it done. The students will likely remember nothing of the mentor, except that he required a lot of work. But the mentor will always remember Brother Cal – his emailed comments on the texts, his Caribbean origins, and the small details of his sequestered, chicken-raising, prayerful life.

Perhaps the Greece course was too minutely designed, without any participation from the students, with too few openings that urged them to make the study their own intellectual inquiry. And so they did not. Perhaps because the students were apparently "told" to take the course for its convenience as a way of fulfilling an academic requirement, they had no interest nor did they expect to develop or receive any. The mentor was unable to overcome this obstacle. Perhaps he lacked sufficient skill and persistence. And, perhaps no matter what he might have done, the students would have chosen not to engage in dialogue.

Free choice is a necessary condition of that engagement; it can not be forced. (See Chapter 2, "The principles of mentoring and the philosophy of dialogue," and also Principle 3, autonomy and collaboration.) And the students had already, before the course began, defined themselves as unfree, except in so far as they could manipulate the situation in which they found themselves to release themselves from it. They made use of the distance virtual reality affords, in order to achieve a kind of hiddenness. They took advantage of the malleability of digits to win as much control as they could. That they were a group and the mentor was more accustomed to working with students individually made the "blindness" of completely pre-packaged "courseware" to individual learners easy to exploit. In the same way, students in huge lecture classes find much freedom to do as they please in the anonymity which their distant professors impose. The *New York Times* recently reports, for example, that students often bring their laptops to class, playing solitaire, surfing the Web or working on course assignments, while the professors lecture. The latter complain about disengagement; students say they are "multi-tasking." Some teachers are trying to make their classes more engaging; some universities, predictably, are testing software able to detect from exactly where on campus students have made even wireless Internet connections (Schwartz 2 January 2003: A1, A14). Mice and mousetraps.

This outcome is not inevitable. Authentic learning communities do appear in virtual reality. The give and take of discussion, collaborative learning, and earnest effort and disclosures of self occur there (cf. the research of Karen Swan and others, e.g. Swan *et al.* 2000). Indeed, as Mary Thorpe describes the current trend in developing "third generation" open and distance learning courses for online delivery, "it is the purpose of the online interaction *to use the learners themselves as a resource*, and to build on their experience, reading and perspectives" (Thorpe 2003: 204). She describes a model of collaborative online course design in which the traditional boundary between "course design," "pedagogy," "learner support," and technology "start to merge" (ibid.: 199). "The social interaction and virtual presence that can be delivered, require the integration of both pedagogy and technology and practical commitment to collaboration in learning" (ibid.: 200). Just as we have discussed, Thorpe observes that in these emerging virtual learning communities students have:

> the choice of how they present themselves, and can to some extent manipulate the kind of personality they present through their words and actions. Studying together will certainly bring their identities into play, possibly more intensively than even face-to-face study opportunities typically allow.
>
> (ibid.: 205)

Both mentors and students have to choose whether to make of learning in virtual reality merely a reproduction of an industrial model classroom or to make that medium into a genuinely collaborative learning environment.

We suggest that it may be the very *mediacy*, the very "distance" of virtual communication, that allows, though it can not guarantee, the emergence and sharing of lifeworld concerns so essential for authentic dialogue. Readers might recall Rianne, from the previous chapter. Online or distance learning was not a practical necessity for her; she could easily meet with her mentor in his office. But she did not feel at home there; his apparent expectation of *im*mediate responses to his questions constricted her ability to think clearly. She wanted separation in space and in time, so that she could reflect, carefully develop her own ideas, and respond articulately. Creating this distance allowed Rianne to say what she really believed and to discuss what she most deeply cared about. To be sure, she could have used the potency of virtual reality to make a mask, to simply offer the mentor what she believed he wanted to see. But that is not what she chose.

Similarly, although Brother Cal was more or less practically stuck with virtual reality in order to do academic learning, he chose to turn the separation it offers to nurture his spiritual lifeworld and then to share his discoveries with his mentor. He took his time to read and write; the very *a*synchronicity of email enabled him to ponder carefully and at leisure the comments and questions his mentor sent him. This temporal distance also enabled his mentor to think carefully about what Brother Cal had sent him, and then to make helpful questions and comments. Indeed, although often touted for its service to speedy communication, virtual reality offers an easily used opportunity for the participants in dialogue to *wait* for each other (Chapter 4, "Waiting as learning").

Can one absolutely tell that one is receiving authentic communications from one's students? Not really. However, as we have suggested throughout, the more mentors individualize the work they do with students, even in groups, the more likely it is that students will contribute their lifeworld concerns to the learning (Principle 4). To achieve this, we must respect and give first place to the curiosity, abilities, and purposes of our students (Principle 2). We must engage them in collaborative inquiry (Principles 3 and 5), encouraging our students to make their own meaningful connections to academic content (Principle 6).

These are the features of authenticity. The Classical Greece course did not achieve this kind of engagement. The longer his students remained opaque, the more discouraged, bored, and suspicious the mentor became. But, working with Brother Cal, he never doubted that they were engaged in authentic dialogue. The lifeworld issues the monk shared – whether obviously profound (the vocation of faith) or seemingly trivial (raising chickens) – brought substance and delight to their virtual companionship.

Nonetheless, one can't be absolutely sure. It's likely that the mentor was not only delighted but also a little relieved when he heard Brother Cal's voice on the phone. He could be quite sure that he was dealing with a real person. But even the little details of identity can be faked, if someone wants to take the trouble to do so. And, of course, the fakery can be detected, if one believes it is necessary to try. Neither fully engaged mentoring nor the most micro-managerial teaching can automatically produce authenticity. If we insist on absolute certainty, we can only chase after lies. The purpose of mentoring has nothing to do with such contests. Intellectual engagement with the student's lifeworld, the dialogical relationship, is the end-in-itself. To the extent that the dialogical process is engaged, the less reason the participants (both mentors and students) will have to turn learning into a power struggle. Just as virtual reality makes such struggles stark and temptingly easy for almost anyone to join, so does it also make clear that anyone is free to choose to be authentic. Mentoring in virtual reality relies on a reciprocal faith that people who can act freely and believe their freedom is respected will make profoundly good choices.

Virtual reality and the immanence of "spiritual" virtues in practical life

But what about Brother Cal's chickens? Are they really trivial? From a practical perspective they are obviously very important. They needed tending so that the monastery could survive in the world; looking after them became Brother Cal's job. In this way, Brother Cal was no different from so many other adult students whose work competes with school. But we might doubt that Brother Cal saw this apparent dissonance between raising chickens and studying metaphysics as a deep and intrinsic conflict between instrumental goals and ends-in-themselves. Brother Cal did not desire to interrupt his academic studies; however, he was not troubled by this. He did not think that he was interrupting his *learning*. It is likely that he regarded raising chickens as simply another way of serving God, of tending the Garden of Creation. For him, we speculate, the particular practical tasks of worldly life could be experienced with the same virtues and immanence of Being he was seeking to encounter, in another way, through dialogical inquiry. From this perspective, raising chickens would be no less fundamental, important or meaningful than academic study. There would be no "contest" at all.

We have offered many examples throughout this book of students trapped in just such a contest. (Faculty too are caught between learning and power, as we will show in our next chapter.) They are beset with multiple practical commitments, which interfere with their studies. Those instrumental needs distract them from tending to the deeper issues of truth, justice, and beauty – issues which, we have argued, require contemplation if one is to live a happy life. We have argued that this conflict can be managed if academic systems are made flexible, and if academic practices accommodate and respect even the most apparently pragmatic students. We have argued that when we dialogically embrace student purposes, we and they will not only make relevant connections between their studies and their practical concerns, but also that the latter will reveal the lively presence of the fundamental issues, "the knowledge most worth having" (Principle 6). Now we suggest that the experience of Brother Cal in virtual reality opens a way not only to manage but also to transcend this conflict between the practical and the contemplative life.

Virtual reality easily gives us this possibility. We have said that because everything can be so immersed and then altered in virtual reality, it very clearly and urgently poses for human beings the question of existential authenticity and meaning: How shall we live? Virtual reality makes easy the manufacture of identity and the control of the identities of others. But it also makes the futility of these efforts easy to see. Why bother, when our efforts at control lead ultimately to boredom, which, at its most extreme, is the desperate emptiness we create when we render our own and others' true selves anonymous?

A large lecture class, where the course material, content, and "discussion" are entirely controlled by the professor, approaches this anonymity. The assemblage of bodies and faces offers and demands little more individual distinction than a sea of water droplets. As to individual need or curiosity, the teacher can delegate that attention to assistants. As to individual "performance," the teacher need only have a reliable and secure system of matching the work students submit to an identifying name or number (a trap for every mouse). Still, we professors, giving our lectures to large audiences, like to know, since we are unable to engage such a mass of people in dialogue, that we have "captured" the students' attention. (This is why professors are upset over the use of laptops in class rooms.) We want the students to "perform," and we try to perform as well. We try to be witty and humorous; we try to excite interest with "multimedia"; and we try to make things quick and easy to understand with Powerpoint displays. Even in the near anonymity of a large lecture hall, we try to project some semblance of personality as though to absorb everyone present in ourselves.

Virtual reality makes it easy to strip away the presence of identity even more completely. For in virtual reality, not even the sea of faces (bored or otherwise) is present. Except for an identification code, the students can be entirely anonymous. Names, questions, comments, worries, and hopes can be ignored. Only the students' "products," their submitted assignments, are required. The "courseware" can tell the students what to do and how; it can allow work to be submitted up to and not beyond a required date. If the assignments are rigidly and minutely designed enough and securely identified, the courseware can match the submitted product to the enrollee, check for plagiarism, and grade the learning. In fact, the teachers need not even participate at all beyond creating the course or, for that matter, authorizing the material a curriculum designer has prepared to their specifications. It is barely necessary to be present. It is hard to imagine that teachers of such courses would be anything but bored, unless they are deeply narcissistic or distract themselves with reveries as factory workers sometimes do.

For the same reason and by the means of the same technology, the students need not participate either. At its most extreme, virtual reality offers the prospect of "learning" and "teaching" being transacted by entirely delegated (or, in infospeak, "dedicated") artificial intelligences. In such a world, what is known? Who teaches? Who learns? Who cares and who knows? We suggest that the existential confusion and anxiety of this environment would be unendurable for human beings. Perhaps it would be normal and in some way satisfying for the indefinitely regenerative silicon and electronic creatures which we might make to replace our frail, organic species (Hardison 1989: 344–348). As we describe below, human beings might achieve a kind of immortality in this way, but we would surely no longer be leading human lives.

But there is a different way to live with and within virtual reality. Rather than disguising or seeking to eliminate authentic identity, people can use the very ease of creative expression virtual reality offers to present themselves and embrace the selves of other participants. And, with the same flexibility virtual reality offers for communication, for scheduling and shaping or reshaping material, both the process and content of learning can easily accommodate almost any practical exigency. Further, learning could also easily embrace the immanently contemplative or (as Brother Cal might call it) "spiritual" potential in the instrumental activities of everyday life. Making money, seeking status, acquiring possessions, participating in one's community, raising one's children or tending one's garden or chickens – all of these activities raise questions about what we believe to be true, call us to do justice, and offer us the chance to experience beauty. They are also ways we enact and communicate our authentic and individual identities. It is through these indefinitely diverse practices that we are identifiable selves attached to and alive in the real world. In the virtual world, these details of individual vitality can thrive and be embraced in learning, if only we choose together to trust what we send to and receive from others.

It may be that from an abstract ontological perspective (or from the point of view of a lecturer or course designer removed from students) the individually distinguishing features of Calvin Smith are merely "accidents" irrelevant to his learning. It is perhaps merely entertaining or a matter of idle curiosity to know that he is a monk, a West Indian, a chicken-farmer, or even passionately and profoundly interested in the study of metaphysics. But if we choose to strip away all these qualities and attachments (or never try to learn about them at all), as virtual reality makes it so easy to do, we create "nobodies." Learning requires learners. Make them and ourselves identity-less, and no one can be sure if anyone is learning anything at all. We can choose to live and "learn" this way too. But why would anyone want such a life?

Learning to live with authentic and virtual realities

Virtual reality makes the meanings and consequences of our choices starkly clear. We can choose to live for power, or we can cultivate our powers for the sake of living good lives. In choosing the latter, we make the detailed, worldly "accidents" into the precious stuff of our lives. Our commitment to them, our "owning" them, defines our individual authenticity and makes them worthy of respectful care in ourselves and others. The authenticity of something (a thing or a person), as Walter Benjamin describes, depends upon its "uniqueness" in a particular time, place, and history. This defining separation is a kind of "distance." No technology of reproduction or representation can overcome this distance without obliterating it, because, necessarily, any such effort to bring something "closer" removes it from its uniqueness (Benjamin 1968: 222–223). Authenticity and thus truthful learning *require distance*, in space, in time, and from the particularity of what or who dwells there. It is this kind of distance which allows us to learn by letting others – whether things, ideas, people – disclose themselves to us; it permits dialogical learning. In this view, even our artifacts have authenticity – our works of art and business, our technologies, and possessions. We can learn from and with them as well. Thus, Trappist chicken farms or whatever other particulars uniquely define us matter. In fact, they make the examined life worth loving.

As we've suggested, virtual reality makes the tension between overcoming distance and preserving authenticity perfectly clear. But the tension itself should not be obliterated. Were it possible for us to fuse with other persons (because we desire to control them, or because, as mentors, our "cognitive love" for our students has gone out of control), we would lose both ourselves and the other. We would be empty. However, if we do not try to transcend the distance, to come closer and apprehend the other, we are alone.

This tension between separation and fusion, revealing and grasping marks the history of human efforts to make things and to create identities. Human authenticity depends upon sustaining the vitality of this tension between restless and settled understanding. We are all learners. And we are granted moments of enchantment in the world, such as the shared experiences of a mentor and, a thousand miles away, of a chicken-raising monk trying, each of us together in earnest dialogue, to explore the mysteries of Being.

Can the academy invite and sustain suspenseful dialogical lives and learning? Universities and other schools are powerful systems. However, they are also the products of human artifice. It is thus part of their authentic nature both to resist and to be subject to purposeful change. In our next chapter, we shall create a fiction, a narrative about the evolving relationship between a student and a professor. By means of this little virtual reality, we shall explore how a traditional university teacher might become a mentor, and thus how the idea of a dialogical community might become accessible and inspiring to the academy.

Chapter 9

Access to and within the academy

> The spirit and meaning of education cannot be enhanced by addition, by the easy method of giving the same dose to more individuals. If learning is to be revivified, quickened so as to become once more an adventure, we shall have need of new concepts, new motives, new methods; we shall need to experiment with the qualitative aspects of education.
>
> Edward Lindeman, *The Meaning of Adult Education* (1961: 4)

More people and more kinds of people than ever before have access to higher education. The opening of tertiary education to "mature" students is significant because in so doing the academy provides access to the material prosperity and security necessary for people to thrive in the world. Clearly, a university degree, a higher education, is not the sole means to a prosperous and good life. However, in both "advanced" and "developing" countries, those who lack access are clearly disadvantaged. Higher education has thus become an essential feature of the national and even the global polity. Indeed, the on-going struggle for access to the academy is a powerful reminder that fundamental social and educational ideals have not yet been achieved.

At its simplest, access means creating opportunities to attend college for people who once had been excluded. But increasing access carries more than numerical consequences. It has also led to the presence of populations of students and faculty increasingly diverse in age, ethnicity, class, and other ascriptions that had been seen as disqualifying. With these new persons, new voices are heard and new experiences become available to the entire academic community. As a result, many basic assumptions of higher education have been opened to question. These include assumptions about curriculum and canon, the organization and process of learning, the constitution of knowledge, the grounds of intellectual authority, and the very purposes of education. What began as a matter of making more room for more people has, necessarily, become a persisting battle over the very architecture of the academy (Herman 1992). That is, what might be seen as narrowly pragmatic aspects of access directly open on to normative perspectives, to questions about our fundamental values.

The practical and the normative: access to and access within

Throughout this book, we have emphasized the necessary interdependence of the practical and the principled or normative aspects of experience. Using the distinction developed by Jürgen Habermas between "system" and "lifeworld," we have tried to point to the "systems" through which humans seek and exercise the means which give them power to prosper in the world. But we have also described how such instrumental understandings, action, and purposes are not sufficient for happiness. It is in and through the "lifeworld" that human beings seek the truth, the moral good and the beauty which gives life meaning and intrinsic value. Without system, we simply suffer and die. Without the lifeworld, we live empty lives.

The question of access can be helpfully understood from the double perspective of system and lifeworld. Access *to* the academy, regardless of students' lifeworlds and their practical needs, inevitably selects for entrants ("inputs") favored by the dominant cultural, political, and economic systems. And those who succeed ("outputs") will largely reproduce, though now in more privileged positions, the larger society from which they originated. Access *within* the academy, a learning community attending as much to the lifeworld as it does to systems, will seek to invite, accommodate and nurture a more genuinely diverse citizenry. A full learning community depends upon the collaboration –the dialogical participation – of all its members, including students. To be a truthful, just, and beautiful polity of learning, the academy needs whom and what it does not know. Opening up the question of educational access thus demands that students and faculty struggle with the tension between succeeding in a harsh world and thriving in a cherishable one.

Openings in the faculty role

It is in the academy's self-interest as a true learning community to open access for others to and within itself. But what about faculty? Why should faculty become more like mentors? How would opening the faculty role be in their interest?

There are clear parallels between student learning, the role of the faculty, and the structures and processes of the academy. Once the academy itself is seen as a polity, a learning community within a larger society, the issues arising from providing institutional access for students also manifest themselves as a sequence of openings in the faculty role. They become fundamental questions about the practical and normative aspects of human learning. In the remainder of this chapter, we shall explore this sequence—these "moments" of inquiry through the interactions between a "professor," a fictional construction based on elements of our own experiences, and "Jim," a student who closely resembles an actual student at our college.

Moment I: the problems of systemic practicality

Jim and his professor

At the beginning of the new academic year, I meet Jim because he's been assigned to me as an academic advisee. His application indicates that he's interested in "facilities management," and that happens to be my specialty in the Department of Business Management where I teach, and the focus of the research and consulting I do. I'm supposed to tell him which courses from his prior college he can transfer here and which courses he needs to take to complete the bachelor's degree in management. I see also that he's worked for many years in manufacturing facilities, first in a steel mill and then for a corporation which makes electronic medical devices. I've consulted for both firms and know them to be very progressive in their products, manufacturing methods, and training procedures. I suppose that they are funding Jim's education, as they have the other students whom they've sent here. I'm curious about Jim's experience maintaining the operations of these advanced facilities, and I wonder how well he will take to becoming a student again. So many adults have difficulty adjusting to university. They never seem to have time to study; their academic skills are rusty; and they don't much like having to take courses which they feel they can't use. Still, they're more serious than I was as a student; they know they have to get those degrees.

Jim is nervous and polite when he comes into my office. He's middle-aged, trim, and dressed in somewhat worn but neatly pressed and clean "shop floor" clothes. A beeper and cell-phone, power lights on, are attached to his wide leather belt. We exchange a few pleasantries and then get down to business. I have a class to teach, and, before that, a meeting with one of my graduate students with whom I'm writing an article. I go over Jim's transcript, telling him which courses he can transfer in. He nods but doesn't take notes. I also give him a copy of the curriculum he'll need to follow: some courses in general management, some in economics and finance, then some advanced courses in current operations and facilities management methodologies. I also tell Jim that he'll probably have to take some more math in order to do those advanced courses, and that he'll need to choose some liberal arts electives. He remains silent while I go over these things.

I ask him if he has any questions, although I'm aware that time is pressing. Jim quietly replies that he thinks he understands what he needs to do. Then, as he's gathering his things (I wonder why he's brought so many papers with him; they look like training records and certificates), he says:

> "I've been a facilities manager for a long time. I know how to do my job and I've taken every training course I can to stay up to date in my field. But my company says I have to get this degree, not just if I want to get promoted, but just to keep the position I have. They'll want me to get a master's degree too, though I'll have to pay for that one myself. I'll do it; I have to work another five to ten years before I can retire. Don't get me wrong, I like to learn. But it's been a long time since I've been in school. And, well, it seems like there are a lot of courses here about things I think I know about already or which aren't going to help me that much. I hope, I mean, do you think that...?"

> "Yes, yes, I understand what you're saying. But these are things you have to do to get a degree and become a college-educated person. We've *all* had to do these things; you just have to make up your mind. Anyhow, you'll see, you can get a lot out of those courses that you don't realize now. We'll talk some more. Just call the departmental secretary and she'll schedule an appointment for you."

I smiled and nodded conclusively, and then turned my head toward the article manuscript waiting on my desk. But as Jim walked to the door, he paused, turned back towards me, and said:

> "Remember that time a year or so back when you came to my company to consult?"

> "Of course I remember."

> "You know, I was the one who recommended you. I'd read an article you'd written on methods of installing lean manufacturing line set-ups while maintaining current operations. I thought we could learn a lot, and we did. See you in class."

I was distracted during the editorial meeting with my graduate student. I now realized that I had met Jim before, at his company. And I remembered that I'd also seen his name on the roster for my class on "Managing the Modern Organization." This wasn't exactly my specialty, but all of us in the department were periodically required to teach some general courses. And even though the prep-time took away from my research and my advanced seminars, I enjoyed this particular class. Some interesting discussions occurred, especially with the older students. They knew what I was talking about, even if they sometimes had trouble remembering the names and explaining the different management theories I lectured on. Also, I had to admit, that they sort of kept me up-to-date on what was going on "in the real world." Sometimes this gave me research ideas, and even contacts for my consulting work. I liked that course because teaching it helped me see how my own expertise fit with what else goes on in companies. My work is very technical and usually I talk with and write for other specialists in my field. I knew that the "neat" methodologies and concepts we developed became "fuzzy" in practice. People and big organizations made things complicated and cumbersome. This could be frustrating, annoying, but I had to be polite and gracious. In the back of my mind, I sometimes uncomfortably wondered, even a little guiltily, if I wasn't just missing something. At conferences, sometimes my colleagues and I would joke about the difference between "the academic" and "the real world." But we never talked about it very seriously.

As I walked from my office toward the lecture hall, I began to wonder about something else, about Jim and me. What if I were in his position? Wouldn't I worry about doing all these courses? In fact, wouldn't I resent having to do so much, especially while still working, in order to get a degree that said I was now "really" qualified to do what I already knew how to do very well? The question was irrelevant because we weren't in the same position at all. So, instead, I mused about the students I'd find awaiting me this term. Maybe there'd be some interesting ones in the usual bunch of non-entities and the "eager beavers" who only seemed to care how much they'd have to read, and what they'd have to do to get a good grade.

During class, I noticed that Jim sat very still. He took notes while I gave my introductory lecture. When I was finished, he, like most students, asked no questions. Later in the day, I began to think about him again and found myself actually comparing the two of us. We were middle-aged adults, working in the same field, facilities management, both of us very serious about our work. But why should I be thinking so much about Jim and bothering to compare us? I was a scholar. I examined and even influenced what people like him did for a living. So what if he worked "in the real world"? Well, I was one of the people who determined what his "real" world would be! *He* read *my* articles; *I* advised his company. Then why was I thinking about him so much? From what did I seem to be defending myself?

These questions rattled my attention over the next several days. I had no answers. Then I remembered a conversation I'd had a couple of years ago with an old friend from undergraduate days; she now taught economics at another university. We'd both recently made full professor. We'd done the publishing, the conferencing, the grant-getting, and we'd sent our students out into the world to become managers, economists, and/or professors just like us.

"Did you ever feel you were running a business?" she asked.

"Sure. We do run businesses, in a way, don't we? We take in students, and teach them. We do research and publish articles. We are well-paid consultants and we have high-status positions in large organizations. What's wrong with that?"

"Nothing's wrong at all. I wonder sometimes if it's enough."

"Enough what? We're well paid and people respect us. We have security...."

"How much security?" she interrupted. "Do you think that we are invulnerable to the social and economic trends that make the work-places we study such unreliable places for long-term employment?"

"Oh, come on. We have tenure, and we are well regarded. We do important work. Anyhow, universities change very slowly; they're attached to their traditions," I replied.

"And don't you think that all those managers and workers, whose inputs and outputs we calculate, believe they're doing important work, or at least behave as though they do because their companies insist on commitment? Don't you think your answer just now was a bit cynical? If our universities took your research on through-put efficiency or mine on added-value as seriously as we mean them, how secure would our own or our colleagues' jobs be? What would happen to academic tenure? You seem to be saying either that our status is dependent upon our institutions' stupidity or that our work isn't really very meaningful after all."

"That's a bit harsh," annoyance creeping into my voice. "Don't you think your work is valuable? I think it is; mine too."

"Do you remember," my friend asked, "when we told one another that we were going into economics and business to do well for our-selves and also to make the world prosper?"

"Not very often," I replied with an ironic smile. "I'm too busy. You know how things are. And we've done pretty well, at least for our-selves," I laughed, "haven't we?"

Our conversation comfortably drifted to other topics. I wondered now about my ironic smile. Was it the friendly condescension with which one treats the naiveté of youthful idealism, one's own and one's students?

Or, was it a way to distance lingering and profound questions? Those questions softly scratch for attention through the veil of one's daily and consuming tasks. Then I thought again about Jim. He stayed with me. I wondered if he believed that he was doing something important, meaningful – all that time and energy he spent everyday and, now that he was a student, would be expending well into every night. I wondered if he thought the expectations imposed upon him were fair, expectations that would never cease. It seemed that for him, a higher education was perhaps a gift to be gratefully received; but it was also a blow to be endured.

Suddenly, I found myself thinking about my own work – the teaching, the research, the consulting. What difference did it make? It was interesting to some students and to fellow experts in the field. I knew that my work helped companies like Jim's, their stockholders and directors, prosper hugely and that sometimes good products found their way more quickly and affordably into more people's lives, which made them healthier, safer, more secure or comfortable. But not necessarily and not for most. I still knew enough economics and history to know that even as the human population, in the aggregate, got richer and that more things and skills became available to make their lives better and better, the distribution of these goods remained wildly uneven and grew ever more so. It was odd that even while the production of wealth and useful knowledge had accelerated tremendously in the last hundred or even fifty years, so had the suffering in people's lives. How come, when we know so much more how to make things better for people, so many more human lives seemed to become more savage? More naiveté. I'd been schooled to spot and criticize the "fuzziness" in such questions. Another effort to eliminate the questions themselves. And now I teach others to do the same.

Comments

For both the policy makers and managers of the higher education system, as well as for its potential "clients," access to educational services increasingly becomes a solely practical goal. But, as critics have so accurately argued, an educational system governed by such practicality is inherently self-contradictory. That is, while the system opens itself to new participants, it simultaneously imposes two practical restrictions: For those people who *do* get in, the requirements for social success and security multiply in terms of continuing (and often expensive) education, certificates, and degrees. Just as more and more people of different kinds are now getting into college, many jobs which had never required degrees at all now do, and those that did now require more advanced degrees and even "lifelong" credentialing. "Jim" exactly exemplifies this trend.

Secondly, for those people who are *excluded*, the social, economic, and personal consequences are more drastic than ever. At the same time that women and "minorities" are more represented in workplaces proportionate to their numbers, permanent job security is increasingly obsolete and productivity requirements have dramatically escalated (Reich 1990). Although Jim is not (yet) educated in economics, he has an accurate sense of the risks he runs by not finishing a degree. He knows that he is expendable, and he knows that it will be enormously difficult for him, especially at his age, to find secure, reasonably paid work and benefits if he is discarded by his employer. In the name of our so-called "knowledge society," learning itself becomes a harsh and uncivil tool in the competition for money, power, and status.

But there is a third restriction as well. This is a normative one, which, whether explicit or taken for granted, accompanies and authorizes the dysfunctions of a wholly pragmatic approach to access. The very claim to openness *justifies* marginalizing those who are altogether excluded and those who never get very far. Deflecting attention from these systemic dysfunctions (which are also social inequities), it is supposed that those who do not prosper, also do not *deserve* to prosper. They fail, it is supposed, for lack of sufficient individual initiative to take advantage of the opportunities available to them. Thus, services to the disadvantaged are reduced even while more responsibility is expected of them. Socio-economic stratifications are then rationalized by ascribing to the disadvantaged complete moral responsibility for their condition. Failure to "move up" thus becomes not only a practical frustration but also a source of *shame*. Behind Jim's quiet, humble manner, we can sense his humiliation.

Even though he condescends to Jim, his professor is aware of these trends. He resides near the top of the status ladder within the academy and, thanks to his publications and consulting, accrues wealth from and commands prestige beyond it. Nonetheless, he is vaguely and uncomfortably aware that something is wrong: that "the system" is not working as his educated beliefs have told him it's supposed to; that there's something unfair going on; and that he himself is both vulnerable to systemic dysfunctions and bothered by a sense of meaninglessness and inequity he can't quite define. He begins to feel some compassion for and a puzzling identification with Jim. The professor's sense of justice is disturbed, however slightly, and so is his complacency in the adequacy of his own expert learning. He is beginning to feel the sting of Meno's "torpedo fish."

Moment II: making the system more friendly

Jim and his professor-as-advisor

After class one evening, I ask Jim how he's doing. He gives me a polite "okay," falls silent but does not move. When I stir, beginning to move away toward my office, he asks if he might see me. Instead of asking him to make an appointment, I say, "Sure, come along now if you have some time." We sit. Jim talks:

"I understand the material pretty well in your management class, not so well in economics. The graphs and formulas go by me too fast. I study them on my own, but I'm usually tired after work, then class. I fall asleep, and there's a lot of other reading to do for both courses. I don't know if I can keep up."

"Well . . ."

Jim interrupts: "I'm frustrated. I think I could learn these things if I had more time to memorize all those names and ideas, and to practice the math parts. I'm sure I have questions, but sometimes in class, I'm embarrassed to be the only one asking. The others – most of them look like they're half my age – seem pretty smart and sure of themselves. And when I try to stop and think about what I want to ask, you and the other teacher have already moved on to something else. Also, it's strange: I often know the topics, even if I don't know the names. In our team meetings at work, we talk all the time about production schedules, efficiency, markets, profit margins, and so on. The examples in your class and in economics are very familiar. And I know how to deal with people, how to motivate them, and get them to participate and contribute whatever they have to offer, just like you talk about. That's my point: I know what you're talking about, I know a lot, but I can't quite connect. I feel we speak similar but still different languages. Don't get me wrong. I know I have a lot to learn and I want to learn it or at least I have to learn it. But I know things too and I can't seem to find a fit for them here."

"You've got a lot on your mind. But what if we talk about your schedule and your energy? I *am* an efficiency expert, after all. That's something I could help you with."

Jim nods with a quick smile. He seems pleased, but also a little amused.

"Yes, yes, I know," I say when I understand his smile. "Having too much to do, being efficient. We *both* know something about that, don't we?"

During the following weeks, Jim and I spoke regularly in my office. We quite easily worked out a study schedule. I asked him about times of day when he felt most energetic and productive. He said he often woke up very, very early anyhow, worrying about his studies. We even did a little experiment. Jim recorded the number of pages he could read attentively at night and in the very early morning. We made a graph, plotting time of day against pages read. He said it looked like some of the graphs he'd seen in his economics book. During the evenings, he began to spend more time with his family, whom he felt he had been neglecting. Once he began to concentrate his study time on the early morning, the line on the graph began to curve steadily and more steeply upwards, "like productivity curves do," as he observed, "when effective cost-savings measures are introduced."

I found myself thinking about Jim more and more. Working on a new article about ergonomic control panels, my mind would drift to Jim. He was still having trouble keeping up. The math aspects of his management and economics courses still gave him trouble, for example. It took him a long time to get a feel for the meaning of a formula, and also for some of the more abstract economic and managerial ideas, but by then, the class would have moved on to another topic, just as Jim had described. He was constantly and realistically worried about falling behind. He would say in one and the same breath that he was worried that he wasn't doing as well as he knew he could if he only had more time and energy, yet that he wasn't sure he was smart enough to be a "real" university student. I didn't know what to say.

I'd listen to Jim's distress, but I was anxious and impatient. I didn't have a "fix" for him, and this is what I was used to knowing how to do – to unclog "production bottlenecks." Jim was serious and committed, no doubt about that. He was pulling a "B" in my management class; he thought he was doing about a "C," a little better than average in economics. I believed him. I was convinced that he could do much better if he had more time, more leisure and more flexibility in his everyday life.

As the term drew to a close and our conversations continued, I made some more suggestions to Jim. What if, next term, he did the second course in economics online? He wouldn't have to go to class. He could take time to recognize more clearly what he didn't understand and formulate his questions. He could ask those questions privately of other students or of the teacher. He liked this idea. He frequently used computers, web sites and email at work. I was pleased, though I wished I had thought of online study much earlier on, even right at the beginning of the first term. Also, I spoke about Jim to some colleagues who taught Web courses, mentioning that he might need some extra help, especially with math and with writing assignments that dealt with abstract ideas. They told me about an online tutorial service for these things. It was staffed by "academic skills" specialists. The "hit" statistics indicated the service to be quite popular with students. Jim said he would give these things a try, though he wondered if they could understand the workplace examples he and I had exchanged when we discussed formulas and managerial philosophies.

I was happy to be helpful to Jim, but also a little frustrated. Was he expecting too much attention? Was he becoming too dependent on me? Other students in my class, most of them older, were following his example. I was used to having fairly empty office hours and to spending this extra time on my own work. In fact, I was so busy, I had missed the deadline for a grant application – something my dean had not failed to observe. He'd dropped by my office, very friendly. He mentioned the application, asked me a joking question about professorial absent-minded-ness, and left with breezy wave and the comment, "You know how much all of us in the department and the university count on you." Yes, I knew the percentage of my consultancy fees and grants the university received as "overhead." Here I was, a full professor, and feeling infantilized, conde-scended to, treated like a mere "employee," and even a little cowed.

Right away, Jim showed up in my thoughts, again! Did he feel upset, disrespected, just as I did? Here was this guy, in the prime of his career and life, and his superiors "suggest" he to go to school – a threat clothed with encouragement.

I shook off these feelings of childish insecurity. I wasn't in Jim's posi-tion. I was relieved that the term was coming to an end and that next term I would have a more efficient approach to dealing with Jim and the other students who wanted extra attention. They'd be more in the hands of people who were more qualified to deal with their special needs.

During the final week of the term, Jim came to see me. He had a spe-cific request. He'd been putting in so much time on his economics course that he'd fallen behind in mine. Also, he'd had to put in extra hours at work and his wife had become ill. He asked if he could have two extra weeks (these would fall over the holiday break) to finish the term paper required for my course. I was uncomfortable, and I told him so. He knew the schedule and the requirements. What if every student wanted a special concession like this?

I changed the subject to something less bothersome:

"What are you doing your term paper on, Jim? I know we talked about it, but, I'm sorry, I don't quite remember."

"It's on de-skilling. You lectured about that topic, and we had some readings to do. We read something by that American Marxist, about the connections between de-skilling and exploitation..."

"Yes, yes, Braverman, the chapter from *Labor and Monopoly Capital*."

"And we read much more up-to-date things, about how companies like mine could train veteran workers, help them learn new skills, while still saving time and money because those employees already knew the products and what you called 'the culture' of the company. That's what interests me."

"Do you have a thesis?" I asked.

"It's more like a question that bothers me," Jim replied. "You see, I've had lots of training. We learn about new equipment; we learn how to install and maintain it. We learn about new techniques of arranging space, lighting, computer hook-ups. But the trainers always present these things as brand-new and the very latest. It often feels like we're starting from scratch, but that's not exactly so." Jim fell silent.

"And what's your question?" I asked, curious now, leaning forward in my chair.

"I wonder why we can't start from what we already know, why we can't be given, you know, credit for it. Wouldn't that be efficient too, if the consultants and trainers spent some more time asking how we already work, what we already knew, to make a kind of bridge to what they are going to teach us? It's like here, in this school. We have to take all these new classes, but they're so often about things we already know something about, even if we can't talk about them in the same way you do. Why can't we be given university credits for what we already know? And, anyhow, when you and I talk, after class, about real examples from my experience, I understand so much better what you're teaching – even the math for my economics class. Wouldn't this be a more efficient way of learning? And, wouldn't that also be, well, more fair, to be given credit, some recognition for what we know?"

"But the university now allows you to take the exams for courses whose contents you think you already know. If you take a challenge exam and pass, you don't have to take that course. You'll get credit for your prior learning. This was a pretty controversial program the university started just a few years ago. I suppose it's okay; it helps students who want to get along quickly. We've talked about that." But I was already sure how Jim would respond.

"Sure, but those exams are all based on the textbooks, not on our experience. I'd have to read the texts on my own, understand all the terms in them. I may as well just take the class; at least there I get some help. Maybe people like me know some important things which aren't in the texts. You said yourself that my experience helped you in your own work."

"Well, that's true, but ... Listen," I said, looking quickly at my watch, "why don't you write up this paper? Explain your question and your experiences, but make sure you back up your ideas with material from the readings. I think you know how to do that now. And about the extra time – well, just do the best you can. I know you're busy and pre-occupied and that some things just can't be helped. We'll talk some more after the holidays. But come in before classes start."

Jim thanked me. He looked relieved and genuinely grateful.

Comments

Jim's professor has taken another step, actually two. Not altogether happily, he's become a much more resourceful advisor for Jim, and a much more conscious critic of the systems in which they both live. He wants to do what he can to help Jim succeed in the university. His discomfiting identification with his advisee sharpens when the dean subtly reminds the professor that he, like Jim, is only an employee, whose worth is not intrinsic but dependent entirely on his instrumental value.

The professor knows enough economics and history to hesitantly realize that his own idle and personal-professional worries are neither trivial nor subjective. He has tried to be a good teacher and advisor, while fulfilling his other obligations. He finds himself opening those roles to something more than he'd supposed they were. Uncustomarily, he has tutored a student outside the classroom, honoring and even learning from that student's "real world" experience; and he has empathetically tried to marshal resources and ideas which can help Jim succeed.

However, the professor also discovers that it's not reasonably possible for him to do everything. Just as Jim has such a hard time fulfilling his simultaneous commitments as a student, worker, and spouse, the professor can't quite manage to be all at once a scholar, teacher, advisor, and ambitious consultant and grant-getter. Moreover, the dean has implicitly scolded and threatened the professor for failing to do the impossible. The dean was much more genial than the professor was in taking Jim to task for the same difficulty. Nonetheless, the message in both instances was unmistakable: The university has expectations; and if you fail to meet them, you will no longer be so welcome here.

Of course Jim is far more vulnerable than the professor, but even the latter catches the fearsome hint of expendability. Not very happily identifying with Jim, the professor has begun to ask if there is something seriously wrong with both the efficacy and the fairness of a system (academic and beyond) which stunts the potential of its own functions and then condemns the functionaries whose very efforts it has impeded. The professor is becoming a critic. Through his very efforts to be a good teacher and advisor, he is on the verge of asking whether it's the system that needs reform, so that it will adapt to people within it, rather than the other way around.

The professor is on the verge, yes. But his uncomfortable wonderings have not yet become projects of inquiry. To be sure, he has opened and expanded the role of "teacher," from lecturing Jim to listening to him, engaging in discussion with him, and using what he hears to help him learn. And he has done the same for his role as "advisor". Instead of telling Jim what he will have to learn, the professor is seeking out and making accessible the available resources of the university: online courses, academic skills services, course challenge exams. Within the system as it is, the professor is becoming an advocate and a resource gatherer for his student. He is providing the beginnings of significant "learner support" (Mills 2003).

And something else is taking place: Jim's professor is beginning to recover his idea of intellectual responsibility by encountering his ignorance. He is starting to ask disturbing questions for which he has no answer. How can he help Jim (and other students like him) and continue to be an influential scholar? How can he re-discover the most profound meanings of his own scholarship if he does not help Jim? The very commitment to the life of the mind requires that we faculty make the university more accessible and that we pay attention to dimensions of student experience we had not carefully considered. Thus, we find ourselves wondering about our basic and proper identity as scholars, as learners and teachers.

Moment III: from doubt to action

Jim and his professor-as-mentor

Throughout the holiday break, I thought frequently about Jim and that conversation with my dean. I was annoyed to be thinking so much of both of them. I didn't like letting myself feel bullied, however subtly, by "an administrator." I didn't like feeling so close to Jim, who was, after all, just another one of the hundreds and hundreds of students I've had. Moreover, I didn't like knowing that I was attracted to Jim and intimidated by my dean for the same reason: I too am an expendable part of "the system."

This was ridiculous and naïve, to be railing against "the system." I know that without systems, there's only chaos and maybe worse. It's not only that systems make group efforts efficient and reliable. They're our best opportunity for increasing everyone's prosperity, and for distributing goods and services fairly, according to rules and with some accountability so that it's less likely that people are subjected to the whims and arbitrary decisions of those in power. Systems create procedures of responsibility. If the rules aren't followed, there are the courts for determining guilt and punishments; and if the rules aren't good, there are legislatures for making them better. We wouldn't like it very much if each time we were wronged – cheated, robbed or worse – we had to find and punish the culprits ourselves and then lived in fear of our enemies' vengeance. Laws, courts, police – these are all systems.

I decided to work within the system we've got, to find a reasonable place in it, and to make it better. Facilities management may not be a very glamorous or righteous-seeming profession. But from my own little corner of the world, I try to make things better. More efficient, more productive, and even fairer too. Aren't consumers entitled to products that are more affordable and reliable for everyone? Aren't workers entitled to work in safe, healthy places – places that are well lit, heated or cooled, where the structures are protected from fire and collapse? Some people might question my social commitment, but aren't all these things part of "justice"? But why am I defending myself? Why am I so bothered? What am I missing?

I went back to work on a new grant application. An industrial lighting systems manufacturer was offering scholars generous support to do *in situ* research on the effectiveness of one of their new products, designed to be easily flexible for teams working in common production cells, such as used at Jim's company. The product was promising and so were the rewards. In addition to receiving the research support, I could probably arrange a nice consulting contract with the places where I tested the system. Maybe Jim's company would be interested; in fact, I could talk with him about the opportunity. And certainly my dean would be pleased to know that I was back in the game. Yes, I *do* love this stuff!

But I had trouble concentrating on the proposal. It wasn't only that I wanted to spend time with my family and friends over the holiday. I just didn't feel motivated. I kept thinking about Jim, and my own "naïve" questions about myself. Moreover, far from being happy or relieved that my dean would be appeased, I continued to resent his intrusion on my autonomy.

Jim's essay, on "Training and Experience," arrived in the mail a couple of weeks late. I'd planned to read it just before the beginning of the new term. I'd put it aside, but now, distracted from the grant application, I picked it up. The essay was more an editorial than a research paper. He argued that trainers had a lot to learn from workers' experience and that if trainers – and managers – listened to what their people had to say, the workplace would become both more efficient and humane. Jim briefly referenced old and newer management concepts I'd covered in the course: quality circles, TQM, workplace engineering, Six Sigma, team design, distributed systems, and so on. But his anecdotes, taken from his own experience as a manager, caught my interest. His stories weren't much of a "data set," but they made me think about our conversations and the questions which had been bothering me.

In one story, a worker who had done poorly elsewhere in the company, was transferred to facilities management, Jim's department. This was pretty much the guy's last chance. If he didn't work out there, he'd be fired. Jim didn't really know what to do with him. The worker lacked specialized maintenance and construction skills. And although apparently willing to do as he was told, he was depressed, apathetic, not interested in anything in particular except keeping his job. Jim began to ask him about his other positions in the company and what he had liked to do. Turned out, this fellow liked being asked to help others who were having problems with their assembly "set-ups" or office equipment. These little efforts weren't part of his job descriptions, and when he took time to assist others, his supervisors criticized him for neglecting his own duties. So, he got into trouble and would transfer to another department.

To make a long story short, Jim made the guy into a kind of roving "fix-it man," someone who would be easily available to help people with trivial but time-wasting problems with chairs, drawers, lamps and bulbs, phone and computer placements. The fellow had a knack for handling these things, and he enjoyed the pleasure of relieving people of the sometimes large frustrations those small problems can cause. Moreover, he turned out, contrary to first impression, to be a good listener and keen observer. Jim's department began to receive fewer exasperated calls for help and fewer requests for minor repairs and replacement items. Jim found that he could keep more of his staff concentrating on larger and more technical projects. He also realized that, thanks to the information his roving fix-it man was supplying, Jim could spend more of his time reliably planning those projects and less on hurriedly replacing consumables in inventory and suddenly having to find somebody to do a small job.

Jim claimed that by listening to this man, he not only had found a useful place for him, but also saved the company money and better understood the many "micro-environments" (a word he'd taken from one of my lectures) in that large and complex organization. It would be useful, Jim asserted, for all supervisors, managers, and trainers to acquire this kind of intimate access or connection.

I wondered if I would have shown so much concern, if I would have been willing, for example, to make a place for an unpromising student. I wasn't sure. The time; the effort; the inevitable frustrations; so many other things to do. The more time I spent with Jim and the other older students, the less I seemed to have for other important things. I wasn't seeing any "efficiencies" in *my* work! What was "the good" Jim was trying to accomplish? Wasn't he busy too? Wasn't he forgetting the big picture, lavishing so much attention on one worker, especially when the results were by no means guaranteed and could easily have come out the other way? But what, I couldn't help asking myself, was "the good" I was trying to do, with my consulting work? And how about that grant application and the lucrative opportunities it could open. I'd be paid by the manufacturer and the test companies would be receiving free lighting systems. How objective would my research be? And who would really care about what I discovered – except for the people who hired me to "discover" results?

I realized I was becoming even more troubled. I decided to call my old friend, the economist, to meet for a leisurely holiday lunch and discussion. She agreed.

We met. She asked:

"What made you call me? It's been a couple of years, you know."

"Yes, we haven't seen each other, but I recently thought about the last time we talked."

And then I began to tell her about Jim, the dean's little visit, about my doubts and questions, about being so distracted. I was gushing, personal, and I didn't care.

"Look," I said as I neared the end of my tale, "I had my mid-life crisis a few years ago. My wife and I are happy, the kids are doing well; I like my work, my self, and all of that. But once I started asking myself what's the good I'm doing, in my scholarship, my teaching, I can't get the question out of my head. You must see, from what I've told you, that I'm not talking about being more successful or helping my students do the same; and I'm not talking about doing volunteer work or something like that. It's not one of those – what's it called? – existential questions. It's basic but more real, more common sense."

"Maybe it's just a practical question," she interrupted. "You know, like Aristotle said, that wealth is good not for its own sake but because it's useful, necessarily and up to a point, so that people have the means and leisure to be happy."

"Aristotle? I didn't know you studied philosophy."

"I don't. But I ran across the quote recently (or something close to it) in an economics book I was reading by Amartya Sen."

"Oh yes, Sen, I read about him when he won the Nobel for economics a couple of years ago."

"He's a real economist, like me, with all the numbers and technical methodologies. But he argues, from within the discipline, so to speak, and not with a political axe to grind, that there's a deep and necessary connection between economics, econometrics, and basic human values like justice and the quality of life. Human 'capabilities' he calls them. These are the freedoms which come from literacy, health care, political participation, and so on. He argues that those values are not uselessly fuzzy at all and not even derivative. They are the important, if not entirely measurable consequences of open markets and income generation and distribution. And those values, those abilities also allow us to *create* markets and sources of income. In other words, these freedoms, those fundamental 'goods,' as you might call them, are both 'constitutive' and 'causal' of prosperity."

" 'Constitutive' and 'causal'? I don't understand."

"It took me a while to get his point. But the basic idea maybe has to do with the kinds of questions which are bothering you. He's talking about what 'wealth' is for: not opulence or luxury, but the means to live prosperously, you know, without having to worry about being able to have good food, health care, housing, personal security, things like that. He's talking about wealth, a decent income, as offering human beings the opportunity to develop all their capacities, to pay attention to what really gives their lives meaning. But, according to Sen, the good reason for human beings to busy themselves creating and acquiring that wealth is to support and enhance those freedoms."

"I think I understand, but . . ."

"Why don't you read his book, the one I was reading, *Development as Freedom*? I know you're not an economist, but you had a lot of the same education I did; and we had to take some philosophy too. It might help you think about your student. The book was especially useful to me. I was bothered by some of the same questions you're wrestling with."

On my way back home, I picked up a copy of *Development as Freedom*. I began reading right away and copied out a paragraph from near the beginning:

If we have reasons to want more wealth, we have to ask: What precisely are these reasons, how do they work, on what are they contingent and what are the things we can "do" with more wealth? In fact, we generally have excellent reasons for wanting more income or wealth. This is not because income and wealth are desirable for their own sake, but because, typically, they are admirable general-purpose means for having more freedom to lead the kind of lives we have reason to value.

(Sen 1999: 14)

I read hardly any farther, then. And the grant application seemed very remote, irrelevant. I even stopped stewing about the dean. I just kept thinking about that phrase "freedom to lead the kind of lives we have reason to value." And what kind of life was that? Maybe just the freedom to decide for myself, whatever it would be? Did Jim, or most people, so pushed and busy, even though reasonably prosperous, like him, have that freedom? Did I? But weren't there some universal values, some things we could all understand and accept, which properly limited our choices, so that we all didn't turn out like many "true believers" I'd seen, telling everyone else what they "had" to do, in the name of some phony "anything goes" type of tolerance? I wanted to talk with Jim.

Comments

The professor is trying to emancipate himself from his own oppression. He's not content to sit and read. He wants to *do* something, though he's not at all sure what that might be. Critical philosophers of education would surely approve of his inevitably painful rise in "consciousness." And they might recommend that direct, organized, political action occur both inside and outside the academy (Collins 1995; Welton 1995; Usher *et al.* 1997; Aronowitz 2000). The professor and his colleagues might lend their clout, privileged status, and expertise to the political, even revolutionary work of public criticism and action. They could guide the transformation of the academy and even of non-academic systems, such as families, workplaces, governments, and the marketplace itself. And certainly at a personal level, the professor is becoming aware that his dean's and his own expediently commercial impulses reciprocate smoothly with all other aspects of a much larger socio-economic system. Perhaps the professor could become a political organizer and act directly on the "steering media," as Habermas might say, of society: money and power (1989: 183).

It remains to be seen whether this professor will choose to use the freedom for which he's groping in such public and political activities. His focus now is on reconsidering the arrangement and the meaning of his professional life. But mostly he's paying attention to how he will behave, as a teacher and as an advisor, toward Jim. He is beginning to wonder how both he and Jim might learn something about "emancipation," about achieving the "freedoms" Sen writes of and the "kind of lives we have reason to value."

The professor is in a difficult but admirable place. He knows that something is missing from the academy and "the system" that would accommodate Jim and that would make them places of genuinely respected diversity and disputation (hooks and West 1991: 27–58) – places where the lifeworld can thrive. And thus he gropes for a more "utopian perspective" (Hart 1992: 200), which he had once dismissed as naïve, to guide his educational practice. But he does not know exactly what this perspective is. His confusion, his discovery of his ignorance, prepares him to learn. He is beginning to be a mentor.

Moment IV: transforming the academy

Jim and his mentor

A week or so before the new term began, Jim came to see me again, as I'd invited him to. I had intended to advise him about the courses he would be taking in the new term and beyond. But after the unsettling and exciting experiences of the holiday, I was more eager to talk with him about his essay.

> "Why did you pay so much attention, Jim, to 'the fix-it man,' the employee whose work record had been so poor?"

> He replied as though he'd been expecting my question, or perhaps thinking about the same things I had: "I believe everyone has a place, everyone has something to offer, everyone can learn. All those things go together. You just have to find out how. So, why not just ask them?"

> "But how do you know? Maybe you were just lucky with this worker. And anyhow, you wrote that he was afraid of losing his job."

> Jim looked silently at the bookcase on the wall behind me before replying, "I don't know, I guess, not in the way you and my economics professor here talk about empirical research. But my experience has taught me that it works out better, more often than not, to at least start out having a lot of faith in what people can do, what they know. I'll bet you could calculate that."

> "What do you mean?"

> "How much time it takes and money it costs to listen to people and let them try. Maybe you gain more in the long run than you do by quickly getting rid of the failures and recruiting replacements. Can't you calculate that?"

I was about to tell Jim something about operationalizing ideas and about the complexities of doing the sort of calculating he seemed to have in mind. But, remembering his essay and the comments he'd made about giving credit to people for what they know and for their ability to learn, I asked,

> "Don't you manage the personnel budget for your department?"

> "Not anymore, not really. Human Resources does that now."

"But do you have to make some estimate or projection of how many people you will need to hire in the coming year or when you are costing out a special project?"

"Yes, right. I do."

"And you can get more specific information from HR, about training costs, salary levels, and so on?"

"Yes."

"Okay, so then how would *you*, Jim, calculate the time you spent helping your fix-it guy find a place and the money that cost? And, to what calculations would you compare this?"

"I'm not sure." Jim looked at the floor, discouraged. Then he responded: "You seem to be pretty interested in this stuff, and you've helped me before with math by connecting to my actual work experiences. How about if you help me with this, and you'd learn something too, about at least one facilities management department?"

My hackles rose a little at Jim's assertiveness. I said, quietly, "Jim, personnel costs are not my field, you know that."

"But you know how to do these calculations, right? And you seemed to be pretty interested. Why does this have to be your field?"

"Jim, I don't think I have the time. And, to be honest, I'm not sure I completely know how to answer at least one of the questions I asked you: to what exactly would you compare the cost of bringing that employee up to speed? But I'll think about it. We can talk some more."

Jim looked unconvinced and discouraged. I changed the subject. "You know we need to discuss these liberal arts courses you're required to do, math, literature, history, and science. You have to decide what to take this coming term."

"Yeah, I know, I have to take them. But I'm not really interested. What I really *have* to do is get this degree."

"Yes you have to get a degree and those courses are university requirements. Everyone has to take them, including *you*."

"Okay, I have to take them; everyone has to take them. But I don't think it's fair. How are they going to help me? Why are they more important than what I know already or than the courses you told me I *have* to take that are at least in my field?"

Becoming exasperated, I replied, "These are subjects which every educated person knows something about."

"But what are they for? I didn't hear you using history or literature in your lectures. Neither did the economics professor. Well, the textbook gave a little history at the beginning, Marx, Adam Smith. They weren't even on the tests. And wouldn't I be learning more math, maybe the kind of math I can really use if I do this calculation project? Also, I'll bet I already know a lot about science from my work experience. I have to know something about building strengths and floor density and heat and cold in order to plan changes in our facilities, at least in order to talk with the architects and engineers who are going to design construction and renovation projects. Maybe it's not exactly the science in the books or on those tests you told me I could take to skip some of the course requirements. But it's still science, isn't it?"

"These courses broaden the mind, Jim, beyond what you use or think about everyday. Maybe there's a lot more out there than you believe, new things you could become interested in."

"There's always more to learn and I'm always learning; that's why I like my job and, partly that's why I'm here. And I know I don't know very much, compared to you and all the other professors and real students at this university. Maybe if my life was different, I'd be like you. But sometimes it just seems like it's all too much, all the things I have to do. I still have two kids at home. Another one's in college; she's an English major, you know. She sometimes tells me things about her studies: Shakespeare, Dickens, Hemingway, other great writers. Someday, I'd like to have the time to read them and enjoy them. I didn't pay much attention to them when I was in school. I wasn't much of a student and the teachers were boring, always talking down to us and sort of threatening us, especially if you weren't one of the smart kids. Then I had to get a job, to support myself and pretty soon a family. You know I first went to work in a steel mill, and we had to learn things, how steel was made, how all the equipment worked. We had to learn; the bosses expected it and for our own safety there was a lot we had to understand. And now, now I work sometimes fifty to sixty hours a week; I have to go to school; my kids are in school; they have all kinds of activities. My wife works. We hardly see each other as it is. At least we go to church together and work on some of the church projects, like the soup kitchen and organizing used clothing drives and so on. And we have other family members to look after. My wife's parents aren't well; we're trying to find out how to get them some assistance, Medicaid or Medicare – I can't keep the two straight."

I wanted to say something, but Jim kept going:

"And you know, Professor, all these things take time and even learning. You tell me that I need to broaden my mind, and probably I do, but life is stretched pretty wide and tight as it is. Also, nobody suggested I get this degree because I'm too narrow-minded or because it's going to make my life better, broader, deeper or something like that. They said I have to get this degree just to keep doing what I'm already doing, and then another degree after that in order to get promoted, to do more management, when they've already told me I'm a good organizer, teacher, planner, and a good 'people person' as they call it. I'm supposed to prove myself, when they already know what I can do. For what, for who? To get a piece of paper that proves that I really know what they know I already know? How broad-minded is that? It doesn't seem fair. Are those liberal arts courses going to teach me about 'fair,' or about how to live with what isn't fair?"

"But Jim..."

"No, no, I'm sorry for interrupting and going on like this. But let me ask you. People are always telling me that this is for my own good, for my benefit. At work, here at school, even you. This thing is going to 'expand my skill-set' or that course is going to 'broaden my mind.' But it really feels like – I don't know – like an after-thought, because what all of you are really saying is that if I want to get ahead, even if I want to stay where I am and survive with my family, I *have* to do these things anyway, no matter what the reasons. Are those liberal arts courses going to teach me about caring for people, I mean really caring about them, not just making them fit? Does Shakespeare talk about that?"

"Well, I think..."

"You always seem pretty rushed when we talk and when you come into and leave class. You're busy and already educated. But what if you had to learn something completely new and different, like doing this calculation project with me or even, I don't know, reading Shakespeare or something from those liberal arts courses, although I guess you probably already know all that. But there must be something.... What if you just had to add some big new thing in your life and you knew it was important or you couldn't get out of it, even if you really didn't know for sure that it was so valuable compared to all the other things you had to do. What if someone told you that you *had* to do it anyhow, to prove yourself, even though you're on top of the heap here and I guess no one can really tell you what to do or threaten you and get away with lying that it's for your own good. I mean, even if it really was for your own good, not that they really cared, wouldn't you, wouldn't you ... wouldn't you get angry, fight back?"

And Jim stopped, his face flushed with embarrassment and frustration. "I'm sorry. Sometimes it's all too much."

I felt that I ought to say something, but I didn't know what. We sat for a few moments – it seemed much longer – in uncomfortable silence. Jim looked exhausted and for some reason I felt drained too. My mind was blank. Then, I asked quietly and without thinking:

"Jim, you remember the fix-it man you wrote about. Do you think you treated him fairly?"

"Yes, I think I really did, as best I could anyhow."

"Do you think you can explain why? I don't mean just why you did what you did, but what you mean by saying your behavior was 'fair'."

"I think I know what you're asking, but I have to think about it."

"Yes, yes, think about it. You don't have to tell me now. And I have to think too. You've said a lot today."

"I know. I'm sorry. I really am. I know you're busy and we're not friends or anything. I just ... I'm just tired and all these things have been building up."

"I think I understand, Jim; at least I hope I do. I've been preoccupied as well. And I'm just wondering if there's something we can do with all the things you've said."

"What do you mean?"

"Actually, I'm not so sure. It's important that you understand that. I need some time to think, to think about how we can use your job experiences in your coursework. And not just what you once learned about making steel or what you know about how to maintain and improve the infrastructure of where you work now. Maybe you understand something really important about fairness too, something you learned about treating people well in all this experience you've had. Would you come back in, say, three days, same time? And could you jot down a few things about what you mean by 'fair'? Also could you make a list of some of the work-related topics you think you know about? I don't mean another essay or revision of this one, just some notes we could look at together."

Jim agreed to try, and also to return.

I really didn't know what I was doing, but I was feeling as though I did, as though something were opening in front of me, still very vague, but pulling me. Shakespeare, Aristotle, Sen, Jim. I was fascinated and excited, the way I felt when a graduate student came up with a research idea I hadn't thought of and I didn't completely understand yet, or when I began conceiving an article on a topic I'd not written about before and for which I hadn't even yet read the literature. I no longer cared about the grant application, but I did want to talk with my dean about fulfilling my undergraduate teaching responsibilities for the next term in a different way.

A long time passed, musing, alone in my office. I returned to this reverie several times over the next couple of days when I wasn't busy with my usual pre-term preparations. My only concrete thoughts were about some course titles: "Honors Seminar in Management"; "Independent Study"; "Research Development." The first two were titles that would allow professors to work with advanced, gifted undergraduates. "Research Development" was usually reserved for graduate students and their professors to work on very current and scholarly projects. In a way, the titles were just labels for empty vessels whose contents the faculty could plan quickly without having to prepare complete syllabi for curriculum committee approval.

I was thinking that somehow I could use these devices with Jim, if the dean would allow it. (I was certainly aware that Jim was neither a graduate nor an "honor" student, nor even, by our normal standards, very "advanced.") But, actually, I didn't need the dean's approval to do an "independent study." I wasn't sure what I would do with Jim in such a course. Yet I felt that if we used some of those authors, Sen and the classics, we could look at this "fairness" issue that was so bothering him – and now me too. Also, we might be able to do something with the topics he believed he'd learned something about from his work experience. I was sure that I could come up with some relevant readings; I could ask colleagues for suggestions. These could help him form a kind of bridge from work to school and honor what he believed he'd learned without his having to take course exams on ostensibly the same subjects but focused on terms and sub-topics alien to him. And wasn't "fairness" a kind of "liberal arts" topic? After all, we'd be reading what my old friend had reminded me used to be called "political economy" and maybe even some literature, some Shakespeare.

Shakespeare? What did he have to do with all this? I hadn't read or seen any Shakespeare in a very long time. But then I remembered a paper a younger colleague, from the English department, had distributed during a presentation she'd made at one of our own departmental meetings. She was interested in developing and teaching "interdisciplinary courses" and was proposing something on "literature and business." Her proposal was still under consideration, but I remembered that she'd talked a lot about literary themes which management theorists, like Peter Drucker, also dealt with, like "leadership," "power," "equity," and "communication." She had talked a lot and written about Shakespeare, about *King Lear*, *The Merchant of Venice,* and one of what she called the "history plays," *Richard II*, I think.

I dug her paper out of my files. I remembered a phrase she quoted from Lear, "reason not the need." I don't know why I remembered the phrase or why it now kept revolving in my head. But after a few minutes, I found the quote:

> O, reason not the need! our basest beggars
> Are in the poorest thing superfluous.
> Allow not nature more than nature needs,
> Man's life is cheap as beast's.
> (Shakespeare 1974: III, i, 264–267)

I wasn't sure I really understood the quote (and I was too excited to read the essay – maybe Jim and I would do that together). But it seemed to have something to do with what happens when decisions are made only according to some tight standard of necessity, to what can be easily measured or calculated: We leave out all the important things, the things that make human life worth living. Or, at least the people making the decisions leave out those values when they're calculating what everyone else "needs." They, the decision-makers, don't do these calculations on themselves. They just go for what they want, what they think they can get. Had I been doing the same, when I did all those productivity and cost-benefit calculations for my research? I think she said some of the characters in the play behaved like that. I began thinking now of CEOs and other senior executives I'd met who defended their very generous stock options and bonuses by saying that they should be rewarded for having to make "the really tough decisions," like cutting "personnel costs" in order to increase net earnings and efficiency. Perhaps we can't measure "fair" very well, but surely any of us can tell when we are treated like "beasts"! Maybe Jim and I could use this quote or even the whole play in the course, *our* course.

When Jim arrived in my office, I knew that I'd have to restrain my excitement and confusion. I didn't want him to be as overwhelmed as I had been feeling. I was his professor and had to show some distance and clarity. Also, I'd almost forgot that I'd asked him to work up some ideas of his own. Wouldn't it be silly, I mean counterproductive or contradictory, if I flooded him with my suggestions and didn't listen to him? After all, it was because I listened to him that all of this started in the first place.

"Jim," I began, "I've been thinking about your idea that we work together. I think we can do it, work on calculating fairness, to see if it can be done. And, at the same time, I think we can work on how to do something with what you say you've learned from your work experience and your concerns about those required liberal arts studies too. In fact, maybe some other students like you, or with interests similar to yours, can join us."

Jim looked puzzled, curious, skeptical, and eager. "That would be great. But how?"

"Yes, I know. It will be a little complicated and strange. I haven't worked out all the departmental details yet, but I'm sure we can do at least some of what you want without your having to do extra course-work. Actually, in order to work this out, I need your help, your collaboration."

"What does that mean?"

"Right now, it means that I'd like to see the notes you've written on what you've learned about fairness and other topics from your work."

Silently, Jim handed me a thin sheaf of papers. Briefly scanning them, I could see that they were filled with what appeared to be notes and arrows pointing from them to lists of brief phrases, like "air and water treatment systems: functional design, health and safety requirements"; "supervision techniques and progressive performance evaluations"; "communication skills, getting the most from employee input." But on the first page, Jim had written only this:

Fairness in the Workplace
Why should what's fair at work be any different from what's fair any-place else? I was taught that being fair means treating others as you would want to be treated yourself. That idea has always been good enough for me.

"Jim," I said, "this looks like a good place for us to begin. Do you think we could spend some time during the coming term talking about your idea, about fairness, I mean, and how you try to apply it to some of these other things, like "communication" and even "air and water treatment systems"?

"Do you mean as part of a course? Sure, I'd like to talk with you, but how is that going to fit into a course, one that will count toward my degree, I mean? Don't courses have textbooks? What's the book? What are the assignments?"

"Well, this course will be a little different from what you and I are used to. It'll be more like what I do with my graduate students. I can explain that. And I can suggest some things to read too. My colleagues have already given me some ideas. But maybe what I have in mind will be clearer – for both of us – if we just sort of try it out, now, for a few minutes. Do you think you could tell me about some of the information you have to have and what you have to think about when you, say, plan to upgrade the air conditioning system in your plant? And, do you ever think about fairness when you're working on a project like that?"

Jim was silent for a few moments. He looked straight at me. Then he began, speaking slowly but breathing rapidly, "Well, it's complicated. There are all sorts of things, technical things of course. I'm sure you already know. And yes, yes, I guess I really do have to think about what's fair, about people's comfort while they work. For example..."

Epilogue

From teaching to mentoring

> If on the other hand I tell you that to let no day pass without discussing goodness and all the other subjects about which you hear me talking and examining both myself and others is really the very best thing a man can do, and that life without this sort of examination is not worth living, you will be even less inclined to believe me. Nevertheless that is how it is, gentlemen.
>
> Plato, Apology (37e–38a)

How successful has the professor been in making the academy, his university, truly accessible to Jim? The professor has opened his role, thanks in part to his intellectual conscience, his adherence to the logic of his ideas and questions, and also thanks in good measure to Jim's persistently presenting his own needs and ideas. The professor has tutored Jim, become a more caring and resourceful advisor, and is entering with him into a process of dialogical inquiry. Within their very small association, the academy is now a very different, far more accommodating place. But we return to the signature question of this book: Has Jim's teacher become a mentor?

We can more precisely understand what is learned during the four "moments" described in our previous chapter, by reviewing them with the six principles of mentoring:

I Authority and uncertainty

The professor begins to doubt his own professional habits. He questions the adequacy of his teaching, scholarship, and consulting to fulfilling the potential of the commitment he had once made (neglected but not forgotten) to an intellectual life. With difficulty, he falls into the habit of wondering whether the success, in terms of money and status, he has made of himself and helped others achieve contributes sufficiently to more fundamental "goods" or meanings of human life. His uncertainties are not selfless. With even more difficulty, he realizes (in part, thanks to his dean's soft but ominous provocation) that he is not much better off than Jim, not less vulnerable to organizationally or "systemically" expedient insults to his capabilities, autonomy, and self-respect.

The professor's uncomfortable but increasingly eager self-reflections confuse him. They also take him to seek new learning and even to using his status within the academy for a potentially radical transformation of his worklife and of Jim's academic experience. In the process, Jim becomes a more effective and more hopeful learner. The professor does not thoroughly understand where he, Jim, and possibly other students will be going. But he is acting from the provisional or tentatively held belief that it has something to do with an exploration of the idea of "fairness." This includes not only fair or respectful associations among people in an academic or industrial workplace, but also respect for understanding the meaning of the idea itself, and respect for a life of the mind to which the professor is reviving his commitment.

2 Diversity of curriculum

The professor's questions about himself make him wonder what he might do to help Jim learn. He starts to take Jim's concerns seriously, not as merely the complaints of a new student having trouble adapting, but as claims upon university resources and policies. He becomes interested in Jim's interests, and (fortunately and easily) finds some common ground between their professions. Jim will learn better because his professor increasingly attends to what Jim is genuinely curious about. It's important to note that the professor himself will also *learn* to become a more open teacher and advisor. He will learn to become a mentor because, he is also genuinely curious for his own reasons about Jim's concerns. Thus, he tries to find ways he can directly help Jim become a more successful student, individually tutoring him by going beyond the textbook, using examples from the latter's work experience. And, knowing that he lacks the capacity and time to be Jim's private teacher, the professor seeks and recommends help from other university services.

But, eventually, he goes further than that. He begins to invent and to improvise curricular content particular to his own and Jim's common curiosity. To do so, he plans to make use of university devices or rubrics, the course designations "Independent Study" or "Honors Seminar," not originally intended for that purpose. The professor's intellectual revolution in thought has led him to a slightly subversive or transformational action.

3 Autonomy and collaboration

By respecting Jim's judgment about his needs and interests, the professor realizes that he is serving his own autonomy as well. Perhaps even deeper than their common professional and practical interest in "facilities management," this care each has for "fairness" and respect forms a moral basis for their intellectual collaboration. Jim of course expects that he needs to learn from the professor; the professor discovers that he needs to learn from Jim. It is only by dialogue that their inquiry can proceed.

The professor is also making other collaborative moves. He calls upon his old friend from college days, now a successful academic economist, for both moral and scholarly advice. He goes back to the presentation a junior professor from the English department had given, in order to enhance the thematic and "liberal arts" significance of the management and professional questions on his mind. And he reports to Jim that he will be seeking suggestions from other colleagues. The interpersonal and internal dialogue on which the professor has embarked is not private; it depends upon and is opening toward an enlarging community. He begins to learn that he is not alone.

4 Learning from the lifeworld

It's not so much Jim's practical or technical difficulties with learning that engage the professor. Much more so, it's the quality of Jim's life: his painstaking and painful efforts to be a good, dutiful worker, student, and even family member. It's Jim's anguish and challenging questions about making life liveable and fair, his overflowing (if not yet completely clear or coherent) presentation of self, his presence as a whole person that both bothers and attracts the professor. And it's these kinds of issues from his own lifeworld that provoke the professor to self-examination, to sustain his attention to Jim, and to discover an intellectual richness which rouses him from his complacency, from, as Kant would have said, his "dogmatic slumbers."

Further, the professor and Jim sense that the inquiry upon which they agree to engage will involve both systemic or technical and fundamentally normative or lifeworld topics. Jim speaks in a rush of words about his practical difficulties as a student and about the unfairness of his situation. The professor asks Jim to make notes both about his technical workplace knowledge and about his ideas of fairness. They are supposing that full learning, both what they believe they have achieved and the learning they seek, will *necessarily* connect "system" and "lifeworld." This reciprocity is crucial. Without systems generating and distributing prosperity, security, and power, the lifeworld is practically unliveable. But if it is forgotten that wealth and other systems-benefits are merely useful, not in themselves, but for the sake of a higher end or more fundamental good (as Aristotle indirectly reminds the professor), then "the system" is meaningless and empty.

5 Evaluation as reflective learning

At first, the professor judges Jim's promise as a student strictly according academic expectations rigidly applied to all students. And when Jim hopes to receive credit for the learning he's achieved through experience and to seek new learning according to his needs, the professor simply expects him to fit his learning, prior and anticipated, into specific, pre-set course requirements. Jim has no voice in the academic decisions that will affect him. It is presumed, in effect, that he lacks the capacity to participate in any way except to adapt himself to what others expect of him. Jim considers this assumption almost impossible to manage and to be unfair.

The professor gradually learns to listen to Jim and to ask himself the same kinds of questions Jim is asking. And he thereby moves toward asking Jim to participate in academic evaluation: what he wants to learn, why and how. Exactly reversing his earlier attitude, the professor realizes that he's outrunning his own clear, and formerly secure, understanding of academic quality. In fact, he nearly outruns Jim's own ideas. Jim's habitual expectations of how schools and teachers behave are so similar to what the professor's had been, that the latter's eager proposals make Jim puzzled and wary. The professor realizes that he has to slow down, restrain his new enthusiasm, *wait* for Jim, if their collaboration is going to work.

Although the professor thereby demonstrates that he is seriously committed to genuinely dialogical inquiry, he will have to be careful, especially when the time comes for him (and Jim will no doubt ask, sooner rather than later) to consider how Jim's learning, old and new, should be evaluated. If the professor is true to his own new insights – and, if he is vigilant – he will ask Jim (who, after all, has years of experience in evaluating both the promise and performance of *his* supervisees) to participate in this process too. It is one more challenge that lies ahead. Collaborative evaluation is simply another aspect of collaborative learning.

6 Individual learning and the knowledge most worth having

The professor might successfully advocate to his dean and colleagues that the learning Jim achieves in their independent study should be credited toward some of the traditional liberal arts requirements (perhaps, for example, sociology and philosophy). And he might also be successful in having some of Jim's workplace learning replace the usual requirements of management majors. Will Jim thus acquire an idiosyncratic education? What will Jim be missing if he and the professor continue on their inquiry venture?

Once the professor's curiosity is awakened and Jim's is honored, both are eager to make connections. Jim does not merely want to "get credit" for what he already believes he knows and then receive his degree.

He's willing to learn what he believes he doesn't know about management and the quantitative tools useful to facilities managers. He's also interested in what his daughter has told him about Shakespeare and other classic authors. The professor is also reaching out, making new connections and reviving old ones – Shakespeare, Aristotle, and the political economics of Amartya Sen. Somewhat to his surprise and distraction, he even finds himself willing to "teach" beyond his field. He becomes eager to explore very unfamiliar material for the sake of helping himself and someone else learn.

Moreover, the professor realizes, for reasons of both practicality and fairness, that he should involve other students and probably other faculty in what he and Jim are doing. The two of them will thus no doubt encounter ideas, questions, and interests neither had anticipated. This neonate community will expand everyone's learning; and the professor's management expertise (perhaps that of the students' as well) will be required to devise an orderly process, a system, so that the surprises of diversity do not make their wonder inchoate.

Finally, another kind of discomfiting but valuable discovery await both Jim and his professor. They are going to connect with the political implications of their enterprise. The professor briefly anticipates that he will have to persuade his colleagues and his superiors to authorize the continuation of this new academic path. The professor will need his students' help, both their testimony and some evidence of their success. Neither Jim nor his professor is very "political." With more and less difficulty, they have managed to come as far as they have without energetically and openly challenging existing institutional arrangements. Jim, in persistently presenting himself to his professor has, unknowingly, made such a change. The professor has so far relied on available openings in the system and his own status to expand his educational ideas and practices.

The professor might have to rely on the example of Jim's unpremeditated courage. If they want to sustain and expand the learning community they are creating, they will be obliged to argue both its efficacy and fairness to greater powers held by people who might well believe they knew as much about what was necessary and valuable as the professor did before he met Jim. The professor knows that the power learning gives is necessary to live well; but he is learning, with great distress, that such power alone is inadequate for a good and full life. Will he also be able to engage his colleagues in such difficult learning?

Jim's professor has embarked on what Lindeman would surely call an "adventure." Though the professor does not yet quite know what he's doing, he, like all mentors and their students, has entered into dialogue. The professor has learned to care about what Jim wants to learn and what he believes he already knows. This "cognitive love" has also caused the professor to ask difficult questions of himself, both about how he will carry out his professional role and about the deepest purposes of his vocation.

He comes to see that he will need to stretch, even subvert, the usual meanings and routines of academic policies. He also anticipates that he will have to engage in a very unfamiliar kind of learning – one that will touch the most basic issues of fairness, truth, and the good life.

This learning will be a political education, for the professor and for his colleagues. If dialogue is to be accessible to all students and faculty, which is only fair, if the collaborative and always provisional emergence of truth is be an academic norm, and if a delightful community of learning is to become open to everyone's curiosity, then the university system itself will have to be transformed into a better lifeworld. The professor will have to learn, as Socrates tried, how to ask his associates to examine themselves. He will disturb them while he engages them in unanswered questions about what they believe they know, the power they possess, what they desire to learn, and how they want to live. As we move from teaching to mentoring, examining our implicit principles and habitual practices, we have to keep asking ourselves what we must still learn in order to live lives that we love – "the very best thing we can do."

Bibliography

Aristotle (1947) *Politics* and *Metaphysics*, in R. McKeon (ed.), B. Jowett (trans.) *The Basic Works of Aristotle*, New York: Random House.

Aronowitz, S. (2000) *The Knowledge Factory: Dismantling the Corporate University and Creating True Higher Learning*, Boston, MA: Beacon Press.

Baktin, M. (1989) *The Dialogic Imagination, Four Essays*, C. Emerson (trans.), M. Holquist (ed.) Austin, TX: University of Texas Press.

Beniger, J. (1986) *The Control Revolution: Technological and Economic Origins of the Information Society*, Cambridge, MA: Harvard University Press.

Benjamin, W. (1968) "The work of art in the age of mechanical reproduction," in H. Arendt (ed.), H. Zohn (trans.) *Illuminations*, New York: Schocken Books.

Berger, P.L. and Luckmann, T. (1966) *The Social Construction of Reality: A Treatise on the Sociology of Knowledge*, New York: Doubleday.

Bohm, D. (1996) *On Dialogue*, London: Routledge.

Brookfield, S. (1991) *Understanding and Facilitating Adult Learning: A Comprehensive Analysis of Principles and Effective Practices*, San Francisco, CA: Jossey-Bass.

Burbules, N. (1993) *Dialogue in Teaching: Theory and Practice*, New York: Teachers College Press.

Colley, H. (2001) "An ABC of mentors' talk about disaffected youth: alternative lifestyles, benefit dependency or complete dunces?," *Youth and Policy*, 72: 1–15.

—— (2002) "A 'Rough Guide' to the history of mentoring from a marxist-feminist perspective," *Journal of Education for Teaching,* 28,3.

Collins, M. (1995) "Critical commentaries on the role of the adult educator: from self-directed learning to postmodernist sensibilities," in M.R. Welton (ed.) *In Defense of the Lifeworld*, Albany, New York: State University of New York Press.

Coulter, X., de Royston, I., Gerardi, J., Herman, L., and Nagler, S. (1992) "Questioning adult learners," conference presentation, Exploring Our Horizons, ACE/Alliance.

——, de Royston, I., Herman, L., and Nagler S. (1993) "Seeing mentoring: understanding and improving mentoring skills by examining videotapes," conference presentation, Sixth Annual Conference on Diversity in Mentoring, International Mentoring Association.

——, de Royston, I., Herman, L., Hodgson, T., and Nagler, S. (1994b) "Mentors of all shapes and sizes: integrating diversity," conference presentation, Seventh

Annual Conference on Diversity in Mentoring, International Mentoring Association.

—— (1994c) "Assessing adults' experiential learning," conference presentation, The National Center on Adult Learning.

—— and Herman, L. (1994a) "Individualization in distance education," in *Proceedings of the International Conference on Distance Education*, Moscow, Russia: Association for International Education.

Cross, K.P. (1992) *Adults as Learners: Increasing Participation and Facilitating Learning*, San Francisco, CA: Jossey-Bass.

Csikszentmihalyi, M. (1991) *Flow: The Psychology of Optimal Experience*, New York: HarperCollins.

Daloz, L. (1999) *Mentor: Guiding the Journey of Adult Learning*, Second Edition, San Francisco, CA: Jossey-Bass.

Dewey, J. (1963) *Experience and Education*, New York: Collier Books.

Dickens, C. (1987) *Great Expectations*, New York: Oxford University Press.

Dickinson, E. (1960) "I'm Nobody! Who are You?," in T.H. Johnson (ed.) *The Complete Poems of Emily Dickinson*, New York: Little, Brown and Company.

Eliot, T.S. (1971) *The Love Song of J. Alfred Prufrock*, in *The Complete Poems and Plays, 1909–1950*, New York: Harcourt, Brace and World, Inc.

Ellinor, L. (1998) *Dialogue: Rediscover the Transforming Power of Conversation: Creating and Sustaining Collaborative Partnerships at Work*, New York: Wiley and Sons, Inc.

Essaytown (10 January 2003) www.Essaytown.com.

Ferrer, J. (2002) "Dialogical inquiry as spiritual practice," *Tikkun*, 18,1: 29–32.

Foucault, M. (1973) *The Order of Things: An Archaeology of the Human Sciences*, New York: Vintage Books.

—— (1977) *Discipline and Punish: The Birth of the Prison*, A. Sheridan (trans.) New York: Pantheon.

Freud, S. (1953) "Fragment of an analysis of a case of hysteria," in J. Strachey (ed. and trans.) *The Standard Edition of the Complete Psychological Works of Sigmund Freud*, 7, London: The Hogarth Press and the Institute of Psychoanalysis.

Fritz, M. (10 March 1999) "Draw conclusions but cite your own work," *Los Angeles Times*.

Gandy, O.H. Jr (1993) *The Panoptic Sort: A Political Economy of Personal Information*, Boulder, CO. Westview Press.

Gleick, J. (1999) *Faster: The Acceleration of Just About Everything*, New York: Pantheon.

Greenway, T. (2003) "FBI eyes," Tgreenwa@Allstate.com, 4 February 2003.

Habermas, J. (1984) *The Theory of Communicative Action, Volume One: Reason and the Rationalization of Society*, T. McCarthy (trans.) Boston, MA: Beacon Press.

—— (1989) *The Theory of Communicative Action, Volume Two: Lifeworld and System: A Critique of Functionalist Reason*, T. McCarthy (trans.) Boston, MA: Beacon Press.

—— (1990) *Moral Consciousness and Communicative Action*, C. Lenhardt and S.W. Nicholsen (trans.) Cambridge, MA: The MIT Press.

Hardison, O.B. Jr (1989) *Disappearing through the Skylight: Culture and Technology in the Twentieth Century*, New York: Viking Penguin.

Harvard Mentoring Project (5 January 2003) *New York Times*.

Hart, M.V. (1992) *Working and Educating for Life: Feminist and International Perspectives on Adult Education*, London: Routledge.

Heim, M. (1998) *Virtual Realism*, New York: Oxford University Press.

Herman, L. (1992) "Making room," *Golden Hill*, 6: 1–4.

—— and Mandell, A. (1996) "The authority of uncertainty," *Educational Foundations*, 10,1: 57–72.

—— (1999) "On access: towards opening the lifeworld within adult higher education systems," in A. Tait and R. Mills (eds) *The Convergence of Distance and Conventional Education: Patterns of Flexibility for the Individual Learner*, London: Routledge.

—— (2000) "The given and the made: authenticity and nature in virtual education," *First Monday* 5, 10. http/firstmonday.org

Hirsch, E.D. (1987) *Cultural Literacy: What Every American Needs to Know*, Boston, MA: Houghton Mifflin Company.

Hobbes, T. (1962) *Leviathan*, M. Oakshott (ed.) New York: Collier Books.

Homer (1967) *Odyssey*, R. Lattimore (trans.) New York: Harper and Row.

—— (1975) *Iliad*, R. Lattimore (trans.) Chicago, IL: University of Chicago Press.

hooks, b. and West, C. (1991) *Breaking Bread: Insurgent Black Intellectual Life*, Boston, MA: South End Press.

Husserl, E. (1970) *The Crisis of European Sciences and Transcendental Phenomenology*, Evanston, IL: Northwestern University Press.

Kant, I. (1965) *Critique of Pure Reason*, N.K. Smith (trans.) New York: St. Martin's Press.

—— (1956) *Critique of Practical Reason*, N.K. Smith (trans.) Indianapolis, IN: The Bobbs-Merrill Company.

Kegan, R. (1995) *In Over Our Heads: The Mental Demands of Modern Life*, Cambridge, MA: Harvard University Press.

Knowles, M. (1990) *The Adult Learner: A Neglected Species*, Fourth Edition, Houston, TX: Gulf Publishing.

Kuhn, T. (1970) *The Structure of Scientific Revolutions*, Chicago, IL: University of Chicago Press.

Kupfer, J.H. (1983) *Experience as Art: Aesthetics in Everyday Life*, Albany, New York: State University of New York Press.

Lasch, C. (1995) *Haven in a Heartless World: The Family Under Siege*, Boston, MA: W.W. Norton.

Lear, J. (1990) *Love and Its Place in Nature: A Philosophical Interpretation of Freudian Psychoanalysis*, New York: Farrar, Straus and Giroux.

Lewis, C.T. and Short, C. (1966) *A Latin Dictionary*, Oxford: Oxford University Press.

Liddell, H.G. and Scott, R.J. (1968) *A Greek-English Lexicon*, Oxford: Oxford University Press.

Lindeman, E. (1961) *The Meaning of Adult Education*, New York: New Republic, Inc.

McCullough, D. (2001) *John Adams*, New York: Simon and Schuster.

MacIntyre, A. (1981) *After Virtue: A Study in Moral Theory*, Notre Dame, IN: University of Notre Dame Press.

Mandell, A. and Herman, L. (1996) "From teachers to mentors: acknowledging openings in the faculty role," in R. Mills and A. Tait (eds) *Supporting the Learner in Open and Distance Learning*, London: Pitman Publishing.

—— (2001) "Review of Aronowitz, *The Knowledge Factory*," *Educational Studies*, Spring: 72–76.

—— (2003) "Remembering our common work: institutional support for open learning," in A. Tait and R. Mills (eds) *Rethinking Learner Support in Distance Education: Change and Continuity in an International Context*, London: RoutledgeFalmer.

—— and Michelson, E. (1991; new edition forthcoming) *Portfolio Development and Adult Learning: Purposes and Strategies*, Dubuque, IA: Kendall/Hunt Publishing, Inc.

Magretta, J. (2002) *What Management Is: How It Works and Why It's Everyone's Business*, New York: The Free Press.

Masters, J.J. (1997) *Finding Freedom: Writings from Death Row*, Junction City, CA: Padma Publishing.

Mezirow, J. (1990) *Critical Reflection in Adulthood: A Guide to Transformative and Emancipatory Learning*, San Francisco, CA: Jossey-Bass.

—— (1991) *Transformative Dimensions of Adult Learning*, San Francisco, CA: Jossey-Bass.

Mills, R. (2003) "The centrality of learner support in open and distance learning systems," in A. Tait and R. Mills (eds) *Rethinking Learner Support in Distance Education: Change and Continuity in an International Context*, London: RoutledgeFalmer.

The New Shorter Oxford English Dictionary (1993) L. Brown (ed.) Oxford: Clarendon Press.

Nussbaum, M. (1994) *The Therapy of Desire: Theory and Practice in Hellenistic Ethics*, Princeton, NJ: Princeton University Press.

—— (2001) *Upheavals of Thought: The Intelligence of Emotions*, Cambridge: Cambridge University Press.

Paley, V.G. (1986) *Mollie is Three: Growing Up in School*, Chicago, IL: University of Chicago Press.

—— (1992) *You Can't Say You Can't Play*, Cambridge, MA: Harvard University Press.

Plato (1963) *Collected Dialogues*, E. Hamilton and H. Cairns (eds) Princeton, NJ: Princeton University Press.

Rao, N. (20 April 1999) "Paper trail," *Village Voice*.

Rawls, J. (1971) *A Theory of Justice*, Cambridge, MA: Harvard University Press.

Reich, R. (1990) *The Work of Nations: Capitalism in the 21st Century*, New York: Alfred A. Knopf.

Rieff, P. (1990) *Triumph of the Therapeutic: Uses of Faith after Freud*, Chicago, IL: University of Chicago Press.

Russo, R. (1994) *Nobody's Fool*, New York: Vintage.

Schon, D.A. (1983) *The Reflective Practitioner: How Professionals Think in Action*, New York: Basic Books.

—— (1990) *Educating the Reflective Practitioner: Toward a New Design for Teaching and Learning in the Professions*, San Francisco, CA: Jossey-Bass.

Schwartz, J. (2 January 2003) "Professors vie with Web for class's attention," *New York Times*.

Sen, A. (1992) *Inequality Reexamined*, New York: Russell Sage Foundation; and Cambridge, MA: Harvard University Press.

—— (1999) *Development as Freedom*, New York: Random House.

Sennett, R. (1977) *The Fall of Public Man*, New York: Norton Books.

—— (1980) *Authority*, New York: Alfred A. Knopf.

—— (2003) *Respect in a World of Inequality*, New York: Norton.

Shakespeare, W. (1974) *King Lear*, in G. Evans (ed.) *The Riverside Shakespeare*, Boston, MA: Houghton Mifflin Company.

Shor, I. (1996) *When Students Have Power: Negotiating Authority in a Critical Pedagogy*, Chicago, IL: University of Chicago Press.

Stone, I.F. (1988) *The Trial of Socrates*, New York: Little Brown and Company.

Swan, K. *et al.* (2000) "Building knowledge building communities: consistency, contact and communication in the virtual classroom," *Journal of Educational Computing Research* 23 (4): 389–413.

Tenner, E. (1996) *Why Things Bite Back: Technology and the Revenge of Unintended Consequences*, New York: Alfred A. Knopf.

Thorpe, M. (2003) "Collaborative on-line learning: transforming learner support and course design," in A. Tait and R. Mills (eds) *Rethinking Learner Support in Distance Education: Change and Continuity in an International Context*, London: RoutledgeFalmer.

Tobin, J. (2001) *Great Projects: The Epic Story of the Building of America, from the Taming of the Mississippi to the Invention of the Internet*, New York: The Free Press.

"turnitin.com" (23 January 2003).

Usher, R., Bryant, I., and Johnston, R. (1997) *Adult Education and the Postmodern Challenge: Learning Beyond the Limits.* London: Routledge.

Weber, M. (1946a) "Religious rejections of the world and their directions," in H.H. Gerth and C.W. Mills (eds) *From Max Weber*, New York: Oxford University Press.

—— (1946b) "Science as a vocation," in H.H. Gerth and C.W. Mills (eds) *From Max Weber*, New York: Oxford University Press.

Weil, S. (1986) "The *Iliad*, or the poem of force," M. McCarthy and D. Macdonald (trans.), in S. Miles (ed.) *Simone Weil, An Anthology*, New York: Weidenfeld and Nicholson.

Weinberg, S. (1992) *Dreams of a Final Theory: The Search for the Fundamental Laws of Nature*, New York: Pantheon.

Welton, M.R. (1995) "In defense of the lifeworld: A Habermasian approach to adult learning," in M.R. Welton (ed.) *In Defense of the Lifeworld*, Albany, New York: State University of New York Press.

Wolff, K.H. (1976) *Surrender and Catch: Experience and Inquiry Today*, New York: Kluwer Academic Publishers.

Zachary, L.J. (2000) *The Mentor's Guide: Facilitating Effective Learning Relationships*, San Francisco, CA: Jossey-Bass.

Index